RUINED FOR LIFE

POST-MISSIONARY IMMERSION, REINTEGRATION, & CONVERSION

*Sharing Amor en Acción's Four Decades of Discerned Wisdom
as a Practical-Theological Guide to Re-Entry*

DAVID MASTERS, D.MIN.

PACEM IN TERRIS PRESS

*Devoted to the global vision of Saint John XXIII,
prophetic founder of Postmodern Catholic Social Teaching,
and in support of the search for a Postmodern Ecological Civilization,
which will seek to learn from the rich spiritual wisdom-traditions
of Christianity and of our entire global human family.*

www.paceminterrispress.com

2019

Cover photo of Caribbean map from Shutterstock

Pacem in Terris Press publishes scholarly books directly or indirectly related to Catholic Social Teaching and its commitment to justice, peace, ecology, and spirituality, and on behalf of the search for a Postmodern Ecological Civilization.

In addition, in order to support ecumenical and interfaith dialogue, as well as dialogue with other spiritual seekers, Pacem in Terris Press publishes scholarly books from other Christian perspectives, from other religious perspectives, and from perspectives of other spiritual seekers that promote justice, peace, ecology, and spirituality for our global human family.

Opinions or claims expressed in publications from Pacem in Terris Press represent the opinions and claims of the authors and do not necessarily represent the official position of Pacem in Terris Press, the Pacem in Terris Ecological Initiative, Pax Romana / Catholic Movement for Intellectual & Cultural Affairs - USA or its officers, directors, members, and staff.

PACEM IN TERRIS PRESS
is the publishing service of

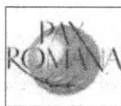

PAX ROMANA
Catholic Movement for Intellectual & Cultural Affairs
USA
1025 Connecticut Avenue NW, Suite 1000,
Washington DC 20036
www.paceminterris.net

I DEDICATE THIS BOOK TO

Dayane Masters, Juliana Taimoorazy, Margaret Ajemian Ahnert,
David & Esther Masters, Hilda Mateo & Chicho Valenzuela, Rubén David, Marcos Luís,
Joseph, Mary, Julie, Thomas, Therese, Chris, John,
Joe & Albina Friedheim, Ambrose & Ruth Masters,

Adriano García, Alicia Marill, Carlos Cueto, Josefina Chirino, Lourdes Rovira, Wayne Cavalier, Joe Holland, Liam Quinn, Julio Giulietti, Teresita González, Mónica Lauzurique, Wendy Lockard, Janelle Jay, Nancy Lizano, Boniface Fils-Aime, Eduardo Álvarez, Angelina Lebrón, Mario Vizcaíno, Alfredo Morales, Jacqueline Picard, Patricia Dillon, Rose Kelly, Nazareth Ybarra, Ignacio Castellót, Ronel Charelus, Alejandro Roque, Margaret G Block, Marzo & Iliana Artime, Ondina Menocal, Lidia Rivera, Ray Rufo, Mary, Caridad, Joe & Mercedes, Cynthia, Tom, Ondina, Terence, Joan & Ed, Tall Rey, Veronica Koperski, John O'Grady, Bryan Walsh, Agustín Román, Nelson Bonet, Andrés Novela, George & María Rodríguez, Oscar Manríquez, Jeffrey Sánchez, Patricia Stout Swanson, Mary Sturm, María Wadsworth,

Ragheed Ganni, Jacques Hamel, Daniel Pearl, James Foley, Steven Sotloff, Anselm, Judith, Marguerite, Reginette, Tom Uzhunnalil, John Hagee, Paul Kengor, Meira Svirsky, Robert Havu Noten, Franklin Graham, Wayne Kopping, Ami Horowitz, Goldwasser, David Barton, Dennis Prager, Sekulow, Haley, Mark Steyn, Nicholson, Bill Federer, Bill French, Ed Burke, Churchill, Thatcher, Wilberforce, Garrison, Lincoln, Yaxley, Tubman, Douglass, King, Parks, Wells-Barnett, Lance Wielder, Washington, Bolton, Neyrey, Owens, Friedman, Shapiro, Maglalang, Raymond Ibrahim, Kirk, Newton McPherson, Wood, Douglass-Williams, Gabriel, Godgiven Aristocrat, Wheeler, Victor Nekhemiyah the Percussionist, Melekh Hhakham Nimehar, Miller, Hanson, Bergman, Crooked Riverbend, Horowitz, West, Cain, Kern, Humberto Fontova, Bozell, Puthusseril, Nabeel Qureshi, Starnes, <u>Rosenwald</u>, Perlman, Littman, Meotti, Reisman, Garthwaite, Malina, Pilch, Rohrbaugh, Sweetspear, Violet Khamoo, Fischler, Renate & Steve Ferrante, Phyllis Schlafly,

*John Olaf, John Edmund, Chris Edel, Wendy, Doris Samanda, Marcos David, Ívar Alejandro, Alicia, Ashley Marie, Henny, Amayah, Alux, Peter Anthony, Bridget Sophía, Mai, Thai, Isabella, Rita & Nick, Jon, Monica, Joe, Dom, Andy, Nick, Chris, Gaby, Dave, Tom, Cecilia, Rachel, Luís, Obdulio, Norma, Nora, Lillian, Yónatan, Karinis, Carolina, Joe & Zum, Chris & David Paul, Mary & Jeff, Jorge Luís & Alondra, Yelisse & Eusebio, Yasilda & Angel, Amarilis, Edilia, Teté, Fedora, Geller, Freddy & Rosaana, Orlandito, Orlando & Evelia, Juan José & Odilia, Corina, Michaela, Scott & Pinina, Milagros & Eric, Andrés & Sylvia, Jowanka, Oso, Victor, Gilberto & Joanne, Adriano & Olguita, Rodolfo & Gisela, Ace & Alicia, Stephen & Hortensia, George & Brenda, Jeff & Annette, Paul & Pilar, Nelson & Norma, Frishu & Ryan, Les & Wendy, Ines & Mark, Elliot & Alma, Sean & Kim Flynn, Pelegri, Rodríguez, Borges, Zylberberg, Johnson, Ireland, Oropeza, Henry, Clive, Kilmeade, diGenova, Sowell, Gullory, Swain, Nedd, Peterson, Valdary, Clarke, Dash, Walker, Reseau, Cuadra, Reigosa, Spadafora, Soto, Mendive, Eimmerman, Domínguez, Román, Barnichta, Rojas, Artiz, Vicky, Chichi, Abraira, Solano, Perdomo, Durán, Bloom, Duffin, Lyman, Raferty, Grembowitz, DeBiase, Carter, Feurstein, Ingraham, Jones, Basulto, Edmundson, Castellanos, Martínez, D'Souza, Aquino, LaMont, Boesen, Ferreiro, Gómez, Fernández, Jebian, Navarro, Tollinche, Bernstein, Cabrera, Acosta, Serro, Giberson, de la Nuez, Rouco, Ecker, Sullivan, Cuthbert, Shea, Aleck, Turley, Jindal, Hannity, Lima, Lloyd, Alegret, Krulik, Montero, Falcón, Hartke, Hughes, Pérez, Dubon, Otero, Marziano, Sánchez, Díaz, Mayo, Li, Andrews, Williams, Calero, Serra, Brannon, Wilmoth-Aguirre, Christophe, Velasco, Pierson, Medvin, Gatens, Sevin, Ramos, Reese, Medved, Levin, Goldman, Blades, TobyMac, 3rd Day, Coffey, Nissim Black, Lecrae, Fountainheads, Imaj, Mandisa, Milton & Mariela, Artemio, Fermín, Bartels, Lucas, Absolon, Korf, Weiss, Vuturo, Eamonn Quinn, Mundet García, Rosita Esquivel, **Spartans**, **Bisons**, **Alfareros**, &*

Everyone targeted for genocide who valiantly resists the jihadists.
May we reject the temptation to aspire to perpetually identify & liberate new
"victims" while we willfully ignore & refuse to shield the obvious targets of evil
in this age of genocide & martyrdom.

TABLE OF CONTENTS

1

INTRODUCTION

Beginning with the
Story of a Returned Missionary

I n the predawn hours of the morning after she arrived home in Florida from her first missionary immersion in the Dominican Republic, Pilar Sofía woke up and walked down the hallway in her parents' house where she had grown up.[1] Upon returning to her bedroom, she opened the door to her armoire with the curiosity of a nosy tourist. Although she knew that she recognized the contents, at that moment, Pilar Sofía could not accept that all those outfits and shoes actually belonged to her, because she perceived herself as a missionary serving in the Dominican Republic, not as a spoiled American brat submersed in opulence.

Her mother, a light sleeper, appeared in the doorway and tenderly asked her daughter why she was gawking at the apparel that adorned her own closet. The young missionary protested to her mom that this was not her wardrobe, nor her personal bathroom, nor her bedroom, nor even her house. She asked her mother how soon her father would awaken, so that they could load their luggage into their car, leave this luxurious hotel, and head home.

---

[1] All names used herein are true and are used with each missionary's permission.

1

Pilar Sofía's disorientation and denials brought tears to her mother's eyes. Pilar Sofía spent the next several weeks feeling judgmental and projecting anger at anyone whom she associated with material opulence, be they other adolescents, adults driving ostentatious automobiles, or anyone remotely related to her local upscale shopping mall (except, of course, for the cleaning and maintenance staff).

When we are recently returned missionaries, it is common for us to believe that we belong to the austere culture in which we were momentarily immersed, and not to the lavish culture of our native USA. A more acute manifestation of this estrangement-phenomenon is the fact that, immediately upon re-entry to their cultures of origin, some recently returned missionaries have testified that they perceive themselves as extraterrestrial visitors to Planet Earth.

During his first-ever short-term missionary immersion with the Jesuits in a slum of Santo Domingo, Adriano felt overwhelmed with a sense of helplessness, because he felt intensely called somehow to alleviate a modicum of the suffering that he had witnessed. When Adriano announced to Jesuit Father Eduardo Álvarez that he was planning to cut short his immersion in order to flee from the source of his distress, Father Álvarez confronted Adriano in order to help him discover the religious purpose for his life. Adriano recalled this beginning of his missionary vocation:

> *And when I went up on the roof of that provincial house, I learned a lesson that changed my life ... God used that priest to convey an idea to my heart and to change my attitude completely. He asked me if I knew what a circus was. At that time, I wasn't very happy about the whole thing and I told him, "Hey, I don't want to talk about dumb things here. What are you trying to say?" The priest said, "I want to talk to you about the circus. "I retorted, "These people don't even have enough to eat, and yet are you going to take me to a circus now?"*

He said, "No, I merely want to talk to you about the guys who perform on the trapeze in a circus." I asked him, "What does that have to do with me being here?" He said, "Everything." And I asked, "Why?" He said, "Let me tell you."

"In order for two people to get up on the trapeze swings, first they have to prepare themselves. And after they learn their act, and after they have exercised and practiced many times, then they climb up onto the trapeze platform, and measure everything. Then, one guy swings out, jumps off the swing, performs a pair of summersaults; and then he extends his hands so that his partner can catch him."

"That is when faith starts. Until the acrobat lets go of the swing and extends his hands, faith has not yet begun. It's only exercise and practice up until that point. Faith begins when he can no longer do anything except hope that that the other guy will catch him."

"That is faith. And that is what you do not want to do." I asked, "What do you mean by saying that I don't want to do that?" "Because ... you want to go home already. And you don't understand that if you leave now, then you are not giving God a chance to catch you."

After Adriano returned from his first missionary immersion, he continued to feel the temptation to despair. Although for almost a month, he attended daily mass in his search for guidance and consolation, he still found himself on the edge of tears nearly every evening. He would plead with God:

Do you understand what I'm feeling? Now, do something about it. I'm waiting for you to open your hands. Lord, do your job. You sent me to Santo Domingo for some reason. Now, show me the way. Show me the next step I need to take.

One night, he drove to Miami Beach with a plan to force God's hand. Adriano swam out about a quarter of a mile, turned to face the lights of the hotels along the shoreline, and began to tread water. When he was all the way out there and the buildings appeared very small, he descended all the way to the bottom, about thirty feet underwater, and sat down there. Then he challenged God directly:

> *Lord, do you remember Jonah and the whale? Well, it's time for you to do something for me because it's not worth continuing to live on this planet if I cannot do anything to help my people. My life has become meaningless because I don't know how you want me to contribute to a solution for all these suffering people to whom you've introduced me. Do something, please. Guide me and do it now.*

Of course, after a bit, Adriano began to run out of air. So he quickly decided to scramble back to the surface because he did not really want to die; he just wanted God to show him how to help suffering people according to God's divine plan.

A few weeks later, he was invited to meet a young lady named Alicia who had also just returned from a year-long missionary immersion in Santo Domingo. Together, they founded Amor en Acción (AeA), a missionary community that, among other commitments, serves as a bridge between the sister-dioceses of Miami, Florida and Port-de-Paix, Haiti.[2]

Amor en Acción

This book, *Ruined for Life*, is based primarily on post-missionary immersion experiences of my friends who are Miami-based and Saginaw-based Amor en Acción missionaries. (Several of them also serve as missionaries with the Missionalis Societas Ioannes Paulus II, Iglesia en Misión, Misión en Acción, and Pax Romana USA.)

Amor en Acción (AeA) refers to a voluntary, primarily lay, missionary community of the Roman Catholic Archdiocese of Miami, Florida and

---

[2] Amor e Acción is a missionary community founded by Cuban exiles in the USA's bicentennial year of 1976. For more information, see this missionary community's websites at: *http://www.amorenaccion.com & https://www.facebook.com/AmorenAccion/.*

the Diocese of Saginaw, Michigan. It serves as a bridge between the sister dioceses of Miami, Florida and Port-de-Paix, Haiti. AeA also faithfully supports several dioceses in the Dominican Republic in their efforts regarding evangelization, education, nutrition, and health promotion. In addition to its long-term, ongoing commitment to these people and projects, AeA members participate in short-term (two- or three-week-long) mission immersions in both the Dominican Republic and Haiti, in order to foster fellowship among ourselves and our Caribbean spiritual siblings.

Founded by Cuban exiles, the organization also enjoys a flourishing relationship with several dioceses of Cuba. As a missionary community, AeA is well aware that it inevitably engages in the transformative phenomenon known as "mission-in-reverse,"[3] whereby visiting missionaries and the people visited mutually evangelize each other toward a deeper level of faith and commitment. Josefina Chirino, a stalwart of AeA, noted the role of this transformative dynamic in her 2001 doctoral dissertation on AeA.[4]

Furthermore, AeA has become a reliable resource upon which the USCMA (United States Catholic Mission Association) and countless other missionary agencies and communities can draw as its members and leaders attempt to both comprehend and contribute to the burgeoning wave of missionary endeavors that feature long-term commitments combined with short-term immersions.

---

[3] Barbour, "Seeking Justice and Shalom in the City," 304; Gittins, *Bread for the Journey,* 55-71.

[4] Josefina Chirino, *The Continued Short-Term Mission Among the Poor of the Developing World: An Effective Tool in Ministry to Young Adults of the Developed World* (Miami Shores, FL: Barry University, 2001), 89.

What This Book Is About

This book is devoted to the need for reintegration by the deepening of conversion among post-immersion missionaries (that is, after they return "home" from the mission field).[5]

---

[5] A number of helpful academic studies are related to this one. Tina Moreau-Jones, in her 2002 survey of U.S. lay missionaries abroad which she compiled on behalf of the Catholic Network of Volunteer Service, the United States Catholic Mission Association, and the Saint Vincent Pallotti Center, categorizes and describes the pre-immersion formation that is currently provided to these missionaries. See Tina Moreau-Jones, *Gathering the Fragments: A Survey of Components for the Formation of International Lay Missioners*. (Washington, DC: Catholic Network of Volunteer Service, United States Catholic Mission Association, and Saint Vincent Palotti Center, 2002), 2-3. Monica Vandergrift, in her 1995 doctoral dissertation on post-immersion re-entry, probes the mental processes that transpire whenever events trigger memories of the immersion experience. See Monica Vandergrift, *Spirituality of Return: Celebrating Our Many Homecomings* (Ann Arbor, MI: UMI, 1991), 1ff. Jo Ann McCaffrey, in her 2005 doctoral dissertation on theological reflection for post-immersion missionaries, stresses the spiritually and emotionally tenuous status of recently returned post-immersion missionaries. McCaffrey also explores the utile role of images and emotions in a post-immersion integration process. See Jo Ann McCaffrey, *At Home in the Journey: Theological Reflection for Missioners in Transition* (Chicago, IL: Chicago Center for Global Ministries, 2005), 8-10. Josefina Chirino, in her 2001 doctoral dissertation on the value of short-term missionary immersions as a tool for evangelizing North American adolescents, emphasizes the vital role of the phenomenon of "mission-in-reverse." See Josefina Chirino, *The Continued Short-Term Mission Among the Poor of the Developing World: An Effective Tool in Ministry to Young Adults of the Developed World* (Miami Shores, FL: Barry University, 2001), 89. See also Claude Marie Barbour, "Seeking Justice and Shalom in the City," *International Review of Mission* 73 (Geneva, Schwyz: World Council of Churches, July 1984): 304; and Anthony Gittins, *Bread for the Journey: The Mission of Transformation and the Transformation of Mission* (Maryknoll, NY: Orbis, 1993), 55-71. Kurt Alan Ver Beek, in his 2006 quantitative study of post-immersion missionaries, observes that external, objective indicators of conversion are only favorably impacted by participation in ongoing post-immersion missionary support communities. See Kurt Alan Ver Beek, *Lessons from the Sapling: Review of Research on Short-term Missions, Study Abroad, and Service Learning*. (Grand Rapids, MI: Calvin College, 2006). Jack Jezreel echoes Ver Beek's findings. See Jack Jezreel, *Just Faith Introductory Seminar* (Miami Gardens, FL: Saint Thomas University, March, 2003). Not coincidentally, the bishops and theologians of the Second Ecumenical Council of the Vatican (Vatican II) reached the same conclusion in their seminal decree on the church's missionary activity, *Ad Gentes Divinitus*. See Vatican Council II, *Ad Gentes Divinitus: Decree on the Church's Missionary Activity* (Città del Vaticano:

Through an intensive study of AeA, I learned to distinguish between methods that tend to succeed in facilitating the deepening of the conversion of returned missionaries and methods that tend to fail. Thus, this book is the result of my practical-theological study of the post-mission conversion experiences of these missionaries.

The thesis of this study is twofold.

- First, the thesis states that, in order for the conversion process of returning short-term missionaries to deepen, greater attention must be paid in the post-immersion period to providing *ongoing support* for sustaining and expanding the process of conversion.

- Second, it states that this ongoing support needs to be grounded in the principle of the *preferential option for the poor*, as found in the Bible and Catholic social doctrine.

By means of this book, I hope to improve our understanding of how post-mission immersion experiences affect the profundity of the

---

Libreria Editrice Vaticana, 1965), 14. Beyond the academic sphere, there are also numerous practical manuals laden with detailed suggestions on how to manage post-mission-immersion re-entry for oneself, or a mission-sending body, or a church congregation or parish. Among them are: Peter Jordan, *Re-Entry: Making the Transition from Missions to Life at Home* (Seattle, WA: Youth With a Mission, 1992); Mack and Leann Stiles, *Mack and Leann's Guide to Short-Term Missions* (Downers Grove, IL: InterVarsity, 2000); Neal Pirolo, *Serving as Senders* (San Diego, CA: Emmaus Road Int'l, 1991); Neal Pirolo, *The Re-Entry Team: Caring for Your Returning Missionaries* (San Diego, CA: Emmaus Road Int'l, 2000); Lisa Espineli Chinn, *Reentry Guide for Short-Term Mission Leaders* (Orlando, FL: Deeper Roots, 1998); Julie Lupien and Michelle Scheidt, *Remaining Faithful: How Do I Keep My Experience Alive? A Manual for Reflection, Integration, and Prayer After a Short-Term Experience in Another Culture* (Longmont, CO: From Mission to Mission, 2005); Mike Daley and Matt Kemper, *Preparing for Your Mission Trip Journey: a Practical and Spiritual Guide for Your Mission Trip* (Cincinnati, OH: Glenmary, 2009); Marion Knell, *Burn Up or Splash Down: Surviving the Culture Shock of Re-Entry* (Tyrone, GA: Authentic, 2007); Melissa Chaplin, *Returning Well: Your Guide to Thriving Back "Home" After Serving Cross-Culturally* (Newton, MA: Newton, 2015); and Amy Young, *Looming Transitions: Starting and Finishing Well in Cross-Cultural Service* (Lawrence, KS: CreateSpace, 2015).

Christian conversion process, and to formulate strategies that can more effectively support that conversion process in the post-immersion stage. My hope is that current and future missionaries will be able to consult this book in order to help themselves understand what really happens to short-term missionaries after immersion. Reading this book might help them to avoid some pitfalls and to navigate more confidently through their initial years of trial and error. It might also help them to design more effective post-immersion programs.

Another Returned Missionary Story

My compadre and former star-student Andrés finally answered God's longstanding missionary call to him in the wake of Haiti's massive earthquake of January 2010. I accompanied him as he explored Haiti for the first time. He was enchanted by the Haitian people, and particularly by the missionary sisters who have dedicated their lives to protecting, accompanying, and guiding young and elderly people alike. While we were immersed, Andrés drank in every place and experience, and genuinely embraced the people.

Because we work together, I was able to observe up-close his attitudes and behaviors ever since we returned. Even though we only spent a week in Haiti, he sorely missed the people and the places day and night, especially the fascinating missionary sisters and lay people of the city of Jean-Rabel.

At work and at home, Andrés was unusually quiet and distant, because he was recalling and pondering the details of our journey. These included visits to orphanages, a poor house for indigent disabled elderly, a flattened technical school where many nuns and young women were crushed to death, a convalescent home for one of the principal priest-mentors of AeA, rural schools and churches, a diocesan Caritas office, convents, and neighborhoods constructed by a church-sponsored housing ministry.

Of course, as his compadre and a veteran missionary, I purposely engaged him in conversations about his post-immersion feelings. Andrés told me that he was surprised how intensely he yearned to return to and linger in Jean-Rabel. His wife Sylvia, my comadre, was worried about this sudden change in her husband. Andrés was in a liminal state after we first returned. His career as a missionary was a chapter not yet written.

However, his immediate prognosis for deeper conversion as a Christian missionary was predictably promising, because his pre-immersion relationships with God, his church, and his family were very strong, and because the school where he works has seven other AeA missionaries who are available to him on a daily basis. Furthermore, our school principal sincerely encourages missionary activity, including travel, consciousness-raising, and fundraising. Each year, she invites us to give post-immersion presentations to the student body, faculty, staff, and administrators. Perhaps most significantly, she and her husband (also a Catholic school principal) boldly endorsed our missionary devotion by taking the AeA missionary plunge and joining us on a recent immersion in Haiti.

Andrés' spiritual progress means so much to me on many levels because he is my true friend, my compadre, my former student, my colleague, and because I patiently conveyed God's missionary call to him for over a decade and a half. We have known each other since 1992, and we are bound together sacramentally because his oldest child is my goddaughter. If God wills it, then we will become two related missionary families (parents and children included); or should I say, one missionary family?

I have been thrilled to witness his ever-increasing spiritual growth, his openness to God, to the people of Haiti, and to the spiritual and moral needs of both his own children and his students. Based on the tremendous fruit that he has consistently borne in his previous endeavors of spiritual leadership, I cannot help but feel delighted regarding the plentiful harvest that Andrés will surely produce – now that he has finally heeded his vocation to become an overseas missionary.[6]

His challenges with post-immersion reintegration call to mind my own initial post-immersion experience when I came back from Venezuela in 1989. I too yearned to return. I too felt out of place. I too thought about Ibero-America and her people day and night. I too was a chapter not yet written, as I tottered on the threshold among geographic and spiritual cultures.

What Led to My Concern

Several years ago, one of the founders of Amor en Acción observed that the movement evolved as a missionary community comprised exclusively of leaders, because those who have not proven capable of crafting their own techniques for keeping their post-immersion missionary spirit and commitment alive had gradually drifted away. Obviously, this is not the ideal post-immersion modus operandi for a missionary community that is an official agent of two US dioceses and several Caribbean dioceses.[7]

What happens to a neophyte short-term missionary who has just returned from that paradigm-shattering initial immersion experience? What will be his or her long-term trajectory as a disciple of Christ in general and as a Christian missionary in particular? I have observed that our respective futures as missionaries and as Christians are in flux when we disembark from the vessel that brings us "home" from the immersion to the land of our childhood and adolescence.

---

[6] Matthew 3:8; Matthew 7:17-19; Luke 3:8.

[7] In the USA: the Archdiocese of Miami, Florida and the Diocese of Saginaw, Michigan; in Haiti: the Archdiocese of Port-au-Prince, and the Dioceses of Port-de-Paix and Gros Morne; in the Dominican Republic: the Dioceses of San Pedro de Macorís and Santiago de los Caballeros; in Cuba: the Dioceses of Santa Clara and Holguín.

As a fervent missionary for more than three decades, I am concerned about the nature and profundity of the Christian conversion process of missionaries after they return from mission immersions. I want to help missionary communities to develop consistent methods for improving our praxis of missionary formation after mission immersions because, despite the fact that my missionary communities consistently excel at the "before" and the "during" of mission immersion, the "after" component emerges as our weakest link in the chain of missionary formation – even though this is often due to factors that are beyond our control, such as the fact that many of our post-immersion missionaries live out of town on university campuses.

First Glance at
Amor en Acción's Returned-Missionary Model

AeA is a diminutive but important and fruitful pioneer of the relatively recent yet potent and burgeoning model of Christian missionary work, which is the lay faithful engaging in long-term commitments coupled with short-term overseas immersions. In fact, AeA was formally founded only a year after Maryknoll began sending laity on short-term missionary immersions.[8]

The prior dominant model among Roman Catholics was that of consecrated sisters, brothers, and priests dwelling for decades in the "missionary fields." In light of this original model, scant attention was paid to post-immersion concerns. Returned missionaries were simply given time to rest, pray, and visit loved ones. However, almost two decades into this new millennium, some missionary communities and agencies have awoken to the conspicuous need for

---

[8] Tom Roberts, "Maryknoll Marks 35 Years of Sending Laity to Foreign Missions," *National Catholic Reporter* 46 (Kansas City, MO: National Catholic Reporter, June 25, 2010): 16; Robert J. Priest, Terry Dischinger, Steve Rasmussen, and C.M. Brown, "Researching the Short-Term Mission Movement, *Missiology* xxxiv (Wilmore, KY: American Society of Missiology, October 2006): 431-450.

intentional and systematic procedures designed to promote post-immersion reintegration and conversion.

Maryknoll, for example, now provides a month-long residential post-immersion re-entry program for its lay missionaries. In fact, nowadays, there are even organizations that specialize in post-immersion debriefing and reintegration. Notable among them are From Mission to Mission in Longmont, Colorado and the Overseas Ministries Study Center in New Haven, Connecticut.

Like many other missionary communities, AeA consistently excels at pre-immersion preparation and planning. The same is true of the quality of our in-field immersions, due mainly to our attention to maintaining communicative and mutually respectful relationships with the local churches with whom we collaborate. Unlike many missionary groups which employ short-term immersions, AeA takes great pains to regularly inquire of the official and unofficial ordained, consecrated, and lay leaders regarding how we can most effectively support their ongoing evangelization and social service efforts.

Over the last forty plus years, we have gradually developed some highly effective methods of facilitating post-immersion reintegration and continuing Christian conversion. The four main planks of AeA's post-immersion platform are:

- Formal post-immersion re-entry debriefing meetings (employing the McCaffrey method[9]) and liturgies;

- Ongoing consciousness-raising and fundraising involvement with AeA throughout the year;

- Weekly missionary formation meetings in the *Pequeña Habana* neighborhood of Miami; and

---

[9] Jo Ann McCaffrey, *At Home in the Journey* (Chicago, IL: Chicago Center for Global Ministries, 2005).

- Weekend reflection days featuring visiting missionaries, clergy, and bishops as guest speakers.

There are three issues on the downside of AeA's post-immersion procedures.

- Firstly, in the old days, numerous first-time post-immersion missionaries were invited to stay involved in AeA's work without the benefit of any specifically focused re-entry debriefing meetings.

- Secondly, our Saginaw community is so shorthanded in terms of leadership resources that post-immersion re-entry meetings are often given short shrift.

- Thirdly, because a significant number of our young missionaries attend out-of-town universities, they miss out on the bulk of our efforts at promoting post-immersion reintegration and conversion.

The most glaring problem is that, due to geographic distance, we do not effectively reach all of our post-immersion missionaries.[10]

Hopes & Claims

After a couple of decades of missionary experience, but before undertaking my formal research, I became convinced that newly returned missionaries, if given the invitation to partake of a comprehensive program of appropriate post-immersion formation activities, will more consistently blossom into Christian disciples who are permeated with the Holy Spirit. As a result, during the post-immersion

---

[10] It is encouraging that AeA's leaders have already solicited our preliminary findings regarding post-immersion conversion and begun to skillfully and successfully implement a number of our most urgent recommendations. Particularly within the Miami Archdiocese, our post-immersion reentry debriefing meetings have been refined, in part, because they have addressed some of the concerns identified by this research project.

phase, their transformative missionary experiences will continue to bear Godly fruit in their local churches and communities.

I will articulate here some of the factors that contribute to the strengthening or weakening of religious fervor of missionaries after they arrive home from mission immersions. I aspire to address these factors in order to devise a system for minimizing the waning and augmenting the waxing of missionary enthusiasm and dedication. In the words of John Kavanaugh, I hope to assist returned missionaries to forge practical "spiritualities of cultural resistance" that are more faithful to the vocation of a Christian missionary.[11]

Before I undertook this study, I surmised that the following post-immersion factors contributed to the weakening of missionary zeal among missionaries:

- The creature comforts of consumerism (such as air conditioning, hot water for bathing, a full refrigerator and kitchen cupboard, gigantic stores and shopping malls packed with merchandise, and a personal automobile);

- Family members and friends who verbally or nonverbally express a pronounced lack of interest in, or even outright hostility toward, repeatedly listening to the missionaries' immersion stories;

- Friends, classmates, co-workers, and neighbors who encourage a lifestyle laden with competition measured only by material success;

- Exposure to the prejudiced opinion that all indigent people merit their respective stations of misery in life because of their own sloth, foolishness, or stupidity.

---

[11] John Francis Kavanaugh, *Still Following Christ in a Consumer Society: The Spirituality of Cultural Resistance* (Maryknoll, NY: Orbis, 1991), i ff.

By contrast, before I began this study, I sensed that spiritual growth among post-immersion missionaries is reinforced when families, friends, fellow parishioners, and coworkers convey understanding and solidarity with the missionaries:

- By encouraging the missionaries to share their immersion narratives and photographs by listening and looking, even repeatedly;

- By pointing out, during conversations with the post-immersion missionaries, injustices and stark inequalities in daily life and the daily news;

- By expressing genuine interest in potentially participating in future mission immersions;

- By facilitating the adaptation of lifestyle and consumption habits that progress toward the goal of simplicity – an objective that can be achieved by reducing the personal consumption of material resources, by exhibiting less selfishness, and by practicing the virtue of generosity more consistently;

- By offering to accompany the post-immersion missionary in local community-service volunteering;

- By encouraging the post-immersion missionary to dedicate more time and effort to regular prayer, meditation, reflection, biblical study, and spiritual formation opportunities; and

- By fostering engagement in some form of enduring local ministerial commitment, whether it be related to the overseas missions or not.

Now, in order to facilitate the reading ahead, it may be helpful to define the most salient terms used in my study.

Defining Pertinent Terms

Ruined for Life

What does the title of this study, *Ruined for Life*, signify? The phrase itself, is the informal slogan of my former missionary association, the Jesuit Volunteers International (JVI) and its umbrella organization, the Jesuit Volunteer Corps (JVC).[12] The phrase was coined by the association's founder, the late Jesuit Father Jack Morris. I have appropriated this phrase for several interrelated reasons.

- First, the concept of "ruination" conveys the truth that missionary immersion experiences permanently "mark" us and "imprint" themselves upon our value systems, much as certain sacraments do. In other words, our consciousnesses are forever "scarred" by God, who seeks to recreate us by beckoning us to emulate his servants Abraham, Moses, Jesus, and Paul by abandoning our comfortable confines and journeying abroad or out into the desert.

- Second, missionary immersions "diminish" our capacity to fit seamlessly and quietly back into our hyper-consumerist U.S. society,[13] because we are haunted, pursued, prodded, and bothered by images, voices, and memories of our friends who are struggling to survive physiologically, spiritually, and emotionally in often subhuman circumstances, while we return to a deluge of superfluous and dependence-inducing material luxuries.

- Third, the slogan further indicates that we missionaries can grow in our willingness to "sacrifice" many of our personal goals, like the parabolic grain of wheat,[14] in order to engender an enhanced

---

[12] Judy Coode, "Ruined for Life," *Sojourners* (Washington, DC: Sojourners, August 2006).

[13] Kavanaugh, *Still Following Christ*, i.

[14] John 12:24.

existence for people who are neglected, abandoned, or systematically marginalized, oppressed, and exploited.

Conversion

In both a poetic and a prophetic sense, mission immersion experiences tend to "ruin" us, so that our hearts and minds may become malleable enough to allow God to reshape them radically like clay in a potter's hands,[15] and so as to better prepare us to nurture a "culture of life"[16] that is congruent with the biblical concept of the Reign of God.[17]

During their conference in Aparecida, Brazil, the Catholic bishops of Ibero-America and the Caribbean (under the spiritual and editorial guidance of both Pope Benedict XVI and the future Pope Francis I) defined missionary "conversion" in simple, straightforward, and radically challenging terms:

> Conversion is the initial response of those who have listened to the Lord with admiration, who believe in Him through the action of the Holy Spirit, and who decide to become his friends and follow Him – changing how they think and live, accepting the cross of Christ, conscious that to die to sin is to attain life.[18]

Immersion

The term "immersion" signifies the period of time spent abroad in the mission field; in the case of AeA, we refer to Haiti, the Dominican

---

[15] Genesis 2:7; Job 10:9; Isaiah 29:15-16; Isaiah 64:7.

[16] Pope John Paul II, *Evangelium Vitae: The Gospel of Life: On the Value and Inviolability of Human Life* (Città del Vaticano: Libreria Editrice Vaticana, 1995), 28.

[17] Matthew 6:33; Mark 1:15; Luke 8:21; John 3:3; Acts 28:31; Romans 14:17; 1 Corinthians 6:9; Colossians 4:11.

[18] Episcopal Conference of Latin America & the Caribbean, *Aparecida Concluding Document* (Città del Vaticano: Libreria Editrice Vaticana, May 2007), 278b.

Republic, and Cuba. The term "post-immersion" refers to the phase that ensues after the missionaries return home to the USA. In that context, the term "post-immersion re-entry meeting" alludes to the first post-immersion meeting hosted by AeA, which is designed to welcome home the missionaries, to debrief them, and to facilitate reflection on their immersion and post-immersion experiences and insights.

In that same vein, the term "post-immersion re-entry Eucharistic liturgy" refers to the annual mass celebrated after all of the summer missionary groups have returned home; its intentions are to welcome the missionaries back home and to foment a sense of community among all the members of AeA and their families.

Liminality

The term "liminal" means threshold. This period of transition or threshold crossing is unique and is referred to by anthropologists Arnold Van Gennep and Victor Turner, as well as by Robert Oden and Jo Ann McCaffrey, as "liminality."[19]

In a real sense, by returning, the missionary goes through a liminal experience; in a sense, he or she becomes a misfit by virtue of shifting from one culture to another. His or her trajectory as a Christian disciple and as a missionary suddenly arrives at an unforeseen yet crucial crossroads. The recently returned missionary typically becomes aware that he or she has experienced a mind-blowing revelation from God, becomes predictably bewildered about how to proceed within his or her homeland in light of this newly discovered paradigm of God's Reign, and consequently is often timorous about communicating his or her narratives to non-missionaries.

---

[19] Arnold Van Gennep, *The Rites of Passage* (Chicago, IL: University of Chicago, 1960), 21; Victor Turner, *The Forest of Symbols* (Ithaca, NY: Cornell, 1967), 93; Robert Oden, *God and Mankind* (Chantilly, VA: Teaching Company, 1998); McCaffrey, *At Home in the Journey,* 1ff.

Mission

The term mission, in its original sense, means "to send." Therefore, the term "missionary" means "someone who is sent." Pope Saint Paul VI, in *Evangelii Nuntiandi*, and the Pontifical Council for Interreligious Dialogue in *Dialogue and Proclamation*, delineate seven principal components of Christian mission: evangelization, proclamation, prophetic witness, dialogue, liberation, conversion, and reconciliation.[20] Maryknoll Father Raymond Finch identifies two legitimate but distinct New Testament paradigms for mission:[21]

- "Go and make disciples of all the nations;"[22] and

- "Sanctify Christ as Lord in your hearts. Always be ready to give an explanation to anyone who asks you for a reason for your hope, but do it with gentleness and reverence, keeping your conscience clear."[23]

The former emphasizes proclamation while the latter leans toward ethical witness.

Missiology, the branch of theology which studies mission, includes the study of all aspects of Christian mission, including evangelization, conversion, mutuality, cultural, familial, and personal impact, unforeseen consequences, conflict, prophetic confrontation of injustice, and advocacy on behalf of voiceless people.

---

[20] Pope Paul VI, *Evangelii Nuntiandi: Apostolic Exhortation on Evangelization in the Modern World* (Città del Vaticano: Liberia Editrice Vaticana, 1975); Pontifical Council for Interreligious Dialogue and the Congregation for the Evangelization of Peoples, *Dialogue and Proclamation: Reflection and Orientations on Interreligious Dialogue and the Proclamation of the Gospel of Jesus Christ* (Città del Vaticano: Libreria Editrice Vaticana, 1991).

[21] Raymond Finch, MM, "Preach Always; When Necessary, Use Words" (Chicago, IL: USCMA Mission Congress, 2000).

[22] Matthew 28:19.

[23] 1st Peter 3:15-16.

Thomas Groome's
Method of Shared Christian Praxis

The principal guiding method of theological-ministerial reflection for this study is Thomas Groome's "Shared Christian Praxis" as delineated in his book titled *Sharing Faith*.[24]

Although his method was developed specifically for religious education, it is adaptable to pastoral ministry, including missionary work.[25]

In the case of AeA (and of most other missionary groups), the natural focusing activity is participation in an initial missionary immersion (known in missionary circles as "baptism by salt water"). This focusing activity serves as our constitutive experience and rite of passage, although not in an exclusive sense.

Let us look at this experience through the lens of Groome's five movements. In examining these five movements in relation to the mission experience, I will weave into the narrative an introductory overview of the chapters of this book as they link to Groome's method.

With the aim of discerning and applying wisdom, Groome's method is organized around a focusing activity followed by five movements.[26]

First Movement

In addressing Groome's first movement, the "naming and expressing of the present praxis,"[27] I focus on my own experiences of mission immersions with both the Jesuit Volunteers International (JVI) and

---

[24] Thomas Groome, *Sharing Faith: A Comprehensive Approach to Religious Education and Pastoral Ministry: The Way of Shared Praxis* (San Francisco, CA: HarperCollins, 1991).

[25] See Groome, *Sharing Faith*, 133-134, 295-297, 302-308, 379-406.

[26] Groome points to Baruch Spinoza as the principal expositor of conatus or conation, which Groome argues is approximately synonymous with wisdom and which intends to foster ongoing conversion. Groome, *Sharing Faith*, 26-29.

[27] Groome, *Sharing Faith*, 146.

AeA, as well as those of my fellow missionaries. In order to document AeA's current praxis, I chose a focus-group interviewing process which is a qualitative method of research appropriated from the discipline of ethnography.[28] To complement this method, I apply Paulo Freire's hermeneutical analysis to discern the "generative themes"[29] expressed by my interview subjects. I preface this segment with a chronological sketch of formative influences that led me to respond to my missionary vocation.

In this first chapter, after describing my compadre's first post-immersion experience as a way of illustrating the factors that provoked my ministerial concern, I introduce AeA's present post-immersion praxis and my resultant concerns, hopes, and claims. I clarify the meaning of this study's title and some pertinent missiological terms. Finally, I delineate Groome's shared Christian praxis as the overall framework for my study, and identify some dialogue-partners, namely Bellah, Kavanaugh, Rambo, Gelpi, Bosch, and the body of magisterial Catholic teaching known as Catholic Social Doctrine (CSD).

In chapter two, I will continue to follow Groome's first movement by laying out my own experiences of missionary endeavors, including every aspect of the missionary life, from early faith formation, to the roots of the missionary vocation, to the pre-immersion, immersion, and post-immersion phases. In chapters three and four, in accord with this first movement, I will document the post-immersion experiences of AeA missionaries.

---

[28] David Fetterman, *Ethnography: Step by Step* (Newbury Park, CA: Sage, 1989), 1.

[29] Paulo Freire, *Pedagogy of the Oppressed* (New York, NY: Continuum, 1995), 61ff, 110ff. A "generative theme" is a crucial component of the "dialogical" method of liberation education. Liberation education chooses "dialogical" (interactive, student-centered, cooperative discovery) models and methods of education over "banking" (passive, teacher-centered, dispensation) models and methods. Groome defines a "generative theme" as a historical issue, question, value, belief, concept, event, or situation that has the power to draw the participants into active engagement because it is already meaningful and important in their lives. Groome, *Sharing Faith*, 156.

Second Movement

Groome's second movement, the "critical reflection on the present action," consists of an interdisciplinary examination of the initial praxis through the lens of select philosophical and social-science literature that explores the comprehensive roles that hyper-materialism and self-absorption play in our US society.[30] This scrutiny yields insights that help to establish the cultural and philosophical context that I subsequently employ to envision a renewed meth-od for promoting the reintegration and ongoing transformation of returned missionaries.

To this end, I draw upon the insights of the late Christian social philosopher Jesuit Father John Kavanaugh and Durkheimian sociologist Robert Bellah and his team.[31] In chapter five, I will undertake the aforementioned critical reflection on AeA's current post-immersion praxis through the lenses of sociology and philosophy.

Third Movement

Groome's third movement, "making accessible the Christian story and vision," entails the exposition and application of conversion theologies.[32] With this goal in mind, I call upon the insights of lay conversion-theologian Lewis Rambo, Jesuit conversion-theologian Father Donald Gelpi, South African missiologist David Bosch, and the corpus of CSD. In chapter six, I will offer an exposition of these conversion theologies as they relate to missiology.

---

[30] Groome, *Sharing Faith*, 147.

[31] Robert Bellah, Richard Madsen, William Sullivan, Ann Swidler, and Steven Tipton, *Habits of the Heart: Individualism and Commitment in American Life* (Berkeley, CA: University of California, 1985), 1ff.

[32] Groome, *Sharing Faith*, 147.

Fourth Movement

In order to accomplish Groome's fourth movement, which is initiating a "dialectical hermeneutic in order to appropriate the Christian vision and story to the participants' stories and visions,"[33] I bring together the experiences of AeA missionaries, the sociological analysis of Bellah et al., the philosophical contributions of Kavanaugh, and the conversion-theologies of Rambo, Gelpi, Bosch, and CSD.

Fifth Movement

In order to address Groome's fifth and final movement, the "decision and response for lived Christian faith,"[34] I suggest some normative principles for the post-immersion re-entry process of missionaries, and I will propose a reform of AeA's methods of guiding the formation of missionaries once they return from immersions.

Therefore, in chapter seven, I conclude with Groome's fourth and fifth movements by continuing to explore the dialectical hermeneutic among the post-immersion experiences of AeA missionaries and the earlier-mentioned conversion-oriented sociological, philosophical, and theological thinkers – all in order to generate insights that might further the holistic reintegration and ongoing conversion of post-immersion missionaries. I also propose some reforms of AeA's current post-immersion conversion-promotion program for returned missionaries.

Now let us turn to a narrative of my own formation and praxis as a missionary.

---

[33] Groome, *Sharing Faith*, 147.

[34] Groome, *Sharing Faith*, 148.

2

MY EXPERIENCES BEFORE, DURING, & AFTER

MISSIONARY IMMERSIONS

I n the introductory chapter, we explored my compadre Andrés's initial missionary immersion and post-immersion experiences, delineated my concern, offered a thumbnail of AeA's current praxis, expressed my hopes and claims, and identified resources that facilitated this study. In this second chapter, we focus on how I have been "ruined for life" – in other words, how I have been transformed into a missionary over time by crucial experiences, crises, and quests, as well as by encounters and interactions with advocates[1] of the Catholic Christian faith.

My conversion can be categorized as one of intensification,[2] which denotes a deeper, revitalized commitment to the faith that I have always espoused. Therefore, I reveal pivotal personal narratives from my own pre-immersion, immersion, and post-immersion missionary experiences that have contributed to my own ongoing conversion as a Christian missionary. Again, this sharing of missionary narratives follows Groome's first movement, namely elaborating a narrative description of the current praxis.

---

[1] In his sequential stage model of conversion, Rambo highlights the importance of the "advocate" of a particular, established religious tradition in the post-crisis phases of conversion. Lewis Ray Rambo, *Understanding Religious Conversion* (New Haven, CT: Yale University, 1993), 17.

[2] Rambo proposes five "Types of Conversion:" apostasy or defection, intensification, affiliation, institutional transition, and tradition transition. Rambo, *Understanding Religious Conversion*, 12-14.

Pre-Immersion Missionary Mentoring
& Discipleship in the Domestic Church in the USA

Missionary calls often testify to the extra-biblical proverb, "Charity begins at home" – in the unconventional sense that missionaries often begin learning how to discern their vocations within their families of origin. So it was with me. I attribute my missionary zeal primarily to the example that my father set for me.

For as long as I knew my father, a former seminarian, he was dedicated to volunteer church ministry, primarily via the Legion of Mary. My father regularly visited and administered the Eucharist to infirm and shut-in people. He engaged in door-to-door evangelization, both locally and in other dioceses, and offered religious instruction and sacramental preparation to people in their homes. My father was generous by nature. He voluntarily did chores and home repairs for indigent, disabled, and elderly people. While they lived in Miami Gardens, my parents spent the better part of each Sunday morning shuttling feeble and elderly people to and from church.

Most of my father's career consisted of teaching the English language to recently arrived adult immigrants from around the globe, at Lindsey Hopkins Vocational-Technical School in the Overtown neighborhood of Miami. While the eight of us children were growing up, my father would bring some of his ethnically diverse students to our home for dinner. After some of us had grown up and moved out, my parents invited one of my father's former Haitian students to move in with them, until he could improve his immigration status, graduate from college, and establish financial independence.

In the summer following my kindergarten year, just after my first school principal, Sister Veronica of the School Sisters of Notre Dame, heeded the call to leave Visitation School near Miami Gardens to serve the Meso-American and Caribbean migrant agricultural workers of Immokalee as a social worker, my parents decided to take us there to visit her so that we could become aware of how these exploited and marginalized children of God were struggling to survive and how the Catholic church was responding holistically to their glaring needs.[3]

As we walked amidst the elevated trailer homes, I remember hearing and watching the toilets flush right out onto the ground; apparently, the trailers had plumbing flowing into them but no septic or sewer systems to handle the outbound waste water. I remember observing wide-eyed the toddlers who were sitting on the ground next to their elevated mobile homes playing with toys, as the sewage was suddenly flushed out of the trailer toilets and splashed up onto the seated children. That glimpse of misery has stuck with me and played a role in influencing me to become a missionary – by engraving upon my conscience an indelible image of my neighbor and by evoking from me basic human compassion.

While in middle school, my siblings and I joined our parents on door-to-door Legion of Mary evangelization campaigns known as *Peregrinationes Pro Christo*. I as I grew older, I continued to cultivate

---

[3] Many biblical books, along with the surfeit of Catholic magisterial social documents, insist upon rights for and solidarity with immigrants. Exodus 12, 22, 23; Leviticus 17, 18, 19, 23, 25; Numbers 15, 19, 35; Deuteronomy 10, 23, 24, 26, 29, 31; Isaiah 14; Jeremiah 7, 22; Ezekiel 22, 47; Zechariah 10; Pope Leo XIII, *Rerum Novarum: On Captial and Labor* (Città del Vaticano: Libreria Editrice Vaticana, 1800), 47; Pope Pius XII, *Exsul Familia Nazarethana: Apostolic Constitution on Migrants* (Città del Vaticano: Libreria Editrice Vaticana, 1952); Vatican Council II, *Gaudium et Spes: The Church in the Modern World* (Città del Vaticano: Libreria Editrice Vaticana, 1965), 27; Pope Paul VI, *Populorum Progressio: On the Development of* Peoples (Città del Vaticano: Libreria Editrice Vaticana, 1967), 69; Pope John Paul II, *Laborem Exercens: On Human Work* (Città del Vaticano: Libreria Editrice Vaticana, 1981), 23; Pope John Paul II, *Centesimus Annus: On the 100th Anniversary of Rerum Novarum* (Città del Vaticano: Libreria Editrice Vaticana, 1991), 48; Pontifical Council for the Pastoral Care of Migrants and Itinerant People, *Refugees: A Challenge to Solidarity* (Città del Vaticano: Libreria Editrice Vaticana, 1992), 6; Pontifical Council for the Pastoral Care of Migrants and Itinerant People, *Erga Migrantes Caritas Christi: The Love of Christ towards Migrants* (Città del Vaticano: Libreria Editrice Vaticana, 2004); Pontifical Council for Justice and Peace, *Compendium*, 298, 308; Pope Benedict XVI, *Caritas in Veritate: Charity in Truth: On Integral Human Development* (Città del Vaticano: Libreria Editrice Vaticana, 2009), 62.

these virtuous habits imparted to me by my parents, through volunteer community service by way of my parish Boy Scout troop and my secondary school Key Club.[4]

While an undergraduate at Boston College, I served in a variety of organizations that focused on the promotion of human rights both domestically and internationally, namely, our Committee to End Apartheid in South Africa, our Human and Civil Rights Lecture Series,[5] our AHANA[6] Caucus, our campus NAACP[7] chapter, and our campus Amnesty International[8] chapter. I also served as a BC Appalachian Volunteer during one Easter vacation.

After college, I served for a year in Central and South America as a member of the Jesuit Volunteers International. After my return from Venezuela in late 1989, I have collaborated with: AeA, Missionary Society of John Paul II, Iglesia en Misión, Misión en Acción, Saint Maurice Parish's Hunger Program, Marianist Living In Faith Experience (LIFE), Phyllis Schlafly Eagles, Turning Point, Susan B. Anthony List, Officer Snook program of Youth Environmental Programs and the US Coast Guard, Saint Stephen Parish's Protectors of God's Creation,

---

[4] Lamentably, some Kiwanis and Rotary branches donate funds to abortion conglomerate Planned Parenthood and abortion promoter UNICEF. Kiwanis sponsors the Key Club and Circle K. Rotary sponsors Inner Wheel, Rotaract, and Interact.

[5] We hosted Dith Pran, Coretta Scott King, Corazon Aquino, Maki Mandela, Donald Woods, Benjamin Hooks, Tony Brown, Dick Gregory, Yolanda King, Bernice King, and Martin Luther King III.

[6] AHANA is an abbreviation of African-, Hispanic-, Asian-, and Native-American.

[7] Regrettably, recent leaders of the National Association for the Advancement of Colored People have veered away from the NAACP's tradition of pioneering advocacy for true liberty, equal opportunity, and justice. For example, their obdurate advocacy of the PROMISE program, which often debilitates school discipline, has tarnished the NAACP. Hopefully, the NAACP will return to its original calling.

[8] I remained an active Amnesty International (AI) member until the worldwide body opted to undermine the essential principles of human rights by promoting the territorial expansion and frequency of abortions of unborn human babies. For that reason, in the summer of 2007, the president of the Pontifical Council for Justice and Peace, Cardinal Renato Martino, ordered all Catholic seminaries, universities, schools, parishes, and dioceses to end collaboration with AI and to shutter their AI chapters.

Pax Romana's International Movement of Catholic Students, International Young Catholic Students (IYCS), Clarion Project, Prager University, Gatestone Institute, Christians United for Israel (CUFI), Young America's Foundation (YAF), American Center for Law and Justice (ACLJ), In Defense of Christians (IDC), and the Philos Project.

Most recently, I have been called to devote my energies to the Iraqi Christian Relief Council (ICRC) which advocates for the survival of Christians (and other religious minorities) and Christianity itself, in the biblical lands of Iraq, Syria, Jordan, Lebanon, and Turkey. The ICRC actively supports the medical, nutritional, educational, orphanage, refugee relief, and rebuilding work of the Assyrian Church of the East Relief Organization (ACERO), the Catholic Near East Welfare Association (CNEWA), Aid to the Church in Need (ACN), the Assyrian Aid Society (AAS), and especially, the faithful and courageous efforts of Catholic missionary sisters such as the Dominican Sisters of Saint Catherine of Siena and the Missionaries of Charity, some of whom have been abducted, raped, and martyred by Islamic jihadists.

Since this chapter documents the trajectory of my missionary conversion, it may be helpful here to sketch the preliminary stages of my spiritual evolution. At home, our parents taught us to pray before and after meals, before bed, as well as to pray a weekly five-decade rosary.

As a kindergartner, I was brazened enough to request permission from both my father and our pastor to receive my first holy communion along with my older brother's second grade class. From kindergarten through twelfth grade, I perennially earned the award as the best student of religion. I served as an acolyte at church and felt profoundly honored to be chosen to serve during weddings, funerals, and especially the Easter Triduum.

Then, while a student at Chaminade High School, I was selected to serve as a peer minister (spiritual youth group leader, retreat leader, and extraordinary Eucharistic minister) and was taken to Dayton, Ohio for training when I was a year younger than my schoolmates.

Despite this uninterrupted string of prestigious roles and credentials, during my early adolescence I experienced a personal existential crisis in which I became intensely puzzled over the meaning and purpose of human life. I remember that this existential crisis arose as the result of the combination of two simple factors.

With ten people sharing one house, there was a pronounced dearth of quiet space suitable for praying, pondering, and meditating in solitude. This was coupled with the fact that I had neither cultivated nor maintained the essential habit of, nor method for, direct, unmediated, one-on-one prayer. I had grown accustomed to communal prayer led by surrogates. In other words, I had allowed my relationship with my Creator to grow vicarious or indirect.

During a seaside group retreat during my first year of secondary school, Marianist Father Robert Backherms reoriented me along the path toward the customs of praying directly to God and at regularly scheduled intervals (a strategy drawn from the transformative tradition of the liturgy of the hours). I still remember the lessons that Father Backherms imparted to me via that lone intervention.

While Father Backherms offered himself as advocate-to-the-rescue during my early adolescence, my father, David Albert Masters, remained the most consistent and influential (though by no means the only) advocate of an established religious tradition that I have encountered and with whom I have interacted throughout the trajectory of my ongoing missionary conversion. I say this because he laid the foundation of my Christian faith via his words and more importantly, via his ample, indefatigable example.

Nevertheless, over the years, I continued to lapse away from the practice of one-on-one daily prayer. I again grew accustomed to seeking and experiencing God indirectly, via intentional visits to natural settings (such as forests, mountainsides, seasides, and deserts), via visits with poor, elderly, and infirm people, via group service projects, via communal retreats, and via communal prayer led by intermediaries.

During my undergraduate career at Boston College, Jesuit Fathers Julio Giulietti and Francis Xavier Clooney, as well as Benedictine Father Sebastian Moore, frequently intervened in my life as advocates-who-led-by-example of a comprehensive constellation of prayer methods, while never neglecting to give prominence to the daily habit of direct, one-on-one prayer. Once a week, in the basement chapel of their residence, Fathers Moore and Clooney led a group of us in the practice of silent Christian contemplation.

When I was thrown into a spiritual-vocational-occupational crisis several months later in Venezuela, I was able to draw upon my familiarity with these prayer and meditation techniques under the guidance of my in-field advocate-in-residence, Jesuit Father Ignacio Castellót.

Immersion Experiences
with JVI in Central America

In 1988, the Boston College International Volunteer Program (BCIVP), which was in the process of merging with the Jesuit Volunteers International (JVI), selected me to serve for three years at a new, and therefore probationary, placement in Venezuela. The BCIVP/JVI afforded me the opportunity to visit and study in Guatemala and Belize for several months, and then to work in Venezuela for nearly a year.

During my first week in Guatemala, I was deeply moved by the legless men and women in the middle of the city streets of Antigua removing weeds from among the cobblestones with metal spoons, in

31

exchange for food. The shopkeepers provided each laborer with one meal each time that he or she succeeded in removing all the weeds from in front of one shop. While amazed at their dexterity and valor, I feared for their lives as they dodged the oncoming traffic by scurrying on their knuckles toward the sidewalks. In spite of their severe physical disabilities, they were indeed providing a useful, income-generating service to their fellow citizens.

Even though I never conversed in depth with them, I sensed that they felt a significant measure of dignity, because they were earning their own living instead of begging for it.[9] Nevertheless, I wondered if such perilous employment might simultaneously represent a humiliating classist manifestation of a society that fails to generate more dignified and safer means of employment.[10]

Immersion Experiences
with JVI in South America

When we were admitted into the BCIVP/JVI, my missionary partners (Brendan Sullivan, Tim Aleck, Tom Turley) and I had been told that we would teach theology and English during the day, tutor and lead spiritual youth groups in the evening, and direct field trips and service projects on the weekends. However, once we arrived in Venezuela, Brendan and I learned that the boarding school to which we had been assigned had a new boss.

We worked full-time at a Jesuit agricultural-technical school, the *Colegio Agropecuario Padre Gumilla*, and part-time at the *Unión Educativa San Ignacio*, a cooperative farm owned by its member families and

---

[9] 2nd Thessalonians3.

[10] Pope John Paul II's *Laborem Exercens* and the *Compendium of the Social Doctrine of the Church* address the needs, rights, and duties of workers with disabilities, giving particular emphasis to their dignity as fully human subjects. Pope John Paul II, *Laborem Exercens*, 22; Pontifical Council for Justice and Peace, *Compendium*, 148. Our Divine Savior himself admonished us that he considers our treatment of the weakest folks in society as the measure of our treatment of him. Matthew 25:31-46.

founded by a visionary, Father Castellót. From Monday through Friday, I felt as if I were imprisoned from eight o'clock each morning until six o'clock each afternoon (with a two-hour-long furlough for lunch and a nap) by a madman.

My direct daytime supervisor at the agricultural-technical school, the new director, was delusional regarding my university training, insisting that I spend my days in a futile effort to compose computer software code so that he could track the daily milk production of the cows and the reproductive and growth patterns of the swine. I had taken neither computer science nor mathematics classes in college; therefore, I was absolutely unequipped to generate computer code of any sort.

My patient attempts at dialogue with my supervisor were punctuated by his accusations that I was indeed a trained computer programmer who was simply selfish and emotionally immature. He insisted that I had surreptitiously talked my way into a multi-year contract with the BCIVP/JVI with the sole goal of pursuing an extended tropical vacation far from the drudgery of a confining cubicle just big enough to facilitate the cranking out of computer code in order to enrich some greedy, heartless conglomerate in cold, gray North America.

I felt a deep sense of frustration. When I communicated my profound feeling of discouragement to Father Castellót, he immediately leapt into action. Father Castellót taught me how to grow deeper and become more joyful day-by-day by relying more heavily on God and on the members of the local Christian community, and by committing myself to a daily discipline that consisted of sharing mass, meals, and conversations with them, whether or I felt like it or not. He also encouraged me to dedicate at least a few minutes every evening to silent meditation and stargazing.

The results were virtually immediate. Under Father Castellót's guidance, I began to appreciate the simple joys of life and my hopeful attitude was renewed. I no longer moped around wishing that I could find someplace where I could hide and wallow in the mire of self-pity. Instead, I began to expect something delightful in every face and around every bend. What a transformation this guided immersion into prayer, worship, contemplation, and human community wrought in me!

In March of 1989, the presidents of Venezuela (Carlos Andrés Pérez) and the International Monetary Fund (Michel Camdessus) abruptly imposed a package of "Structural Adjustment Programs" (SAPs) upon the Venezuelan people and their economic system. In a desperate move, uncharacteristic among the famously docile pre-Chávez Venezuelans, many citizens of the lower and middle economic classes erupted from their hillside apartments and shanties in order to join in the most widespread street riots and looting sprees since the violent ouster of a previous dictator, Marcos Pérez Jiménez, shortly after World War II.

One local consequence of these SAPs was that the government ordered the bank to boost the interest rate on our farming cooperative's mortgage and capital improvement loans from eight and a half percent to forty percent – literally overnight. The young adult members of the cooperative farm instinctively huddled around Father Castellót in search of spiritual and logistical guidance, because without a miracle, they realized that they were on the verge of permanently losing the farm.

Father Castellót turned to me and told me that he needed me to become his bilingual grant writer, translator, and liaison with Father Giulietti in Boston. Out of the blue, I had a renewed purpose – something productive, significant, and rewarding, something worth getting up in the morning to strive to accomplish. After a few short months of corresponding with Boston, and commuting between San

Fernando de Apure and Caracas, the life-sustaining funds arrived from the Thomas White Foundation and we were able to pay off both of the loans.

JVI Post-Immersion Experiences

Since our placement was new and therefore probationary as far as the JVI was concerned, our director, Father Giulietti, instructed my partner and I to evaluate the new placement. We informed him that it was untenable to continue to send more JVI missionaries to labor under this particular supervisor, and we recommended that he suspend our placement at least until a new supervisor was installed.

As a result, my dream of a three-year-long missionary placement was abruptly truncated down to one year. As soon as I returned from my JVI placement in Venezuela, I took a three-week-long trip to Costa Rica and Nicaragua to assuage my profound disappointment. I was left wanting another shot at missionary life. I felt truncated, deprived, and sorry for myself. I was a hundred percent convinced that God was still calling me to serve him as a missionary.

Only a month after I returned from Central America, I began teaching theology and doing campus ministry at Monsignor Edward Pace High School in Miami Gardens. The teacher who was moderating the Mission Club asked me to take it over and informed me about what she dubbed a "ghost organization" known as AeA, whose representatives rarely made contact, through which our school was affiliated with a Catholic sister school in rural Haiti. When I approached my former principal with the idea of taking some select students on an overseas summer mission immersion with AeA, he paid me only lip service.

However, just one semester later, when Father Liam Quinn arrived as the school's new spiritual director, he secured instant approval for AeA mission immersions and numerous other vital, transformative ministerial endeavors. As it turned out, AeA members (especially founders Alicia Marill, Adriano García, and Carlos Cueto) and Father Liam Quinn threw me a spiritual lifeline by affirming my continued missionary aspirations.[11]

While in Central and South America, I had witnessed the effects of the weight of long-term poverty upon regular folks, spiritually, emotionally, intellectually, and physically. Toward the end of my year in the JVI, I resolved to find a way to remain connected to some of the materially poorest people in the world for the rest of my life, and I have implored God to guide me and to sustain me regarding this commitment.

This is why AeA has proven to be so essential to my spiritual life and identity. I have made and maintained this resolution because my sense of compassion is always activated whenever I witness my spiritual siblings in heart-wrenching circumstances; because my conscience literally wakes me up at night whenever I turn my back on the least of human society; and because I explicitly sense God's presence whenever I listen to or observe my spiritual siblings who suffer

---

[11] Numerous Msgr. Pace HS teachers, staff members, administrators, parents, students, and alumni have actively contributed to our missionary endeavors by joining us on mission immersions and by raising awareness and funds to provide salaries to the teachers at our AeA sister schools, as well as to finance our immersion travel expenses. As I mentioned previously, recently, our principal Ana Mundet García and her husband Eduardo García (himself a Catholic school principal) immersed themselves by visiting our sister schools in Haiti. I profoundly hope that when the word and the images from their immersion get out, this type of engaged self-sacrificial leadership will serve to challenge and invite their fellow Catholic administrators to take the plunge and to deepen their own commitment to the eager and talented, yet materially needy, teachers and students of the Caribbean and beyond. Kudos are also in order for the local missionary leadership provided by Alicia Marill of Barry University, and Anthony Vinciguerra, Mary Carter Waren, Ondina Cortés RMI, Judith Bachay, Elisabetta Ferrero, and Joe Holland of Saint Thomas University. These leaders deserve to be lauded for their generous efforts, especially because, believe it or not, there are Catholic schools and universities whose administrators refuse to extend such intensive and consistent solidarity toward our most vulnerable spiritual siblings beyond our national boundaries. Perhaps we all ought to remind ourselves periodically of the meaning of the label "catholic."

abjectly and whenever I see someone in a better situation reach out to share with or to shield them.

Immersion Experiences with
AeA in Quisqueya[12]

In my dual capacities as a secondary school theology teacher and an AeA missionary (focusing on the Gros Morne region of Haiti where Monsignor Edward Pace High School's three AeA sister schools of Moulen, Pewou, and Lormand are located), I co-moderate our school's Mission Club. We dedicate most of our efforts toward fund-raising in order to pay the salaries of all twenty-five teachers at our three sister schools. In order to practice solidarity and partake of the benefits of the phenomenon of mission-in-reverse, we endeavor to travel to Haiti with AeA on at least an annual basis, when political, security, and safety conditions permit.[13]

Because I frequently give oral presentations after returning from mission immersions, I prefer to seek quotes from people whom I meet in eye-opening situations, instead of putting my words into their mouths by imposing on them my own interpretations or supposi-tions. This approach more often than not results in a more vivid and higher impact presentation, which in turn normally elicits a more profound and committed response from my various audiences (high school and college students, retreat groups, youth and young adult groups, parish social concern groups, and pre-immersion missionar-ies). Therefore, one morning at an outdoor market in rural Haiti, I asked a woman selling mud cookies why people would choose to spend hard-earned money on mud. She angrily asked me whether I

---

[12] *Quisqueya* or *Kiskeya* (the mother of all lands) is the indigenous Taíno name of the island that the Dominican Republic and Haiti share.

[13] I dedicate so much time and energy to consciousness raising and fundraising be-cause I concur with Rambo that true conversion ultimately leads to consequences, re-sults, outcomes, and responses. Rambo, *Understanding Religious Conversion*, 17.

would prefer to endure a whole day with something or with nothing in my digestive system. She punctuated her response by stomping off in disgust after dramatically waving and throwing her hand towel to the ground. A few minutes later, she returned to her stall.

I felt a twinge of regret at having exasperated this unsuspecting merchant. So, after our visit to the school, Monfortian Father Ronel Charelus helped me to apologize and to explain my intentions to her. She listened patiently, nodded, shook my hand, and even smiled.

The most astonishing scenario that I have ever encountered during my missionary career is currently being lived out in some rural zones of the Northwestern corner of the Dominican Republic, close to the border with Haiti. Some villages are now totally bereft of children because, ever since the government decided to eliminate rural elementary schools in sparsely populated regions, the only educational option made available to the children of the impoverished villagers is to hand their children over to the administrators at the Adventist boarding school and orphanage in the provincial capital of San Fernando de Monte Cristi.[14]

At no point in the children's lives, from age seven until graduation from the Adventist secondary school, are the children returned home; not even for holidays, vacations, or familial funerals. This is

---

[14] When I first encountered this rueful phenomenon, I could not help but empathize with the fictional parents of Hamelin (of *Pied Piper* fame), as well as with the fictional father, Caractacus Potts (of *Chitty Chitty Bang Bang* fame), when they realized that all the children of their respective cities had been kidnapped. What a demoralizing pair of options in the Dominican Republic's arid Northwest, either literacy or an intact family. This heartrending predicament has been vigorously critiqued by Pope Saint John Paul II and the Pontifical Commission on Justice & Peace which have asserted that: every child has the right to live in a united family; every family has the right to have and rear children; in fact the family's role in raising children is irreplaceable and inalienable; furthermore, all parents have the essential right and duty to educate their children in close and vigilant cooperation with civil and ecclesial agencies. Pope John Paul II, *Centesimus Annus: On the 100th Anniversary of Rerum Novarum* (Città del Vaticano: Libreria Editrice Vaticana, 1991), 47; Pope John Paul II, *Familiaris Consortio: On the Role of the Christian Family in the Modern World* (Città del Vaticano: Libreria Editrice Vaticana, 1981), 36, 40; Pontifical Council for Justice & Peace, *Compendium*, 155, 238-241.

not to say that their parents and guardians cannot sign them out in-person whenever they see fit. On the bright side, the villagers are not obliged to pay anything for their children's education, nutrition, medical attention, housing, clothing, or miscellaneous expenditures, because everything is subsidized by Seventh Day Adventist benefactors.

On the opposite side of the central Dominican mountain range, in the Southwestern region of the Dominican Republic, adjacent to Haiti, many parents hand over their severely malnourished children (from infants to toddlers) to the sisters of Mother Teresa of Skopje and Kolkata, the Missionaries of Charity, with the intention of offering them survival and eventually a better long-term future in the household of a loving, adoptive family. Children, who appear to be mentally retarded on the morning of the first day of each round of visits to the orphanage by AeA missionaries, are up and talking within two hours after our arrival. By the second afternoon, they are running around and enthusiastically shouting out our names. For the first few years, these nearly instantaneous cognitive and communicative transformations seemed quite miraculous to me.

In a far corner of the men's ward of the public hospital in Port-de-Paix, I noticed a man who was covered from head-to-toe with a white sheet as if he were already dead. When I pointed this out to the doctors and nurses, one Cuban physician explained that the patient was still alive but was dying of tuberculosis.

The physician apologized for the mistake and promised that the sheet would be adjusted promptly, but informed me that it mattered little because, since his wife had abandoned him, there was no one available to buy him medications or even to feed him. He explained to me that since the patient had not eaten regularly for a couple of weeks, that even if he had been receiving the prescribed drug therapy, the lack of basic nutrition would have negated the efficacy of the medications. So I gave some money to the nurse who was the most solicitous and asked her to promise me that she would purchase and personally administer him some food and medication, if any happened to arrive in Port-de-Paix before he perished.

The general lack of sympathy demonstrated by the patient's wife, physicians, nurses, and orderlies left me bewildered and disappointed by the apparent absence of brotherly and sisterly love. I wanted to do my part; but since we were scheduled to leave town the next morning, I did not know what my appropriate part was.

Before we left the hospital that afternoon, I recalled the numerous Dominican parish-based volunteer-hospital-visitation ministry groups that I have encountered. With these vivid images in mind, I asked several nurses and physicians, and later, the diocesan vicar general himself, if any of the parishes had religious sisters, lay people, or clergy who paid regular visits to the patients in the public hospital. They all answered in the negative and acted as if the idea had never crossed their minds. They informed me that their hospital-chaplaincy ministries were focused on convalescent and nursing homes administered by the church.

AeA Post-Immersion Experiences

Whenever I return from immersions, I feel the impulse to counsel everyone to conserve water, food, electricity, and fuel. Students at the secondary school where I teach seem interested in hearing my tales about the missionary lands. But I have noticed that only some are truly interested, while others just want to waste class time in the hope of avoiding academic work.

My mother and father always listened to me patiently and without interruption. Two of my younger siblings have joined me on mission immersions in the Dominican Republic. Most of my friends from secondary school and college have treated me fine and are willing to listen to me. However, sometimes when I would point out what I perceived to be an injustice or an affront to basic human rights, several of my friends fell into the habit of feigning hostility (albeit in a superficial way) and spewing overly judgmental maxims against genuine victims. Some of them jokingly labeled me a "granola" (meaning hippie) and nicknamed me "Sandinista Sammy" (meaning communist).

As a result, I sometimes felt like avoiding them, because their teasing drained my spiritual and emotional energy. I could not see the wisdom in continuing to expose myself to social situations in which I was constantly wrangling rhetorically, even though I eventually realized that they were mainly ribbing me simply to entertain themselves.

Whenever I return home from immersions, the departure airports tend to shock me.[15] Two particular aspects of airports normally seize my attention. The first is the stark classism (a dualism between the "haves" versus the "have-nots," or in this case, the "ins" versus the "outs"); and the second is the exclusive, air-conditioned interior sanctuaries of the airport boarding parlors, shops, and restaurants.

I perceive that whole artificially chilled indoor ambience as a barrier, as a kind of social and psychological barricade which excludes the common folk while allowing in the few, precious aristocrats who are dutifully and deferentially served by their discreet and docile lackeys.[16] It disturbs me that, while I am always admitted into that protective bubble, most of the population is forever barred.[17]

---

[15] I feel unique and isolated in that regard because I rarely encounter other missionaries who seem to share airport-induced alienation.

[16] In Haiti, beyond the exclusive inner sectors of the Port-au-Prince International Airport, the only air-conditioned locales that I have encountered are banks and some hotel rooms; while in the Dominican Republic, select department stores, shopping malls, discotheques, resort hotels, and luxury apartments should be added to the list.

[17] It is my perception that the physical barriers (air conditioners, walls, fences, hedges, guardhouses) which insulate those inside from the heat, smoke, dust, noise, distractions, and chaos of the Ibero-American metropoles, simultaneously serve to insulate

Myself as Minister & Educator

I am a husband, a father, a full-time secondary school teacher of Catholic social doctrine and the religions of the world, an adjunct university professor of theology and ministry, an environmental conservationist, and a part-time missionary.

By virtue of my role as a short-term immersion missionary,[18] I feel morally obligated to serve as a witness or spokesperson on behalf of my Caribbean and Central American friends as well as Florida's migrant agricultural workers — to all who know me, be they my family, my students, local church groups, my pastors, or my fellow parishioners. I intentionally perforate walls of ignorance and indifference for my students, my colleagues, and my supervisors so that they can perceive and ponder what transpires in the lives of marginalized folks who are struggling to survive and thrive both locally and around the globe.

After I introduce them to these slices of other people's realities, I invite them to exhibit solidarity by contributing to some measure of amelioration. I exhort them to donate their money, to travel and read with the goal of discovery, and to raise awareness and funds among others.

As I noted earlier, I co-moderate our school's Mission Club, a student missionary and human rights club affiliated with both AeA and IYCS, which undertakes consciousness-raising campaigns like our annual "Mission and Human Rights Week." Our club dedicates the bulk of the school year to raising money to pay the teachers' salaries at our AeA sister schools, in addition to responding to natural

---

the consciences of the people who benefit from the unjust social-economic-political systems.

[18] I am active in several communities with missionary aims: Amor en Acción, Missionalis Societas Ioannes Paulus II, Iglesia en Misión/Misión en Acción, Pax Romana, the International Young Catholic Students, and the Iraqi Christian Relief Council.

disasters. I engage in such projects because my conscience drives me to act on behalf of people who are in great need.

My social conscience was formed by my evangelizing Catholic parents and my professors of Catholic social doctrine, particularly Julio Giulietti, Ignacio Castellót, Joe Holland, Megan McKenna, Alicia Marill, Liam Quinn, Adriano García, Carlos Cueto, Robert Noten, David Barton, George Rodríguez, Mark Steyn, Alejandro Roque, Lourdes Rovira, William Federer, Oscar Manríquez, Nelson Bonet, Patricia Stout Swanson, Josefina Chirino, Dennis Prager, Paul Kengor, Stephen Millán, Mary Carter Waren, Ronald Musto, James O'Donohoe, Gisela Pastrana, Mary Sturm, Gerard Vanderhaar, Ron Robinson, Ray Rufo, John Hagee, Franklin Graham, Phyllis Schlafly, Charles Kirk, David Horowitz, Wendy Lockard, Renate Ferrante, Ed Martin, Jay Sekulow, Candace Owens, Raymond Ibrahim, Elaine Sevin, Ami Horowitz, Daniel Dreisbach, Humberto Fontova, Ben Shapiro, María Wadsworth, Todd Starnes, Christine Douglass-Williams, Bill French, and Juliana Taimoorazy. Indeed, just as my teachers have done so in me, the awakening of other people's social consciences has proven to be an integral component of my ministerial career.

Critical Analysis as Participant-Researcher

I am a Native Floridian whose family descends from Alsatian-Lorrainian Jews, French Canadian Catholics, Native Canadians, and indentured-servant Menorcan-Balearic-Spanish Islanders who arrived in the Timukwa region of the Pascua Florida Peninsula in 1768. Both of my parents are also native Floridians. I was raised as a Roman Catholic European-American Southerner in an English-speaking household (despite the fact that, my mother grew up knowing conversational French and being able to read Spanish, and my father could speak, read, and write English, Spanish, Haitian Creole, Latin, and some German).

I am the second of eight children of a seminarian-turned-teacher and a homemaker. I was blessed and privileged to be able to attend high-caliber Catholic schools and universities my entire life. I am married to a Dominican woman who is also a part-time missionary, and I am a proud father of two sons. We live among West Indians, Haitians, African-Americans, Caribbeans, and Central Americans of the middle and lower-middle economic strata.

We worship regularly with a wide variety of Ibero-Americans and West Indians, mostly of the lower-middle economic stratum, at Visitation, Saint Stephen Protomartyr, Saint Lawrence, and Annunciation parishes, near the borders of the adjoining cities of Miami Gardens, Miramar, West Park, Pembroke Park, Hallandale, Sky Lake, and North Miami Beach. I work and minister among Cubans, Haitians, South Americans, West Indians, Puerto Ricans, Dominicans, and Central Americans of every economic stratum.

Some of my students have been sons, nephews, and grandsons of presidents, vice presidents, and dictators of Caribbean nations while others have been able to enroll thanks to need-based grants. Owing to my missionary endeavors in various countries around the Caribbean basin, some of my immigrant neighbors have dubbed me an honorary Haitian, an honorary Dominican, an honorary Cuban, an honorary Nicaraguan, an honorary Guatemalan, and an honorary Venezuelan.

Despite my extensive on-the-job and in-the-classroom missionary training, until I read Roberto Goizueta's *Caminemos con Jesús*,[19] I was somewhat of a theological snob. Although I have always been a Roman Catholic, I privately viewed myself as spiritually and intellectually superior to the many Ibero-Americans who employ statues, medallions, portraits, and other images in their worship. As if I were a

---

[19] Roberto Goizueta, *Caminemos con Jesús: Toward a Hispanic/Latino Theology of Accompaniment* (Maryknoll, NY: Orbis, 1995).

strident Reformation-Era iconoclast, I used to view such practices as obvious contraventions of the first commandment of the Decalogue.

However, Goizueta convinced me that, although the faith of many Ibero-Americans often appears to be image-laden and focused on saints instead of directly on God, it would be a mistake to judge them categorically and conclude that they are all misguided idolaters. By listening to the Mexican-American Catholics of San Antonio, Texas with a genuinely discerning intent, Goizueta (a Cuban-American raised in Atlanta, Georgia) allowed his Catholic faith to be renewed by the example of these intensely faithful pilgrims, who believe that they mystically touch and lend a hand to God during his passion by joining in the processions and rites of Holy Week.

While reading about Goizueta's epiphanies, I too underwent my own epiphany. I abruptly realized that sincerity of heart totally undermines any accusation of idolatry, because Christians believe that people can only sin intentionally, not as a result of confusion, ignorance, or inherited traditions. I suddenly felt guilty and repentant for my decades of judgmental theological conceit. This revelation has helped me as a missionary by melting away many of my paternalistic biases and simultaneously opening my heart and mind to all kinds of people as well as to the validity of their respective manifestations of faith. Goizueta sowed transformative seeds in me that have yielded a rich harvest of mission-in-reverse.

As with any minister, my upbringing, education, and early formative experiences have equipped me with both advantages and disadvantages, with horizons as well as blind spots. Because I was raised by a former-seminarian-turned-evangelist who frequently took me door-to-door with him since my childhood, I have a pro-clivity toward Christian mission deeply ingrained in me. I have observed that my colleagues and students, who have been raised by parents who intentionally chose to introduce them from an early age to materially poor people, to the work of missionaries, to people of varied ethnicities, or to any combination thereof, tend to respond more eagerly to our missionary invitations and appeals than do folks who have lived more insulated lives.

In other words, people's upbringing ranks among the most enduring determinants affecting their openness to missionary invitations. For example, I realized long ago that some folks tend to react to unwanted and unsettling contact with the extreme privation of others by choosing to ignore reality and to further widen their own blinders. Nevertheless, this fact does not preclude the possibility of missionary vocations late in life, because I have witnessed quite a few of them.

As far back as I can remember, I have been action-oriented. My most natural response to witnessing deprivation or injustice is to launch some type of campaign of assistance and to solicit the collaboration of others. I recall that as an undergraduate in a CSD class, the professor told me to postpone my action-oriented responses to his questions in order to allow some of my classmates to emotionally and mentally process the expository material which he had assigned us to read. The professor explained to me that not everyone was yet ready to do something about the injustices that had been brought to our attention only recently.

Preachers, teachers, evangelists, and missionaries have confided in me that they often feel impatient and frustrated when they perceive that they are achieving only limited success in terms of motivating their colleagues, students, congregations, and target audiences to respond to their exhortations with commensurate compassion and generosity. However, this is not the case with me.

While I do not always see all of my missionary goals realized to the degree to which I aspire, I have never felt any negative reaction more extreme than a mild and fleeting sense of disappointment. I am pragmatic in that sense because I have learned that the quality of our appeals, in terms of both planning and delivery, has a definite effect upon their respective results. When our appeals are fresher and more enthusiastic, the responses are correspondingly more enthusiastic. Furthermore, if we ask or invite too often, then we usually witness more donor- and compassion-fatigue; as a result, we now intentionally space out our appeals.

In summary, while I recognize that I personally fall near the extreme along both the indifference-compassion and paralysis-action spectra, I am nonetheless patient with the people who surround me because I comprehend the pivotal role that parenting and previous life experience play in the development of altruistic compassion.

Generative Themes

As signaled earlier, to effectively utilize Groome's method of shared Christian praxis, it is necessary to identify generative themes. Borrowing from Freire's lexicon, Groome defines a generative theme as a historical issue, question, value, belief, concept, event, or situation that has the power to draw the participants into active engagement because it is already meaningful and important in their own lives.[20] This is precisely why these generative themes possess the greatest potential to promote conversion.

Pre-Immersion Generative Themes

In retrospect, it is plain to see that in my most formative pre-overseas-missionary-immersion years, my parents taught me not only compassion but also the values of prayer, evangelization, volunteer service, and openness to ethnic variety. More importantly, through their consistent, selfless, evangelically inspired example, my parents taught me to actively love marginalized people beyond our biological family and beyond the boundaries of our nation. They taught me to be truly catholic, that is, universal, in my outlook.

---

[20] Freire, *Pedagogy of the Oppressed*, 61ff, 110ff; Groome, *Sharing Faith*, 156.

Immersion Generative Themes

The dominant theme that I have culled from my mission immersions is the rampant degree of deep-seated classism in the societies where I have served. In response to my intermittent queries regarding the blatant exclusionary classism accompanied by wretched material and spiritual deprivation in the lands that I visit as a missionary, some members of the local aristocracies have chosen to espouse the boot-straps-laziness-blaming-the-victim justification that is also axiomatic elsewhere.

Linguistic duplicity soothes the consciences of some of the gentry with regard to the unequal plight of their juxtaposed domestic serv-ants whose own children and aspirations for advancement are dras-tically marginalized. In Central America, South America, and the Caribbean, many families that employ domestic servants refer to them as *muchachas* (girls) or *criadas* (girls who are raised by their neighbors), irrespective of their age and even after they become grandmothers in their own right.[21]

Post-Immersion Generative Themes

Three generative themes are revealed by my personal post-immer-sion experiences. They are: 1) the impulse to continue to heed a mis-sionary vocation despite obstacles; 2) alienation from friends whose perspectives have not been widened by a personal missionary im-mersion experience; and 3) discomfort regarding the disparities of classism. Now that we have examined my own formative pre-immer-sion, immersion, and post-immersion praxes, in the next chapter, we will document the rich and diverse post-mission immersion experi-ences of the AeA community.

---

[21] In some cases, such terminology indicates the deprivation of human equality and dignity. According to CSD, all workers have the right to rest periodically and the right to raise and educate their own families.

3

DISCOURAGEMENTS TO CONVERSION

I n this chapter and the next, we will hear the reflections and insights of post-immersion Amor en Acción missionaries, with particular emphasis on the people, conversations, situations, conflicts, and events that either engender commitment to, or abandonment of, the continuing pursuit of spiritual conversion by Christian missionaries.[1]

To infuse a logical structure into the ample testimony of the missionaries, I parsed the impediments to further conversion according to both decreasing scale and increasing proximity with regard to the individual missionary. Therefore, I will present the testimonies that deal with these obstacles in the following five-tiered sequence: societal, ecclesial, interpersonal, familial, and intrapersonal.

Nevertheless, this five-tiered structure did not prove as useful when examining the encouragements to further conversion. Therefore, in Chapter 4, I will categorize the testimonies that promote deeper missionary conversion according to their respective subject matter.

---

[1] The missionaries I interviewed were enthusiastic at the opportunity to contribute to the renovation and enhancement of our post-immersion conversion-promotion processes.

Further, in both Chapter 3 and Chapter 4, I will identify and examine the generative themes within the narrative testimony. Chapter 3 will examine generative themes that discourage the deepening of Christian missionary conversion, while Chapter 4 will examine generative themes that encourage such deepening.

Focus Group Questions

Immediately prior to each interview, I read the following statement out loud to the assembled missionaries:

> *The aims of this interview are: to increase understanding of how post-immersion experiences affect the profundity of the Christian conversion process; and to propose and devise methods and systems to more consistently facilitate the post-immersion conversion process.*

Within the focus group format, I then proceeded to interview the missionaries by employing the following questions:

> *1a. What did you feel when you got home from the mission immersion experience?*
>
> *1b. Describe any sense of disorientation or anxiety or of feeling misunderstood or out-of-place that you experienced on your way home or after you returned home.*
>
> *1c. How did your family, friends, coworkers, fellow students, pastors, and fellow parishioners treat you after you returned, and how did you treat them?*
>
> *2. Did you experience any profound spiritual changes while you were immersed (during the mission)? Did you make any resolutions (promises to yourself or to God to change something about yourself or a about a given situation, be it, social, economic, political, et cetera)? If so, describe them briefly.*

3a. After you returned home, what people and experiences helped you to pursue the resolutions for conversion that you had made during your immersion (while on the mission), and how?

3b. Describe any alterations that your values underwent during your immersion (while on the mission) that were then affirmed or deepened after you arrived home.

4a. After you returned home, what people and experiences impeded your pursuit of the resolutions for conversion that you had made during your immersion (while on the mission) and how?

4b. Describe any alterations that your values underwent during your immersion (while on the mission) that were then challenged, contradicted, abandoned, or forgotten after you arrived home.

5a. What impact did your first re-entry debriefing meeting for recently returned missionaries have upon you, and why?

5b. What impact did the welcome home liturgy for recently returned missionaries have upon you, and why?

6. In what ways are you and your life different now as a result of your missionary experience? What new directions have you discovered or been led to by the Holy Spirit as a result of your missionary experience, directly or indirectly?

7. Based on your experience, how might your missionary community, better support and guide missionaries once they return home, especially after their first missionary immersion journey abroad?

What follows are overviews of the answers to my focus group questions, with some choice quotes arranged according to the five aforementioned degrees of decreasing scale and increasing proximity: society, church, friends, family, and self.

Societal Discouragements

The preponderance of the AeA missionaries of each age stratum that participated in my focus groups believe that the superstructure of North American society effectively tends to lead its residents away from the values of the Holy Spirit, as delineated in the New Testament, and toward the values of the "flesh."[2] Kavanaugh brands Christianity as boldly countercultural within our contemporary hyperconsumerist United States of America.[3] The testimonies of missionaries burst with examples of the temptation-laden moral minefield that is today's US culture.

Now let us look at an assortment of first-person verbatim testimonies. Jennifer, a young AeA missionary, reported cognitive dissonance when her immersion was immediately followed by luxury:

> *When I first came home, my aunt and uncle met me at the airport, and they thought they were going to do something special for me by taking me to this town for a mini-vacation. I just got off the plane, and boom, we went to a very touristy, well-to-do area. I would compare it to Saint Augustine, Florida. I hated it. I felt so terrible. I ended up with a migraine headache. I was in tears. They ended up just taking me home. I could not go from being in a slum of San Pedro de Macorís, where they barely have enough to eat, to this touristy town where people are spending five hundred dollars for a handbag. It disgusted me. My aunt and uncle were interested in hearing my stories. But trying to sit there and tell them in that place; I just couldn't do it.*

Adriano, an AeA founder, echoed the observation that post-immersion cross-cultural transitions can be abrupt and disconcerting:

---

[2] Galatians 5:13 – 6:10.

[3] Kavanaugh, *Still Following Christ*, 83.

Here we are discussing the children and their situation, but mean-
while children are dying of starvation, ladies, and gentlemen.
Therefore, that was how we felt, a feeling of not belonging to the
reality here that everyone else was living. We were part of it, and
we knew everybody here, and everything was fine. But we had just
returned from Mars, and from speaking with the Martians, and the
Martians had shown us another world, and no one here could un-
derstand us, even if we had told them about it.

Michaela, an AeA immersion leader, revealed the ubiquity of the
guilt impulse that accosts her whenever she returns from a missionary immersion:

I always feel guilt when I come back. I cannot help but feel guilty.
We complain. We try to live simple lives, but our simple lives are
not simple in contrast to the lives that we just left behind in Haiti
or the Dominican Republic. I have a roof over my head. I have a
table. I have chairs. I have food in the cupboard. It's not really a
simple life. I can go out and replace something if it breaks. I always
feel guilt.

One AeA missionary described her initial post-immersion disorientation as follows:

The airport always gets me, just making that immediate change
from the developing world to the artificially advanced, developed
world. But the disorientation does not stop there. It is a constant
battle to try to live in the two worlds. That's where the confusion
starts for me.

Michaela, again an AeA immersion leader, noted that her estrangement sometimes manifests itself as suspicion toward tourists:

Well, it's strange because we arrive at the airport, fresh from a mis-
sion immersion and here you have all these tourists, mostly North
Americans, carrying all their souvenirs, talking about all the par-
ties that they attended, and all the beaches that they visited. And I

wonder whether they were among those tourists who came through on the tour buses, stopped in the bateys,[4] and threw candy out of the windows at the children.

One AeA veteran recalled her negative emotions upon re-entry:

When I get back, I do feel disoriented, anxious, and some measure of sadness. Looking back over the culmination of all my years, that is what I have felt at different stages. Definitely, every year when I get back, I'm out of place. I'm almost caught between two worlds. Okay, I'm here with my family and I'm happy to see everybody, but I want to be back over there. So, it is definitely a mix of feelings. Luckily, I've never felt depressed. I've felt sadder and maybe more anxious, anxious about what I should do about all of the over-whelming difficulties that my Dominican friends are facing. I think it's probably because I'm at a different stage of my life, that I say: This is great; but we need to do something about this. I'm not going to be angry about it and just sit around because that produces frus-tration. You feel frustrated because you ask, Okay, Now, what do you do? Because life goes on and you're going to school and you're going to work and you're doing a million things. So, to what degree am I going to be able to do something about this?

Josefina, an AeA founder, confessed that her post-immersion transitions are anything but smooth:

It's as if I've been away for a very, very long time, for years. It feels like forever and sometimes I wonder, Will I remember how to drive my automobile? Sometimes, after I come back home, the first time I sit behind the wheel, I ask myself, Will I be able to drive? Then I

---

[4]The term "batey" refers to a rural slum situated amidst sugarcane fields whose residents are the families of the poor immigrants who manually harvest the sugarcane. Dominican bateyes are inhabited by indigent Haitians. This term is derived from the Caribbean Taíno word that originally described the open area in front of a Taíno chief's residence where most religious ceremonies were conducted.

think, I drove just the other day, just a few weeks ago. What's wrong with me? I feel very, very strange and very out of place.

Lourdes, another AeA founder, lamented the painful and bewildering nature of her post-immersion re-entries:

Regarding the returns, even though they are different for me now, after so many years of experience, they continue to be very abrupt, as if I have mounted a rocket ship and, suddenly, I have landed on a new planet. And this is a planet to which I don't want to return. Home, even though it's home, it's an alien place where I feel out of place.

It takes a while, but for me, coming back to Miami, I feel out of place here. Moreover, I have to go back to work in an environment that is completely political and cutthroat. So, for me, going back to work so suddenly is traumatic, like having open heart surgery without anesthesia. For me, it is horrible to have to go back to work, having just come from the simplicity, from the prayer life, from the community, to the mayhem, to the rat race.

I don't even know how to describe that environment in words. It's very difficult. Only when I can get into the groove of pondering of how can I use my life and position here to figure out what I can do to make a difference for children?

Whenever I return from a mission immersion, I always try to get out of my office and schedule visits to schools so that I can see children and converse with teachers and have that more gradual transition back to the office work.

But no matter how many years I do this or how frequently I travel, I continue to come home to an alien place. And for me each transition takes weeks and then, once I've adjusted to be being home again, I start longing for another immersion.

Josefina, again an AeA founder, noticed a magnified sense of loneliness whenever she returns home alone, as opposed to returning with a group of fellow missionaries:

I have always felt very lonely when returning home, and I have felt very lonely even in the work that I have done with the ETC [Encuentro Total con Cristo] communities over in the Dominican Republic for the past twenty something years. I've done it consistently for over twenty years.

It is not like the work of building or launching a project in the sense that you have to pour money into it. And you don't have to give reports, and you don't have to count the number of people that are eating daily as a result of your work. It cannot be measured in numbers.

It has meant working with teams that offer the retreats and then building community among the retreat alumni. Therefore, the results of much of my work have been ephemeral, intangible, and not concrete, visible, measurable. And when I return from those immersion trips in particular, I feel especially lonely.

One AeA veteran spoke of the incisive social critique offered by a visiting preacher:

A missionary Oblate of Mary Immaculate, Father Darrell Rupiper, who lived and worked among the poor people of Brazil and was expelled by the government back in the 1960s, and who later traveled the USA as an environmental ambassador, recently asked the congregation at a local parish, Do you know what the fastest growing industry in the USA is now?

It's storage warehouses, self-storage. In other words, we're in a hyper-consumer culture. We're the most consumerist culture in history. Now we've gotten so extreme that we don't have enough room to store all our stuff.

We've acquired so much stuff that we can't fit it all in our houses, in our garages, in our attics any more. So, we've got to go rent extra space instead of giving it away or sharing it with somebody. The fastest growing industry right now in the USA is constructing buildings to hold our extra junk. Amazing!

Carlos, yet another AeA founder, echoed the experience of observing his guilt convert itself into a conviction of responsibility:

I struggled for years and years with all of these guilt complexes regarding having and not having. I dated a girlfriend here who was from a wealthy family. And I thought that it would be wrong for me to buy new pants. And then I would go work as a professional with pants that had obviously been let out and you could notice the seams down the back, and it was definitely not professional looking.

But I was just trying to deal with all of these clashes of principles and values and priorities and conflicts and so on and so forth. It took me the better part of twenty-seven years before I was able to put it all into context and to not have to worry so much about these issues. I still have a conscience. But the guilt complexes for me were finally overcome. But it took forever for me to put into perspective who I am, what God wants me to do, how God wants me to pursue saintliness, and live my vocation, and be totally dedicated to him one hundred percent, from the inside out, not from the outside in.

It took me forever to realize that because I was going from the outside in. Should I take this off? Should I wear this? The chain? The watch? Is this too expensive? The whole thing. And then I realized that spiritual life is lived from the inside out and that what is important is a sense of priorities and what you live for. If you happen to have it, then you have it; but if you're living to have it, then that's a problem. That is a real problem. I clashed and conflicted internally and spiritually forever and ever and ever and ever and ever.

With the exception of my dad, clashes over spending and lifestyles were rarely spoken about. My father always said that I was obsessive and compulsive and that I was totally out of kilter and that I was totally overdoing all of the work that I was dedicating to AeA. I probably was doing forty hours of work as a professional and forty-eight hours a week of AeA. And then I did burn out around 1983. There was just too much work and no vacations, and I felt burnt out, and then I took a little bit of time off.

Pilar, a young AeA missionary, experienced intense guilt upon her post-immersion re-entries:

The first two years I came back, I felt very guilty, very, very guilty, like a hypocrite. When I was over there, I pretended to be on an equal economic level, and then I came home, and the first time I walked into my house after the mission, everything seemed so sterile, after being in a place where everything was so dirty and things were so much more raw; having the roads paved and everything clean, it almost seemed that it was antiseptic, like you couldn't touch anything. I walked into my room and I felt everything was huge, huge, huge. My closet, I can't believe I have this much clothing. So it was guilt that I didn't know what to do with.

The second time I came back, two days later, we left on a family vacation to Beverly Hills. I just could not enjoy it at all because the whole time I felt like I was selling out.

I felt that if I was a missionary, that I could only be a missionary. I did not understand at that point that being a missionary didn't just mean everyone living at that level. It meant changing the way I live my life, not everyone living in poverty; because what does that help?

So, I think the first years I just felt very guilty with myself and angry at everyone else, and angry at anyone that hadn't gone on a mission and angry at people that had money and didn't help. I think

I saw things as pretty much black and white; either you were poor and good or rich and bad. And that's definitely not the right way of seeing things. But I just came back very full of anger, but not pro-active energy at all.

I also came back the first time, I would say, very atheistic. I think a lot of people have always said that, when they went on mission, they felt a lot more religious, but when I came back, for that whole year, I said, I don't believe in God, because how can a God allow these people to suffer so much? We were there, we would go to mass in this huge cathedral and I would walk outside, and the kids were dying, and I thought, how can I believe in a God that allows this to happen? So, I would say that it made me question my faith completely.

And the second year, while I was on mission, I even had a hard time, at camp, doing the Bible stories because I questioned, Do I even believe in this? Do I even believe in God at all? and I call myself a missionary; because it was such a hard reality; and me, saying I'm a missionary, I'm of the church, and me asking, But how does this happen?

Then the third year was very different, because I think that by talking to other people that went on mission and also family members, it kind of helped me realize that anger was going to do nothing and was just going to kill me because me feeling guilty about having a big house was not going to give another person a bigger house.

The first year I came back and said, I'm not going to college; I'm just going to be on mission all the time. But then my father asked me, How much more of an impact can you make after going to school and seeing the bigger picture? So, the third time I came back, I didn't feel as guilty as much as misunderstood.

When people would see my pictures, they would say, Oh, they have clothes on. Oh, they look happy. That's why, even now, I haven't shown my pictures to anyone that aren't mission people. And my mom is always telling me, Show them to everybody! But there's a story behind every person; but people only see the clothes they're wearing.

Our executive director, Teresita, said it very well: When you come back, you feel like a fish out of water. That's exactly what I felt, especially the first few times. There are new jobs and going back to school. But I still know that, not very far away, people are waking up to a reality where they don't have a bathroom.

Sofía, a young AeA missionary, identified consumerism as the principal obstacle to the deepening of her Christian conversion:

Consumerism is something that I think is a big obstacle and something that I was very guilty of falling into after my first mission. I can't talk about now this year, because I just got back; it's still too soon.

I was no less consumeristic a few months after my first mission than I was before. I completely fell into the consumerism again. And this year, coming back from mission, I realized I spend so much money on stupid stuff that I don't need to, and I can save that money so that next year I can go on mission for five weeks instead of two weeks or for other things or even to give it away. And I become more aware.

That has even been a wake-up call the second time, because the consumerism is something that is completely easy to fall into, the culture of wanting more things, and more clothes, and more this, and more that, the new mobile phone that came out.

When you go on mission, you feel that you want to leave all your stuff, things that I know I will need again; even things that I tell myself that I probably will keep like the air pump and the air mattress, the bigger things, and they say, Just take it all, take it all; and they ask, Aren't you going to need this?

No, I don't care; just take it all; I don't need it. Nothing matters; you're not attached to the material things; you're free. It's a freedom that you have over there that you don't have here. That's something that I feel also, when I come back, instead of fearing losing my things or my possessions, most of which I leave behind, I feel really afraid, when I come back, of losing those relationships with those people.

Pilar pointed to creature comforts, and to the fast pace of life and intensity of competition at her Ivy League-caliber Catholic university, as impediments to her ongoing Christian conversion:

Not what has a necessarily bad influence on me, but what takes me away from this road that I'm on when I come back from mission, is the fast-paced North American life in general. I don't think it's just Miami because I live in DC during the school year, and it's a very unique situation. You're talking to all college students. We're a very specific population.

At least for me, at school, it becomes so much more about competitiveness among people and I think it's just the nature of my school, an elite Catholic university.

I am very passionate about the subject I'm learning. I'm learning it because I can put it into practice and then help the people I met in Consuelito, as opposed to a lot of my classmates who never had a missionary experience and are just worried about taking the easiest professor, which to me, seems so ridiculous after I've had this experience. Which is not to say that I don't get sucked into it. I'm not this person sitting on the outside who's immune to this culture. It's very hard not to get sucked into the same lifestyle.

I think that the fast pace, that's one thing, filling every minute of the day with something and being completely efficient, is what I feel is stressed, especially in the United States. We learn that we must grow up to be efficient beings.

During a mission immersion, it's not about the fastest way to do things. It's about the best way to do things, which is the process. It's not about where you go, but how you go about doing it.

I think that in school, I really lose sight of that sometimes. I worry more about just the solution or my end goal, as opposed to, how I go about doing it. Do I really take time to talk and listen to people? So, I think the fast-paced life is a huge obstacle for returned missionaries.

And also something you said earlier, things like: being in the air conditioning all the time; not ever going without food; not ever experiencing the heat. Miami is just as hot as the Dominican Republic, but yet I have been here the whole summer and I have never once said, I am so hot, because I get in the car, and I turn on the air conditioner here. I am living in the same city as someone in Overtown and I am experiencing something completely different because I have air conditioning and they might not. So, I think that just the comforts that I have make me forget.

Another hindrance for me is people who challenge the resolutions and changes that I try to implement when I return from my immersions. For example, I had a big problem this year in communal bathrooms when people left the water running while they were brushing their teeth. I would get close to them and ask why don't you turn it off? Do you want to waste the water? And people would ask me what difference does it make?

People would question the difference that you're going to make by saving this much water because the bigger picture isn't that that water is going to go to that specific family that I know. The bigger picture is about what our formation leader, Fefita, asks: Are you really going to change your daily way of life?

Am I just going use this much water in the Dominican Republic because I have to? Am I going to be super wasteful here in the USA just because I have more water available? I think just being sur-rounded by commodities, and by people who question what differ-ence is it going to make? I think that makes me stray away from my resolutions.

I think it's about this culture of constantly trying to impress each other. This is what I'm studying. This is what I'm going to do. This is what I'm doing. When we go to the Dominican Republic it's not about "look at all that I have and look at all I've accomplished.: The question is first: How are you? The Dominicans that I know try to find some way to relate to you, to make you both equal.

Sometimes in college I can get sucked into that competition, as op-posed to trying to find common ground. We're always trying to find out how to upstage other people. We meet but I'm always ahead of you. Somebody always has to be at a different level, as opposed to trying to find the common ground.

I think that's a phenomenon of highly competitive universities filled with people that all have type A personalities and who were all like that in high school. There are great things about it; like a lot of these people are the ones who really care about the world and are some-how going to make a difference.

That intense degree of consumerism, I think that was one of the biggest wake-up calls that I got this year on the mission trip. I no-ticed the difference between the generosity I experienced amongst those who don't have and the selfishness among those who are very attached to objects, to things.

For example, when I was there, this happens to me every year and I always forget, I would say: Oh my God, your hair clip is so beau-tiful. The next day it was wrapped up in a bag for me, the next day, no questions asked. Here! And I knew she only owned one hair clip. It's just my nature to say, That's so pretty. Here it is! Don't complement anything. A six-year-old gave me her one ring, and I thought, I have so many.

And when I got back, I realized it's not just the people that are around me; it includes even me. How hard is it for me to lend someone something? Give it back! I need it. I really need it. That's my biggest flaw, even among my family and my sisters. I think that, definitely, the more I have, the more concerned I am about the stuff that I have, and I'm worried about. Keep it clean and it has to be here when I look for it.

When you go on mission, you feel that you don't need it anymore. It doesn't matter. For example, I don't need so many garments. Being attached to material things, as opposed to being attached to relationships. The people with whom we come in contact value more the relationship that I have with them because maybe they have experienced times when money has completely gone away.

I mean when you have nothing, I think you understand better the fact that things come and go. That's what makes the difference. I think that since I haven't had that experience of losing everything and not having, I think that it makes me more materialistic. It's not just about a material object that you own. But that's really something that I guess is my biggest obstacle to conversion. I come back and say, I need this for my house, and I need this for my room. That's the difference. I really do not need so much.

I'm not saying to just give everything away like these people do. Nobody should live in poverty. But, how much time do I really spend thinking about material things throughout my day, as opposed to thinking about other issues that are not material things? And I would say that as the months progress from when I go on mission, and even as the days progress, it's really more about what do I need to buy and what do I need to get? As opposed to, how often do I really think who do I need to talk to? That's what I'm thinking right now. I really spend more time focusing on objects than on the people around me.

A young AeA missionary lamented the multiple obstacles to Christian conversion that the culture of Miami features. She also pointed out the negative influence of some of her blatantly anti-Christian college professors:

Well, number one, definitely the culture in every way, this culture, American culture, and even more so, and I don't know if you guys feel the same way, because I haven't lived anywhere else, I feel that Miami culture sucks. Why? Because I feel Miami individuals are a very fake kind of people.

And also, even sad to say, private school people, like the people we went to school with, not all of them, but a lot of them. Some of the ways in which we've been brought up, and some of the people we've been surrounded with, and that are our peers in Miami, I find are an obstacle.

Although, as I said, I see some of those obstacles as opportunities, as challenges; but they are nevertheless discouraging. They are obstacles. So, the culture definitely, everyone's lifestyle, everyone's measure of what is important.

Like you said, college for me was an obstacle. When I came back the first time from a mission, college was terrible for me. Why? Number one, you see the people that are choosing their fields of study because of what's going to make me the most money. What's going to give me power and fame and money, and not what's going to help other people?

College was something that was very negative for me. Why? Because I personally got involved in the social atmosphere, sorority life, partying, and things that completely distracted me from my renewed commitment to AeA. This was the first year. Also, they were organizations that were not spiritual in nature. There was no room for that in that kind of a lifestyle.

Also, a lot of the classes that I had were detrimental too; they worsened my faith. I had a lot of professors who would talk badly about the church, badly about Catholicism, who would confuse me, who would talk badly about religion in general. A lot of people with some very, very liberal mentalities. But it was bad for me, particularly at that moment, because it was feeding me all these negative things, and things that were contrary to what was going to help me fulfill my commitments. So, college for me, the first year, was very bad.

Laura, a young AeA missionary, found that her newly transformed attitudes toward materially poor people have placed her in opposition to the biases of US mainstream culture:

As for the values, I know that I had a different attitude, because of the way that I was raised, specifically toward the guy on the corner a little way from the house, who stands there with the sign that says, I'm a Vietnam Vet; I will Work for Food, whom I would completely ignore before I went on mission because I was told that, and I believed it, that he could work if he wanted to.

I was told lots of stuff about that poor guy, about him being into drugs and all this stuff. I don't look at him that same way anymore. Instead, I look at this man who might need a friend. He might need someone to listen to his story. And now, I'm always trying to think of ways that I can help him.

When I share my ideas with people, they shoot them down but ... These are ideas about ways that might help him. I don't know. I don't have the financial ability to help in that sense, but I just look at him differently. I don't see him as this guy who's trying to cheat the system and as someone who's lazy and doesn't want to work and all this kind of stuff. I don't see any of those people like that anymore.

And I share that with everybody who makes that comment and I don't always get good reactions from them; but I'm not afraid to say it anymore either. That's one incident that always sticks with me because I use him as an example; but there's a lot more than just him.

There are quite a few people in Saginaw that need help, and people act as if they created that situation themselves, and so they just have to deal with it. I know better now. I went on mission. I saw how, through no fault of their own, many people's lives are unfair. I guess I don't judge their situations anymore.

Carlos, an AeA founder, was the object of his boss' eugenic invective:

My boss at work, with whom I had seldom engaged in talk of a religious or missionary nature, because that's not what you do with your boss at work, and I'll never forget it, it was in 1985 or 1986, told me that I was a hindrance to Nature because I was going to Haiti to give food to the Haitians.

He said to me, You are a hindrance to Nature because you are interrupting the natural process of Nature's attempt to eliminate all of those people. At that point in time, I didn't tell him to go eat feces because with him it would not have made a difference. I am a hindrance to Nature.

I think that he was trying to be cute more than anything else, but the fact that he said it meant that, well God only knows. He was probably a little bit of a racist, a little bit of a social Darwinist, a eugenicist, and felt a little bit guilty that he perceived himself as being more selfish than me. But I don't know for sure.

Ecclesial Discouragements

When missionaries identify the church itself as an impediment to post-immersion conversion and commitment, they often include, as components of that same church, their own missionary community, parish, parochial school, or Christian university, in addition to their bishops, pastors, administrators, consecrated and lay ministers, teachers, and assorted personnel.

Many folks feel especially defrauded whenever malfeasance, neglect, callousness, or imprudence emanates from any church entity because they perceive it as the apex of hypocrisy due to the claim that churches speak for and receive guidance from God. Moreover, since many people tend to place their trust more readily in their churches than in other societal institutions, they simultaneously render themselves more vulnerable to the potential effects of any negative experiences.

Below are samples taken from the responses in this category, along with an overview of other responses.

One veteran AeA missionary asserted the cross-cultural unifying power of the Eucharistic liturgy, in spite of the flagrant pastoral negligence exhibited by a handful of ministers who fail to make the effort to minister to folks of a certain ethnicity:

> *I traveled to the batey of Consuelito, and came back angry at my own religion, questioning God, and at the lowest spiritual point that I have ever been. But I returned to Miami more motivated than ever to make a change, just without the church!*

> *What burned me? Well, believe it or not, there is a small minority of priests in the Dominican Republic who totally turn their backs on batey dwellers, most of whom are Haitian born or of Haitian descent. These callous priests ignore these very materially poor*

Haitians, refuse to make the pastoral effort to minister to them, and deny them access to the sacraments.

But somehow, perhaps by the guidance of the Holy Spirit, I have continued to travel there to Consuelito with AeA, and slowly my faith life has returned.

One AeA veteran missionary reported the decision of the trustees of a Catholic university to rescind approval for university-sponsored missionary immersions in Haiti in conjunction with AeA, as the result of legal advice that they received:

At one Catholic university, the administration cancelled the Alternative Spring Break to Haiti because their attorneys advised them that Haiti wasn't safe. So, then we managed to get in to speak to the Board of Trustees. We were each given a minute to speak in front of the Board of Trustees, and they decided to reinstitute the Alternative Spring Break. But they would not approve it for Haiti. Instead, they shifted it to the Dominican Republic.

That's an example of the bureaucracy that must be navigated. Yes, it's better than nothing. But our whole intention was to go to Haiti in order to build and maintain those relationships. Therefore, we have to keep returning to Haiti. But the alternative that they approved was not with AeA. Instead, it was with another organization, with which they went in, built a house, and left; that's it.

However, now that some time has passed, I should probably ask the priest who's currently in charge of campus ministry about re-starting a partnership with AeA.

One AeA missionary who leads secondary-school students on short-term AeA immersions lamented the hardheartedness of some administrators, colleagues, and students at one particular Catholic high school:

I would say that getting back to school and getting back to work are obstacles to my conversion. I often return with my own students. Then we have to deal with the bureaucracy to find the time and the place for the students to present their experiences to the whole school. We have to deal with so many little details. We make you, the administration, look good because we are taking students overseas.

But now we bring back the message. The message we bring back is: This is what we did. This is what we saw. This is what we experienced. This is what we need to do. Each time we go, other students, as a community, donate all the supplies that we take with us. It is very important that they see that, even if the whole student body cannot travel with us, that they are still part of this mission.

Some of the faculty purposely skip the presentations. The administration doesn't really care. They won't show up to listen to the presentations. As long as we can make them look good. As long as we can include that in our admissions brochures for next year.

Our principal lets us speak at the faculty meetings as well after we return from each immersion, which is good. He lets the students come in, but he tells us that we may only have one minute to speak. How can these kids possibly share their experiences in less than a minute? We usually show slides in the background while they're talking so that the faculty sees them. But he reminds me, before we start, that we're running late and that their presentation must be kept to a minute. How can I tell these kids that? This is how they treat us.

I try to say: But this is our faith. But they disconnect themselves. I think that students are more open to it because they're young and they want to make a difference. But the school where I teach has become more upper middle class, so some are open, but some become so attached to their vehicles, like their Hummers. I think some are more open than others; but they all want to make a difference. I think they're generally open. So, it's easier to share with them.

I think that it's most effective when students who have been immersed on a mission share with their fellow students, student-to-student. I don't necessarily share in those settings; but I leave it up to the students to share their experiences. Because I'm an adult, they already expect me to express how I've been changed by the experience in various ways. But I think hearing how the immersion changed a peer makes a bigger impact. So, at school, I leave the sharing more to my students. But among the faculty, I do share despite the jaded attitudes of some colleagues.

Wendy, a young AeA missionary, perceived her peers in a religious youth group to be spiritually shallow and callous to the plight of abjectly poor Caribbean people:

I was really involved in the youth group at my parish during my first three years of high school. However, after I had gone on mission, I felt that this was the only cause, AeA. Missionary work with the poor is the only way. This youth group is a waste of time.

I've done all these talks. I've done all this stuff, all these retreats. It doesn't get anyone anywhere. Look at these kids; they do the same thing over and over again. This isn't for me; I want to quit. My mom said, I think you should finish your commitment; but she didn't make me. Especially for the second half of my senior year, I really just completely shut out the youth group, after my first mission. I was really just closed off to it.

Before I had gone on mission, I had applied to be a campus peer minister at my high school, and I just was so mad because I perceived these youth leaders to be spiritually shallow and stagnant. It was a trend to be religious. I said: You don't understand what's real, what is really important, what's really service. And I thought that I really did. And I also had the frustration of feeling that I knew but I couldn't do anything about it. And like my friend said, I had all these things going on. I'm so young.

There's this overwhelming amount of poverty. What can I really do about it? I wanted to fix it. I swore that I was going to change the world. I did; I swore. And I think that it affected my second year. I had a really good immersion experience my second year, but at the same time, I went into it saying, I'm not going to react the same way; I am not. I had not even thought about it.

But when my missionary sister was talking, I remembered that after my parents picked me up at the airport, I was crying in the back seat. To now think about how my parents must have seen that, how that appeared, scared me, and really, I did not want to go through that again. I was completely wrapped within my own little bubble of sadness.

And even though I was impacted by my second year, I still had a certain amount of protection that I had placed there. And I think that, among the many reasons that I did not go on mission this year, I think that that did affect my decision in some ways. So, I have to say that I thought that it would make it a religious experience. When I was on mission, and right after I returned, I was very prayerful. But then afterward, it wasn't helping me. I didn't feel that it was doing anything for me. I think that God really was in it.

I feel that my involvement in AeA now is for a different reason than religion. I think I got involved because of that connection because I was involved in the youth group and in service, and then they came and spoke at my school and I was really intrigued. Oh, look at these people. They're really faithful and I can learn a lot. And then post-immersion, I felt that I was really just closed off. Especially because I was attending a Catholic high school, and no one, out of all of those Catholics, seemed to want to understand or hear about it or anything, even teachers.

Some teachers, however, were supportive. Especially a Marist brother who is a guidance counselor; he was awesome. He even helped me do a school-wide shoe and school supply drive. So, there was a lot of support, despite my perception that no one wanted to help me. And I was convinced that no amount of projects is ever enough. It's never enough.

Lindsay, a young veteran AeA missionary, complained of parish indifference:

Most of the people in our parish didn't even know that we had left. We had a mission send-off mass, but it wasn't at our parish. Some people knew we were going, but I didn't feel that, in our parish, they felt we were making a difference. We felt we were making a difference; but it wasn't really viewed as anything, I felt, to our church.

A young veteran AeA missionary lamented the indifference of her pastor toward missionary endeavors:

I think it would have been helpful for the priest to show some interest, or if he would have shown interest and invited us to speak, instead of making us feel that he's subjected to having us speak.

Another young veteran AeA missionary echoed the complaint of pastoral indifference:

I felt similarly about our priest. The director of religious education asked me to write a report and give a little talk, which I did. But the priest kept postponing when I was supposed to do this. So, then I felt that he doesn't really want me to get up there and give this, like I'm in the way or he's just trying to make the lady happy. I imagined her bugging the priest, Let her give her talk, nobody wants to hear about it, but .... So, I did end up giving the talk, and that did help because that's how I express myself, through writing.

Jennifer, a young veteran AeA missionary, was publicly insulted by a judgmental non-AeA missionary:

After one summer mission immersion, I attended a Catholic social doctrine class that my missionary mentor, Carmen Mora, was teaching. A lady at our table who had gone on mission to South America was telling about her experience.

The people there knew that I had gone on mission, so they were asking me questions. So, I began sharing my experience; and I tend to be kind of positive, the glass is half full type of person. So, I was telling my story, and she stopped me and told me that I was romanticizing poverty.

I was crushed. I am serious. I went home and cried about it because I thought, Oh, my gosh, I missed the whole point of mission. I was completely devastated because I thought that I totally misunderstood the experience I had, and I was not going to go back. I wrote about it in my journal, and I prayed about it, and I cried about it, because it just totally threw me. I was so bummed.

Fortunately, the weekend after, we had a mission meeting and I shared it, and Carmen was the one who helped heal that hurt. She told me that I wasn't the one who had missed the boat because that lady had had a bad experience. She was the one who wasn't really meant to go on mission. Through the things she said to me, she helped heal me.

I felt so much better because I was seriously thinking, I am not getting it apparently, because I was telling my beautiful little story about the chapel and I could see what she was saying, and I thought: That's right because that's the kind of person I am. I love fairy tales. I want a happy ending. My favorite book is Jane Eyre. My favorite movie is Sense & Sensibility. I love poetry. I love to read it. I love to write it. I am that kind of a person. So, I thought she was right.

But then Carmen helped me to see that the lady had no authority to judge me. She was an older lady who had gone on a long-term mission. I won't forget that, nor will I forget how my missionary mentor helped me either. Boy, that was hard. She certainly did impede my missionary trajectory. I was just convinced by her. I was devastated. You can't even imagine the weight that was on me until I talked with you guys. And I guess it wasn't just my missionary mentor but the whole group who understood me and from where I was coming.

Of course, I saw the poverty when I was there. A couple of incidences in particular that really, really got to me were when I had to visit these kids' homes after I had been getting to know them and I saw where they lived. That was so hard. Then again, I saw so much beauty in them too, and that's what I was sharing about.

I wasn't sharing the horrible poverty that I saw because I guess that wasn't the main point of what I experienced there. Maybe I didn't primarily feel pity. I felt more the beauty of our common humanity and their simple joy. AeA has always taught us that, as missionaries, we prefer to approach issues of poverty and injustice through human relationships more than through political-economic denunciations.

One AeA founder spoke of the pain that she feels at the airport whenever she returns from immersions alone, and in doing so, shined light on the unintentional tendency in AeA to ignore the post-immersion needs of our most veteran missionaries:

I have recently made it a point that, whenever I am in Miami, whenever some AeA member returns from the Dominican Republic, I go to the airport to receive them. I have done so now several times because when I arrive at that airport myself after an immersion and there is nobody there from AeA to receive me, it feels horrible because, on top of the fact that when we return, we feel that we have returned to an alien land, at that moment, I feel all alone, and I ask myself, What the hell is this?

Carlos, an AeA founder, remembered that AeA began as a missionary community exclusively comprised of leaders who could launch and execute their own projects. In its infancy, AeA did not take the time to provide guidance and formation to newcomers:

Back in those days, AeA did not have the structure or the patience or the acumen or the insight or the fortitude to be able to take somebody who was not an independent thinker or who could not contribute his or her own ideas, and tell him or her, If you want to help us, then this is what you can do.

You either got it and immediately jumped on this already moving train and started doing stuff, or we would just thank you for your monetary contribution and continue what we were doing, and that was it. It was neither good nor bad. That's just the way it was. AeA, at that stage, was an organization for born leaders. There is no value statement in that. That's just how it was.

A fellow AeA founder echoed the fact that AeA began as a missionary community consisting only of leaders, not followers:

It was such that the task at hand required oomph; it required self-starters.

Lourdes, an AeA founder, remembered the growing pains of AeA's early years:

At the beginning of our AeA trips, we did not have this consciousness about re-entry. We didn't have any of that. It was preparation to go. Once you went on an immersion and came back, that was it; you had already accomplished your mission.

It was only later when our theologian friends, Alicita and Fefita, began to talk about it and to raise our awareness about re-entry and the mission-in-reverse process. And now it has become a formalized part of our formation process over the past decade, after about thirty years of AeA traveling to and from the Dominican Republic, Haiti, Colombia, and México, without having focused on the aftermath of the mission immersions. Now, we meet post-immersion in order to talk and debrief.

Another AeA founder reiterated the growing pains during AeA's infancy:

Immediately after coming back, I found my first teaching job and went to teach and all of a sudden all of that experience was bottled and silenced for a long, long time. Other than a handful of spiritual people, there was really no one to guide us. We did not have a process for this debriefing or unpacking of everything that we had lived through.

So, I maintained silence at home and silence at work. I only spoke about my missionary immersion with people who had gone with me to Colombia. So, it was a very fragmented experience which did not become integrated into my life as a whole until later.

Back then, it was a completely different experience from nowadays, that is, after the birth, formalization, and evolution of AeA. Pre-immersion preparation and post-immersion debriefing are handled more systematically now.

A Saginaw AeA missionary expressed dissatisfaction with the inadequacy of the AeA Saginaw re-entry process:

I don't remember having a re-entry meeting really. I think we might have shown each other our pictures. We held a picture party.

Another Saginaw AeA missionary echoed dissatisfaction with the inadequacy of the AeA Saginaw re-entry process:

There's no real re-entry program in Saginaw. Well, we attempted to start a re-entry process this year. But the photo parties have no spiritual component. There was no reflection. It was a re-entry meeting but without any structure to it. We were able to go through our photos and share and relive our stories.

That's the only support that we get. There's no structure and no meetings. Not everybody attends them. You don't get to talk about your feelings or what you experienced spiritually. All you talk about are stories about what happened during the day camp, and the stories that usually get shared at the picture parties are usually about the fun times and the visits to the houses of sick people and the houses of the families of the children who participate in the day camps.

We have none of that in Michigan. We tend to informally share our pictures with the people who were with us on the mission. We always have to rush because somebody has to leave early, so you can't really fulfill the re-entry agenda.

One veteran AeA immersion leader noted the need for patience when leading post-immersion meetings that include missionaries of diverse ages and levels of experience:

Sometimes the post-immersion responses of some of the high school students who have only participated in their first immersion experience don't seem as profound and they may tend to hover at the level of just wanting to share photographs. But that's to be expected. They are young. They will deepen over time. They are the future.

Margaret, a young veteran AeA missionary, indicated that there are distinct ways to conduct post-immersion re-entry meetings, some of which are beneficial and others that are futile:

Re-entry meetings can be helpful, if there are others that have had experiences of comparable impact and if the meetings are led correctly. Sometimes those meetings can devolve into picture swapping sessions, but other times I remember sharing some of my most vivid images and memories while trying to make the formation leaders understand my gratitude.

I have attended a couple of them where the dominating sentiment could be summarized by statements such as: Look at this! Remember this? Yeah, I had so much fun, fun, fun! Let's remember all the nice stuff! Whoopee!

But I've been to some other meetings in which Fefita, one of our formation leaders, has slowed us all down and has told us to transition into a prayerful mode. Then, she always asks us to describe the most vivid image that is locked in our heads and hearts from the immersion trip.

There is always something from each trip that my heart holds onto. One example was from Berita Mystique, where I saw a baby drinking from a cup filled with mud and so she had mud-stained lips. That was one of those images that stuck with me.

One AeA veteran lamented the inconsistencies and scheduling problems regarding post-immersion community liturgies:

Some people say that it's not a re-entry mass and others say that of course it is intended to be both a reunion of the whole AeA family as well as a liturgy via which the larger AeA community welcomes the missionaries back.

However, many people are already on out-of-town vacations with their families when those masses are held; the parents of the young missionaries often schedule their familial vacations right after the immersions each summer and the parents whisk them away as soon as they return.

So, they inevitably miss the re-entry meetings and the re-entry mass. Therefore, the re-entry welcoming liturgy is often not all that it could be or should be without them.

A young but experienced AeA missionary critiqued the incomplete nature of our post-immersion liturgies:

> But does anyone invite us to share any reflections or feelings during those masses? How can it be considered, at least in part, a re-entry mass if we are not invited to share anything? Meeting with the whole AeA community does definitely help and encourage the returned missionaries, but it seems stunted or incomplete by the lack of sharing on the part of those who have just returned from their immersions.

Another young but experienced AeA missionary echoed the critique about the incomplete nature of our post-immersion liturgies:

> Nor does anyone tend to offer a formal welcome to those have recently returned from immersions. What I have noticed is that when we have discussed the re-entry aspect of that liturgy, we rattle off the names of the abundance of recently returned missionaries who will not attend the mass because they are already out-of-town on familial vacations. So, generally, the masses are attended by the elders and young missionaries who have been immersed in previous years.

Another AeA founder contrasted the Eucharistic habits of AeA's early days to those of today:

> Back in those days, we never had a Eucharistic liturgy to welcome us home. Now, we try to have a Eucharistic celebration to start each academic year. In addition, we always have a beautiful send-off mass or commissioning liturgy.

An AeA veteran complained about low attendance at re-entry meetings due to scheduling conflicts:

> In Miami, we have attendance problems at our re-entry meetings and masses too, because we schedule them when most everybody is on post-summer-immersion vacations with their families.

One AeA founder observed the difficulty of ensuring the participation of immediate post-immersion missionaries in re-entry meetings:

> *Sometimes we haven't been able to do it. We've just can't get the people together because they go away on vacation or back to college.*

Justin, a young AeA veteran, longingly commented that his immersion experiences are so much more spiritually intense than any of his post-immersion periods:

> *The whole religious aspect of my life got turned around. I don't think that for myself they were ever affirmed because that change that occurred was because of the experiences that I had on mission, and I did not continue to have those experiences when I got back. They're kind of unique on mission, and I didn't have that when I got back. It doesn't get affirmed or deepened until I go back again.*

Margaret, another young veteran AeA missionary, lamented the post-immersion loss of spiritual momentum regarding her pursuit of the resolutions that she envisioned and made during immersions:

> *In AeA, we structure our evening prayers during the immersions so that we can speak and discuss the day's events and insights every night together. When we're there, we always hear people express this urge to get started, to do something, to change something. But after we come back, without having that nightly meeting, without those people around us who understand us because we have shared the missionary experiences together, without having them to talk to all the time, our hearts still want to do something but it seems that we lose that support, that circle of prayer that we had while we were immersed, giving us all those ideas and the backbone to go ahead and make that make that change, start that program, to help however we can. It's totally different when we're back here. Plus, we're juggling work and the demands of daily life back here.*

Carlos, an AeA founder, opined on the necessity of holding more frequent meetings:

An isolated re-entry meeting is a flash-in-the-pan one-time event. If there is not a community in place, and a structure that meets very frequently, onto which you can jump onboard and find spiritual nourishment, social nourishment, missionary and vocational formation, avenues of release, then it all peters out. Then you don't have a life in the Holy Spirit. We need to hold a meeting one night every week, either on a Friday or a Saturday.

An AeA founder concurred on the need to return to the habit of meeting frequently in order to regain our communal vigor:

I think that we need to do a much better job of gathering. We've lost that sense of convening, of gathering people for prayer, of gathering people for sharing, not just for the business side of AeA. Nowadays, we tend to gather for business. But this gathering for prayer, gathering to listen to each other, gathering to share experiences, gathering to laugh, to sing; I think that we can improve on that. We can make prayer and sharing a more integral part of the daily, weekly, and monthly life of AeA and our members. We have lost the community life.

Another AeA founder concurred on the necessity of holding more frequent meetings in order to promote cohesion and vitality:

I agree that we have lost a lot of our communal energy and we have to revive that by meeting, by meeting, by spending time together, praying together, and playing together. For God's sake, not everything has to be a retreat. We could play dominoes together or have a pool party or a barbecue; many of us have pools in our backyards.

Two young yet experienced AeA missionaries tendered the most disputable opinion out of all the interview participants by espousing the belief that the founders and leaders of AeA intentionally allow post-immersion neophytes to struggle on their own in order to prompt them to discover their own methods for resolving the post-immersion blues. In other words, they are convinced that AeA's leaders purposely deny post-immersion guidance for a little while in order to fortify the young missionaries spiritually. Wendy opined that:

I think that AeA kind of allows us to struggle a little bit and to be frustrated, to be sad. I think that each and every member of AeA realizes that that is a struggle that we need to go through. It's kind of like being in that tight cocoon so that you can become a butterfly. It's true. They let us struggle. They let us be sad. They let us be frustrated.

They don't necessarily try so hard to protect us emotionally, like our parents do. They don't say, I want to feed you, and I want to clothe you, and I want to make you feel better. I want to make you happy. Let's go to the movies. Let's go here. Let's go there. AeA does not do that. They allow us to be sad and experience those negative feelings of re-entry when we come back because I think that they feel that that is essential to our growth as missionaries and to our discernment process also regarding what we ourselves should do.

And because they're each different, because the individual founding members of AeA are very diverse individuals, and they have different professions, and different lifestyles, that opens up a lot of room for diverse paths in AeA. And that's something that I've always appreciated. It's a very wide circle of all different kinds of people of all different ages, different interests, and different professions.

Pilar, another young yet experienced AeA missionary, concurred regarding this most controversial point by also championing the belief that the founders and directors of AeA intentionally allow the post-immersion neophytes to struggle on their own for a while in order to encourage them to discover their own methods for resolving post-immersion disorientation and challenges. She interprets the nonjudgmental post-immersion guidance style as a purposeful decision to promote the spiritual autonomy of new missionaries via a policy of non-imposition of templates upon them:

> *I think the way that I've found AeA to be most helpful is to realize that they give you the tools, like with the formation meetings before and during the immersions, to then have you, by yourself, decide how you're going to change whatever things you identify in your life.*

> *If I came home and all of a sudden, they came and asked me: What are you going to do now? How are you going to change? Pressuring me to give premature concrete answers, and holding me up to a certain standard, I think would be very intimidating. And I think that giving us the freedom to keep in touch as much as we want and to get away from the missionary milieu sometimes, and even being supportive of someone who goes away to college for a year, and then comes back and says, I've been doing this and that, and hearing someone say, Oh I want to hear about it, and always being willing to take you back, even if you haven't been there for a whole year. It's not as if, if you temporarily veer off of the road of AeA, then you're gone forever.*

> *I think that the fact that they give us freedom to discern on our own, and to figure that we're going to have doubts and struggles, and still refuse to spoon feed us, I think that's the best thing. They care about our transformation, about our spiritual growth, but they don't say, I care about your spiritual growth, Now, what are you doing? But they take a genuine interest in us and invite us back to the meetings.*

> *It's a subtle, patient way. And they don't treat you like children. And they don't trivialize your experience, which I think is important. They've gone on, God knows, how many mission immersions. If I talk to my AeA mentor, she'll sit there for an hour and listen to me go on about an insight that I've discovered for the first*

time. But she doesn't ask, Well, have you thought about this other country? They don't trivialize the realizations that we've made at our age. And they don't try to impose the paths that they've chosen, their ways of life, on us.

I think something has happened to me in other groups that has not happened in this group, which is that I haven't felt, Well, if I walk into this group's meeting wearing a certain outfit, they'll think, You hypocrite. They do expect for me to somehow change my lifestyle, but they don't think it's just going to be manifested by the way I dress. They do not impose any mold on new missionaries.

They know that you can decide to give your whole entire life to God via consecrated religious life or you can decide to have a family. You can decide to have a career. They're not interested in turning you into one narrow type of person. They're just interested in helping you transform yourself into the best instrument of God that you can be, however you can be, not just how they are or how they've been.

I think they're able to do that very well because of experience and because they're really smart. I think that the different age strata within AeA are so important. I think that's what I like the most. In the beginning, it was what made me the most uncomfortable. It made me feel awkward at first when I was at the meetings. I don't think I've ever been, as a seventeen-year-old or an eighteen-year-old, because we're all used to peer ministry where everybody was the same age. I wasn't used to being in the room with a fifty-five-year-old talking about his or her faith.

But I think that it was the best thing because even with my experience this year, I think having an older community, having people ranging from eighteen to thirty-nine, I think that it really helped develop me a lot more because a person who's thirty-nine has a completely different perspective than me and that's great, and that's something that AeA has that's really great, that I can see someone at sixty-five questioning God.

And I can say, It's okay that I'm questioning God now because he or she is sixty-five and I see him or her as a more faithful person that I am, and he or she is saying, Sometimes I don't believe and sometimes I question. I think that the fact that they're not patronizing is very important. Instead, they're so open about what they feel, and they make us feel like equals.

That's what I feel. Even though I'm only twenty, when I talk to them, they don't make me feel like I'm only twenty and like I've only been on three mission immersions. Instead, in AeA, I am a missionary and that makes us equal and so we can share just as much.

Interpersonal Discouragements

The medieval French poet Eustache Deschamps opined that, "Friends are the family that you choose for yourself."[5] Adolescents in the USA tend to pass through a stage during which they trust their friends more than their families and prefer the company of their friends over that of their families. However, adolescents are not the only demographic group who display the proclivity to absorb and manifest the values and habits of their friends; hence, the observation by Hellenic philosopher Democritus that, "Birds of a feather flock together."[6]

Many post-immersion missionaries express an impulse, and even a need, to distance themselves from non-missionary friends whose ethics and behaviors they perceive as antithetical to their own newly

---

[5] Eustache Deschamps, (http://thinkexist.com/quotes/eustache_deschamps/), 2010; (http://www.brainyquote.com/quotes/authors/e/eustache_deschamps.html), 2010.

[6] Democritus, (http://wiki.answers.com/Q/Who_said_the_famous_quote_birds_of_a_feather_flock_together).

acquired or newly renewed missionary virtues and practices. As I mentioned in the second chapter, I too felt and acted upon this impulse.

Laura, a young veteran AeA missionary, realized the stark contrast between her rate of growth during her overseas missionary immersions and her friends' relative stagnation during their stateside materialistic immersions:

> *Of all my values, the one that has changed the most for me is just materialism in general, the materialistic shallow life that a lot of times I would lead with my friends. And now I just realize it. I had changed so much because of some of the experiences I had.*

> *It felt as if I had been gone for a year. All of that experience was packed into what would be a year's worth at home. And when I would come home, my friends would say, Oh, we did so much this summer. And then they would just talk about going to a party or something.*

> *And I would say to myself, God, I'm glad I left! So, I guess that was a value or a lack of value that was affirmed. The realization that that was not where I wanted to be was reaffirmed by the fact that while I was gone and changed so much, they didn't change at all and they experienced no growth.*

Wendy, a young AeA missionary, felt profoundly disillusioned with the egotistical values of her non-missionary friends:

> *It was hard to relate to people. I felt that I couldn't relate to people that were in my own society now. I felt that I couldn't talk to my friends from high school. I felt that I couldn't talk to them about my immersion because they couldn't understand. I did feel mis-understood. I felt that they saw me as a crazy person that just had experienced something totally abnormal. That's pretty much how I felt.*

If I felt that you were receptive toward listening to what I had to say or what I had experienced, then I was pretty polite or welcoming, but if you were immediately uninterested, then I didn't really have time for you or I didn't care to converse with you.

It wasn't that I didn't want to spend time with people, I really just couldn't emotionally. I was really emotionally down and depressed. The guilt had a lot to do with the stuff inside. I was feeling that I had learned something about the world that was so obvious and yet there were so many people that just didn't care to know, and I was shocked that I associated with people that didn't care.

I was shocked that I had lived and would live a life of vanity and shallowness and all that, and that the majority of people in my life based their lives on selfish things and selfish thoughts. And I wanted to change that.

So, I wasn't able to talk about it with anybody except for the mission group, and that included my parents, who were very supportive, and my best friends. It took me time to slowly warm up and share my experience.

I feel that my first-year experience also affected my second-year experience in the sense that I was really stuck on the anger and I really couldn't let it go. Like my friend said, I was angry at anyone that had never gone on a mission, and angry at everyone that had money, including my own family.

Wendy recognized that her immersion experiences inevitably separated her from her friends who never had such an experience:

I would say that my friends from high school really didn't support me at all. They didn't want to hear about it and they wanted me to forget about it, and they said, Why do we always have to talk about this? Get over it. You were there. You went. Let it go.

They didn't want to listen because it makes people uncomfortable. It makes them feel guilty. Why would I want to tell you suddenly that you're selfish? Not that I was telling them that, but that's the message they take. It's not their interest. It's not their priority.

It's also not fair for me to criticize them because two weeks before I left, I was totally cool with doing the things that they wanted to do, talking about the things they wanted to talk about, or indulging in gossip, or whatever. And then all of a sudden, I come back from having this experience which they don't understand or cannot even imagine.

Then, how can I expect them to comprehend what I went through? Honestly, it's unrealistic for me to expect them to really understand or relate. At my age, it's impossible to relate without having the experience. They felt like, I didn't go, so I'm not interested.

One veteran AeA missionary did not hesitate to identify his friends as impediments to his spiritual advancement as a missionary:

My friends were an impediment, not that they knew what they were doing, not that they were purposely impeding me, but it was just the fact that they weren't going on mission. I would say that none of my friends are religious, none of them. Fewer than a handful of them are Catholic. So, for one thing, that makes it all harder to talk to them about my mission experience.

But these are the people that I'm with most of the time and these are the people with whom I do things. So, when it comes to my friends getting together, or my friends going on vacation, or my friends doing things, it's always in contradiction to mission meetings or mission trips.

So they always present that choice, because my resolution was to stay committed to AeA. They know that this is important to me. Nevertheless, they always try to convince me to skip missionary meetings. Not only that, but there is also the fact that mission isn't a part of their life.

Laura, a young veteran AeA missionary, noticed the underlying indifference of her friends when she tried to share her missionary anecdotes with them:

When I returned from my earliest mission immersions, my friends would say, I want to hear all about your trip. Go get your pictures. Then they would say, Yeah, Stop talking, and let me look at the pictures. When you have your pictures, you have a story behind each one, so it takes time to go through them. They kept flipping through the photographs, so as to get it over with quickly.

Justin, a former full-time AeA missionary, echoed the frustration and isolation that he felt due to the underlying indifference of his friends when he tried to share his missionary anecdotes with them:

I went on my first missionary immersion during a transitional period for me because I had left high school, and this was my first year away in college. I wasn't really in connection with all of my really good friends from high school because we all went different ways, and so I didn't have them around to talk to about it and I wasn't yet really close to anyone in college to the point where I felt that I could share.

I did feel the whole rejection because when you get back you really want to express your feelings; you really want to tell your stories about the people that you met, about the friends that you have, not just through the pictures but through the memories that you have that you keep with you.

And so, when I was in that transitional period, I was still in contact with my friends from high school, but I didn't see them a lot. So we were usually catching up on things that were going on in our lives, and when I got to that part, I always felt that they were indifferent. So, what did you do over the summer? I went on this mission. Oh yeah cool. Where did you go? And I'd tell them. Did you have fun? Yeah, but it's not the fun that made the experience.

They didn't really want to hear the stories, I guess. They just wanted to know if it was a good experience or not. So, I felt that frustration with my friends.

One young veteran AeA missionary registered her post-immersion sense of frustration when she attempted to communicate with her friends back at home:

I would show pictures to my friends and they would say, Well, they're dressed pretty nice. Yeah, those were the clothes we took from the United States. Those were the type of comments that I got. Then I just stopped trying to share with them, and I was starting to get angry because they weren't understanding.

A young AeA missionary switched friends post immersion in order to avoid negative influences:

Whereas, the first year, I was just starting college; for me, it was a pretty bad influence. The first year, I actually lost some of my friends because we had differences when I got back from mission. I didn't really want to hang out with them for a while, so they got mad at me. It was just petty arguments that became big deals because of our ideological differences.

I actually chose not to be their friend anymore because I thought that they were bad influences on me. The friends that I have now I think are all either positive influences on me or no influence at all; so the friendship thing is not as much of an issue.

And now, the second year around, I feel a little bad about that. I feel that, Wow, I lost an opportunity again to maybe, I don't want to say, change certain people who were my close friends, the people that I dropped. Maybe I shouldn't have dropped them; maybe I should have continued my friendships with them. On the contrary, who knows? Maybe I could have been a positive influence on them. I don't want to say, change them, but good things may have come out of those friendships in the future that now I'll never know about.

Wendy, a young AeA missionary, criticized herself and her friends in the USA because they seem only willing to share a portion of their excess money, but not a bit of what they believe they need:

I find that unlike here, when people there who don't have anything, are able to give something away, even if it hurts them, they consider it a really good gift. For them, when it's a sacrifice, when it really affects you, when it hurts, when you say, Damn, I'm going to miss it.

Those people, they give it anyway. Here, it's, Well, I'll give you some, if I have extra, or if it's something that I don't wear anyway or if it doesn't fit me anymore, or if I have enough extra; I need some extra, just in case I'll need some for later. So, I need extra extra. There, people give out of their need.

And people here, well, for example, we had a fundraising gala this past year. I didn't even ask several of my friends because it's discouraging when they say, No, no, no. They have some silly excuses for why they can't go. It costs fifty dollars for a ticket, which is not cheap. It can be a lot for a nineteen-year-old, but when you see them wearing designer clothing and following the latest trends, you wonder because you see that they have the fifty dollars. They just don't want to spend it on that; they want to spend it on something else.

So that's very discouraging, and at the same time, it doesn't push me away from AeA or mission. It pushes me away from those people. It makes me question why are we friends? Are you really helping me grow as a person? Because when I surround myself with people like that, I get easily sucked into that same way of life. And it's not to say that I can blame them because it's inside of me.

We are equals in the sense of our humanity and our tendencies. I just happen to be open to going on this mission trip and to being changed by it. But at the same time, I have a certain responsibility to keep myself aware of the reality of the situation.

Regarding the gala, the people that didn't have the money, like my aunts and uncles. My aunt is divorced. She's a second-grade teacher. She has three daughters. She just recently bought a townhouse. She really does not have a lot of money at all; and she bought two tickets for her and a date, and it's not her typical social event. She didn't know anybody that was going to be there. She had never been before. She wasn't necessarily familiar with the culture of AeA. She did it mostly because she loves me and cares about me.

But that's important; that's how people get involved in these sorts of things, through their connections with people, and that's the key. The people you don't expect, the people whom you would excuse more easily, saying, Oh I'm not going to ask them because it's really hard for them financially. And they're the ones who are the quickest to give you the money for the ticket.

It's interesting to see how people react when you ask them for some help, because we can't do it by ourselves. So that's discouraging, when people say, No, no, no. But then, it's really encouraging when somebody you didn't expect says, Yes.

Familial Discouragements

Perhaps the most heartbreaking source of obstacles for a recently returned missionary can be his or her family, particularly his or her own parents. While patient dialogue can reveal that parents are usually motivated by comprehensible concerns, nevertheless, their verbal critique or condemnation can be particularly poignant for an inexperienced missionary whose sensitivity level is always height-ened immediately before and after each mission immersion.

Like many of the early Christian martyrs, AeA's founders should be regarded as true pioneers because they struggled against the overt opposition of their own parents in order to heed God's call to forge this enduring missionary community.

One AeA veteran described her family's lack of support regarding her missionary call:

> When I participated in my first mission immersion with AeA, we headed for the inner-city slums of Santo Domingo. There I met peo-ple who profoundly moved me and changed me in a way that took me by surprise and in a way that I cannot exactly describe. I don't know what happened. But the return for me was, and still is, very disconcerting and this hasn't changed over the years.
>
> In the beginning, after my first couple of trips, I remember that my mother was still alive, I would bring my pictures home, and this whole idea of going abroad with missionary intentions was so for-eign to my whole family that would ask me: What is this for? Why do you go there? No one in my family embraced my missionary vocation. Whenever I showed them my photos, they said, Okay, that's nice. They criticized me back then and they still do now.
>
> In the beginning, they treated my missionary endeavors as a fad. In the beginning, my family said, It will pass. Her interest and zeal will eventually fade away. And then, as the years passed, and I con-tinued making these missionary journeys, they began to ask me why I had not gotten this out of my system already. They said: You should have gotten over this by now. Don't you think it's time that you should give these mission immersions up? Now, that I'm over fifty, they tell me, You're getting too old for this. Don't you see? You shouldn't be doing this at your age.

My family has never, never supported me in terms of me answering my missionary vocation. They don't understand it. It is completely foreign to them. "Foreign" is the word that I use, and not just regarding the missionary aspect of my life. They don't comprehend any bit of my religious vocation. The whole thing is foreign to them. They ask: Why are you like this? Why are you teaching theology? You should be working at a bank and earning money.

So, I am an enigma to them, and I have always been so. And I become more of an enigma to them every time that I choose to travel. So, that's my family. So, my family is nothing in terms of comprehension or support ... I have a very good family and they love me, and I love them. It's just that this particular area of my life is incomprehensible to them, despite the fact that they raised us as Catholics. Our parents' attitude has always been, Yes, it's fine for other people to give some of their children to the church, but not us.

Although I never received any verbal support from them, the very few times that I solicited their aid, both my brother and my sister chipped in significantly to help AeA raise funds to keep some of our vital Dominican projects afloat.

One AeA founder recalled how worried and upset his father was because of his conviction that the founders were excessively committed to AeA and the church:

My father and I had a great relationship until AeA. Interestingly enough, in today's gospel reading, Jesus says, I must come before family and friends. My father started getting on my case when I joined AeA, and I started getting very involved, and it became AeA seven nights a week.

My father asked me, What the hell is wrong with you? You used to go out. You used to go out to clubs every night. Because I used to club every night before Cursillo and AeA and do all the things that young guys at the tender age of twenty-seven try to do when they go to clubs every night. And my father felt that that was wonderful, that that was a fine existence.

And then all of a sudden, we started having some tremendous spats. What the hell was I doing dedicating all my time to the church? He said that that obviously was not right. But my father wanted me to quit wasting my life by going to church seven days a week. He thought I should be clubbing every night. He was upset that I was giving all of my energy to the church. He was not upset that I was getting involved with poor people.

In my first few years with AeA, I would always go on the mission immersions for a week or a week and a half per year. And then I would return to Miami, and then go on a family vacation with my parents as well. But I would still dedicate a week or a week and a half to vacation trips each summer. The problem wasn't that I was involved with poor people. The problem was that I was doing AeA seven nights a week. It was a full-time job.

My father wanted me to be more balanced, which meant going to church only on Sundays. It was consuming. It was consuming. There abounded some sort of Cuban anticlericalism. My father would say, Keep giving yourself to the church and the day that you get sick, they will give you nothing. Being too religious is not so good.

An AeA founder censored her own post-immersion sharing with her family as an emotional and spiritual self-defensive tactic:

I didn't share with my family. I stayed silent and I did not share. I sometimes showed them my pictures at the beginning of my missionary career; and after later journeys, I would not even show them my pictures.

They would have died of a heart attack when they learned that I had to deal with fleas and lice and, had gone hungry for a while, and had to arise at 5:00 in the morning to pray, and that I had cut my fingers from scrubbing laundry by hand.

In their view, they had emigrated from Cuba with us precisely so that we wouldn't have to live like slaves. And now, is this your choice to return to a fate from which we labored so hard to save you? This life of servitude would be a regression for our families. They had taken us out of Cuba in order to protect us from the prospects of such a horrible fate as servitude.

Another AeA founder echoed the phenomenon of encountering resistance to her missionary call from her parents:

Typically, in the Cuban family, the aspiration and the hope is that your girls will marry and give you grandchildren and that your sons will get married and thereby ensure the continuation of the family's name. Sometimes, when the son joins a religious congregation or becomes a priest, it is considered prestigious and an honor. But when a daughter opts for the religious life, they presume that she'll be treated like a maid to the priests and spend her whole life like a slave.

It's true; that does indeed happen in some countries in Africa and the Caribbean. Some nuns live like slaves or maids. So that's not for my daughter. My family was pretty much the same as hers. They never understood. In the beginning, they were very, very, very opposed. Later, they resigned themselves to it, but my missionary call never resonated inside of them.

Both of our families are very Catholic and very devout. Now, my parents even host the annual AeA re-entry mass and meeting at the end of each summer, because, later they became very proud of me after they finally overcame the dreaded threat that I might become a nun. A missionary, maybe; but a nun, never.

Margaret, a young AeA veteran, found it difficult to communicate about her immersion to her parents and friends:

Everyone always tries to compare the volunteer work that they, or someone in their family, have done with whatever you tell them. It is almost like people feel they have to prove themselves to you. I have found that it is often hardest to share with the people closest to me. They have seen the change in me, but they have never really asked for the details.

I find it much easier to go speak to large groups of students or parishioners about my experience while formally representing AeA. I don't know why it's easier for me to get up and tell my whole story to those people. I guess because then I'm still disconnected from those people. I'm not seeking that heart-to-heart connection with them. You've seen me with the kids. I love to tell the stories. It's really meaningful for me to get that out.

But for me to tell it to my close friends; I've never really told my parents the details about it or anything. It's hard. It's strange. I don't know if that's a widespread phenomenon among returned missionaries. It might just be me.

One AeA veteran noticed that her family members neither want to invest themselves personally in the lives of poor people in the Caribbean, nor in facing any potentially prophetic challenges to their own habits that might arise from such engagement:

Our families and friends think that we're do-gooders and they ask us what they can give us to take down there to give away to the poor people. It reminds me of when the tourists go to the bateys and throw stuff to the kids. They don't get personally involved. They don't invest themselves. They just offer material items from a distance. I might preach at my family and friends and say: This is why we need to change this or that. But they don't take my challenges seriously.

Another AeA founder echoed the fact that his parents were worried that the founders were overly committed to AeA and the church:

My parents were not happy with me either ... We were too serious for our parents and they were highly concerned that we were involved way too much in the church.

One young AeA missionary complained about being labeled as morally superior by her parents because she had become a missionary:

Ever since I started going on missions, I've been labeled the good one in the family; and it stinks because that carries a negative connotation. Because people are even afraid to say, I'm a missionary, because the image that comes to mind is someone pounding on a Bible telling you that you need to repent from your sins, so you'll be saved, and if not, then you're going to hell.

Actually, I was told that on mission this year. ... I don't even know if my family feels this way, that they think of someone who perceives herself as holier than thou, as someone who is looking down upon them. I go on mission because it's something that's fulfilling to me. It has nothing to do with how it will make others feel. I guess a lot of times that impedes me because I get the impression that sometimes my title as a missionary might do that to some people. But if it does, then obviously that's something that that person needs to deal with. It's something unintentional on my part.

One AeA veteran missionary expressed the extra angst that she used to feel upon returning from mission immersions, due to her former beau's indifference to her missionary experiences and the incumbent emotions that they elicit:

For many years I was in a relationship with a person who did not support my efforts and failed to understand the depth of the impact the missionary experience had on me. Such a relationship can be very detrimental to the re-entry process and cause much more confusion than necessary.

When you're with a person who just doesn't have that in his heart, who just doesn't have the thirst for social justice in his blood, then you are totally lost when you get back from a mission immersion experience. You're returning home with a wide-open heart to someone who doesn't understand what you've just been through.

Intrapersonal Discouragements

The Nipponese martial artist and founder of Aikido, Morihei Ueshiba, acknowledged the vital significance of each person's internal struggles when he declared that, "True victory is victory over oneself."[7] Young missionaries who participate in short-term immersions often find, after they re-enter their society of origin, that their best-laid plans for conversion are undermined by the twin temptations toward lethargy and self-indulgence.

One young AeA veteran missionary placed the blame for her own lack of post-immersion missionary conversion squarely upon her own shoulders:

I don't think that I can say that anyone except myself impeded my pursuit of the resolutions because I think that's a cop-out. And I know that I have made some small changes. And I've had enough transformative experiences to motivate me. And I've been immersed in a culture where I've let myself sometimes forget the lessons learned during those missionary immersions, and it's not because my friend wants to go shopping.

It's because I say, Okay. And I think that, as a result of my culture, I justify that. No one else does it for me. Maybe others justify it for me. I work hard. I earn my own money. I can buy what I want. People say that. But at the end of the day, it comes down to the fact that it's my resolution. It's my resolve. That's where my impediment lies.

[7]Morihei Ueshiba, (http://www.seidokan.org/princ_of_aikido.htm) 2010; (http://www.fightingmaster.com/masters/ueshiba/quotes.htm), 2010.

There are things that can dissuade me, like college. There's the whole party scene and wanting to feel like you belong. I was the do-gooder; that was my nickname in college; that's what I was labeled. But I think that the college party scene was something that did impede my sense of mission and my pursuit of my resolutions because I think it took my focus away from something that was important to me and placed it on socializing. Because that's what you do in college, you drink, you go out, and you party, you meet people ...

The competition that I felt was over my values. I wasn't a very spiritual person when I was around that group of people. I didn't consider when I got home at three in the morning that I was going to go pray in my bed before going to sleep. For a few years, going to mass was not a priority for me. I made excuses. I studied on Sunday. But I could have studied on Saturday night instead of going out. But now on Sunday I have to study instead of going to church. I don't know how to explain it, but I just feel that that skewed my values in some way, and I let them become skewed.

Another young AeA veteran missionary also took responsibility for her own lack of post-immersion missionary conversion:

I can make all the excuses that I want, but it's me. In the end, it's yourself who will impede you from whatever, unless you're being physically forced. This past summer, while I was in Cutupú and Consuelito too, we had a few prayer reflections about this and about what keeps you away from your relationship with God or from following through on what your resolutions will be when you get home.

And always, my top one was fear, because if I did go home and attempt to be the perfect person, and go to church all the time, and not go out with friends as much to drink, and change my lifestyle to the way I'm sure that God would prefer I live, then I would have to stay that way because once you're good then you can't go back.

I'm already in my comfort zone with the lifestyle that I have, and so it would mean stepping out of my comfort zone.

We were thinking of small steps that we could take back home to better our lives, and there were some people who had been wanting me to join a prayer group. And I don't want to, because once I'm in it, how am I going to find an excuse to get out if I don't like it? So, it's just easier not to do it. I said that maybe a small step would be just to try that, to try the prayer group to better myself.

Because I always figured that you're young to have fun, and when you get older, you can do good. What if I died tomorrow? I would have messed myself up. That's my fear from the other angle.

One veteran AeA missionary also spoke of her own struggles to advance her post-immersion missionary conversion via the pursuit of her ascetic resolutions:

As far as resolutions go, I made a ton. I was going to do this, that, and the other thing. The first year was the worst because I was going to change the world or my little world by conserving water, by being less materialistic, and less into consumerism, less into myself, less selfish, by giving up soda pop, by giving up this, and giving up that. Obviously, I didn't succeed [as she lifted a bottle of a carbonated beverage].

That first year, I only lasted a month or two. But with each successive mission immersion, I find myself being more careful and more aware in terms of my spending, my wastefulness, my selfishness. I think that each year, I grow a little more. I take baby steps, but they are definite changes.

Another young AeA missionary described her internal struggles to follow through on the spiritual resolutions that she made during her latest immersion:

During the mission, I made the decision to pray a lot more, to be a lot more meditative, to be more dedicated to growing and becoming a stronger, bigger person. By that, I mean a person with a bigger heart, who is very loving, so that I could choose a career that would make a difference.

When I came back home, I believed that I needed to do something that was going to help the situation. I wanted to dedicate myself to growing as a person so that I would never forget that goal. Now, looking back, I definitely see that it's definitely a hard thing, especially for people who go away to school.

How many people choose careers because of the money and because of the benefits for themselves and that temptation? There are times that I have thought wait, why did I say that I wanted to do something positive? I still don't know what I want to do. Really, I'm pretty clueless about it. I've always known that it was going to be something that would benefit someone other than myself, and also myself included, because you never can help someone else without helping yourself.

So, those were some of my goals, some of my changes. Definitely, I wanted to pray more after I came back. But it didn't necessarily happen. I wanted to share my experience with my youth group and my high school campus ministry team, and when I didn't feel that it was well received, then that went down the drain too. Those have been some of my goals, just to save the world from itself.

One young AeA missionary has struggled with her Christian faith after her immersions:

I kind of believe that eventually my faith life is going to deepen and improve. But we always talk about how it's a change in our way of life. I see people differently. I believe in people's humanity. Strangely, I believe in the good in people, but at the same time, it's really strange, like a two-sided coin, I think that people have a lot of potential, but at the same, I feel that there's nothing that I can do to solve this problem, this particular problem. Now, it's easier for me to see people that are suffering in my day-to-day life. I'm slower to be compassionate toward people that are arrogant and have money. I feel distanced from God. I can't just say that it's because of mission. It's a personal thing. I guess, with all the changes that accompany adolescence, my missionary experiences didn't push me toward God. But maybe in the long run, it will. I think that, for now, it has pushed me further away from God. I question the validity of Catholic Christian faith because although it is inspiring to see these people with a lot of faith, at the same time, I have to wonder: Do they have a lot faith because they need it and do we attend Catholic school because it looks good? What really are our motives? What are people's motives? I think it comes down to that. I guess I took a lot of things personally. So, if someone that claimed to be religious didn't want to hear my stories, then I conclude that all his philosophies are wrong. Maybe it's just my perception that they don't want to hear my stories, because four years ago, someone might have said, Hey, Listen to my story. And I could have said, Oh that's cool. It might have been interesting to me. But I would have looked at someone's pictures. And even now, since I didn't experience it, so to me, for most of those kids, there's no story behind those pictures. Even though I know that deep inside there is, I have no emotional connection to them. The perception that others are closed to the narratives of missionaries may be different from the reality. That's why it's hard for me to answer the question: Did your missionary experience push you further from God? Because although I question a lot of what I had believed in the past, blindly believed, now I do feel that it's going to take me somewhere further in my faith. My doubt and my questions, I believe, will take me further in my faith, but I'm still skeptical.

Another young AeA missionary concluded that post-immersion spiritual questioning leads to deeper faith in the long term:

What she was going through, growing more distant from God, which is what I did for my first two years, I don't see as a negative thing. Because even if I got more distant from God, I think that faith became a much bigger deal in my life because I was thinking about how I didn't believe, and I was questioning. Whereas, if I hadn't gone on mission, and I wouldn't have questioned, then faith would have just been something I took for granted. So, I think that once I was faced with the reality of poverty and then began asking, Do I believe in a God? Do I believe that I'm really a missionary? Even if I had said, I'm an atheist, I don't believe in this, whatever. At least I was taking a position. And I felt that being a missionary made me take that position. Either I did, or I didn't, but at least I didn't just not care. Now, when I can say that now I do believe, and I do look at it differently, it's because I have gone through that pe-riod, which I also think has a lot to do with my faith and the age we're at as freshmen in college. But I don't think it's necessarily a bad thing that mission sometimes makes people, makes me, question and reject certain philosophies.

Lourdes, an AeA founder, described her internal struggles to main-tain her long-term missionary commitments:

Regarding post-immersion resolutions, since I have been a member of AeA, I have always believed that I have got to do something about what I'm seeing and what I'm experiencing, and regarding how the people we meet and visit are forced to live. And I have felt exhausted and wanted to give up and to say, To hell with all of this. But then I think of the faces of the people who are waiting and hoping to find something to eat tomorrow. So, I get up out of bed and I go back to work and I do whatever I can do for them, like selling the dough-nuts, and preparing for the dinner-dances, and preaching at the masses, and attending planning meetings, and coming here to this interview so that our missionary brother can finish this dissertation and graduate, and so that people can read it and be further inspired to act in solidarity and keep doing generous things on behalf of materially poor people. Sometimes I participate in all these things because I truly want to, and at other times I have to force myself. I have the sense that I own the responsibility. I wouldn't be able to sleep tranquilly if I were to give it all up and drop my commitment to AeA. I get angry every other day about it, but then I am driven by what I have witnessed, to answer the call of God and the cry of the poor.

Carlos, an AeA founder, confessed that he has felt spiritually distressed because he has never perceived God in poor people:

Observing my cofounders created a tremendous conflict inside me and tremendous angst because these people loved the Christ in the poor and I never saw Christ in any other human being. And I never have to this day. And they would love the poor because of the love of Christ that they encountered in the poor. And I thought, Well, I keep going on these trips and I don't see Christ in the poor. I wish that I was like them. I'm not like that. That created some very, very serious questioning within me regarding whether or not I was ever meant to be a missionary. I did not discover that I was indeed a missionary until many years later while I was engaged in prison ministry. But I hate poverty. I don't want to become a poor person. I try to live simplicity in my life, and so on and so forth. I don't work for money. But I could never relate to them. And it took me many, many, many years of dualities and conflicts before I could sort it out. What did drive me during the Cursillo and post-Cursillo and in all of my spiritual exercises is that I am absolutely head-over-heels in love with Christ. And for me, God did not create poverty. Poverty was created by humans, and it was a headache for God, and I had to resolve God's problems. And now, it is incumbent upon me to fix something that humanity has screwed up for God.

106

God is trying to figure it out, and I am God's hands and feet, and damn it, I'm going to go out and resolve these problems for God. He did not create them. He doesn't want them. Every night that a child goes to bed hungry, that's a headache for God, and I've got to be here to resolve those headaches for God. But I don't love the poor. I can't relate to poverty. I don't want to be poor. And my fellow missionaries would work for the love of the poor and the love of the God in the poor, and I would exclaim, I don't see God in the poor!

One young AeA veteran also spoke of her own struggles to advance her post-immersion missionary conversion via the pursuit of her resolutions to intentionally set aside time to listen to others, instead of rushing to fulfill her multiple commitments:

It's hard to put a name on the values because that could also be just a part of me growing as a person, and it's hard to name which ones actually come from mission because the mission experience also affects you throughout the whole year... So, it depends upon how much energy or effort I put into it, which is hard. And the further in time that I get away from that mission immersion experience, the less energy and effort I put into it. And then it comes back around, so that when I go on mission again, I regain the impulse.

A young AeA missionary admitted that she isolated herself from her family after her immersion:

I guess I presumed I was going to be all happy and excited when I got home and actually, I didn't feel that way. I felt heavy-hearted or sad. I just kind of stayed by myself for a long period of time after my re-entry, in my room or at home. I just stayed away from people. I never told anybody in my family why I was upset. I didn't feel they would understand.

One AeA founder also imposed post-immersion silence on herself:

After I went with AeA to urban slums in La Vega, I never discussed my own experience with my students or colleagues. It was a little bit later, when I started to think that it would be a good experience for my students to be immersed with AeA, that I began to share my own experiences, feelings, thoughts, and reflections. Of course, now I do. Once in a while, I share on that level with my high school students. I'll pull out a picture in class and tell them a story. The reactions to my sharing vary widely. Sometimes, a boy will approach me immediately after class and tell me that he wants to go with us on an immersion. Others don't seem to be affected by it. Sometimes I say that I do not receive support at work for the advancement of my missionary conversion. But that's because I don't talk about it, and because I am not open with them about my missionary insights and issues. And because they don't know about it, therefore, they don't care about it. It has to do with my own character and my own personality. And part of my silence on the issue has to do with the degree of the sacredness of my missionary commitments and reflections. I don't even think that the priests that we have at the school where I work know about the degree of my involvement with AeA, because I haven't told them so. They know generally about AeA. They once invited a couple of us to go to their house to inform them about AeA, but they don't know. Father Eduardo Álvarez, our Jesuit mentor, knows. But I don't sit there all day long talking incessantly about my AeA immersion experiences and reflections.

Upon return from her initial immersion, Sofía, a young AeA missionary, felt intense estrangement from her material belongings, from her family, and from her hometown. A year later, it became obvious that she had matured much:

My feelings were pretty different between the first year and the second year. The first year, I can describe it in one-word, complete, complete estrangement. I came back, and I felt that my house wasn't my house anymore. My things were not mine. I didn't feel that I owned these things anymore. I think that I had become so immersed in my first mission experience and in that lifestyle that I had almost adopted that lifestyle as my own. It felt that that very poor house where I had lived was my house, and that those were my things, and that that was my city. And when I came back to Miami, I felt completely estranged, like this wasn't my life anymore and that this was not my city, this was not my home. I remember looking at my room and at my bathroom and feeling that my house was a foreign place. I didn't feel like it was mine. It just felt like a hotel or something that was not personal. I felt really, really depressed the first year. I was just miserable, just sad. I would cry all the time. I didn't want to talk to my family about it. I just wanted to be left alone because almost anything would prompt me to start crying again. So that's why I didn't want to share the stories at first. I didn't want to show the pictures because I was still so emotionally connected that I needed some time to be able to at least break away from it a little bit to be able to start to share my stories. I was also kind of impatient with people. I was bitter. I was angry. For me, my first mission experience was not a religious experience at all. I also questioned my faith a lot. I was depressed for a long time. My second mission experience was completely different in terms of my feelings during re-entry. I did feel a little bit estranged. I did feel sad, a little bit depressed, especially the first two days, but nothing like the first time. I didn't feel angry toward my family and friends. In fact, I was very, very eager to share the stories the second time I came back. I couldn't wait. On the car ride home, I was sharing stories right away. I wanted to develop the film right away. I wanted to talk about the experience and everything that had happened. I didn't feel angry. It was easier to get back into the swing of things the second time as well. I also didn't feel as guilty as I did the year before about having things and using hot water and things like that. I kind of embraced a little more the things that I had been given. I appreciated them, I guess you could say, a little bit more. The second year, I felt sad and I was missing the people and I felt a little

109

bit depressed, but at the same time I felt a sense of joy. I felt happy. I treated people better than I did before. I had a smile on. I wanted to share all the stories all the time. I felt much happier and better the second year. I forgot to mention that my second-year immersion was also a much more religious experience. It was a very religious experience. I think that my faith has definitely deepened during the second mission and even after, even more; it was much more positive. On that mission, I was constantly in prayer. I would pray a lot. I recognized things as mystical or holy. I noticed spiritual people and spiritual moments that I did not experience the first year. After I returned the first year, since it was not a religious experience at all and since I was just so caught up in my own feelings of sadness, depression, frustration, I did not turn to God at all the first year. I didn't pray since that just didn't even seem like an option to me. After the second immersion, I have been much more in prayer since I came back. I feel that my prayer life has grown; it has deepened my faith. I turn to God to help me answer certain questions and to help guide me as to: What am I going to do now? How do I react? What is my role now back here?

Conversion-Impeding Generative Themes

It is propitious to pause here in order to identify the themes which have been unearthed by the narratives in the foregoing segment on post-immersion impediments to conversion. If addressed intentionally, these hindering themes can be transformed into the potent generative themes that are the crucial tools for the efficacious implementation of Groome's shared praxis method of practical theology because they radiate the energy of divine wisdom that is capable of producing profound conversion.

Culture Shock

From the perspective of a recently returned missionary, culture shock can be characterized as a sudden sensation of disorientation and alienation from one's culture of origin. The feeling of culture shock begins to affect some post-immersion missionaries as soon they enter the airport from which they will depart the mission field bound for home.

In my own case, I feel the most intensely discouraged and alienated from God when I have to pass through international airports on my way home to the USA from a missionary destination, be it in the Caribbean, Central, or South America. To me, it seems as if these transitional portals are designed by human beings in such a way that they are so spiritually impermeable that they are capable, in some respects, of walling out God's Holy Spirit. As I stated in the previous chapter, these airports definitely wall in the "haves" and wall out the "have-nots" – and this design feature appears to be intentional.

Others begin to experience the estrangement at the arrival airport. Still others are confronted by this spiritual-emotional-cognitive chasm as soon as they arrive at an overtly opulent destination, such as a lavish shopping mall or a luxurious resort hotel. Other short-term missionaries feel the bewilderment and anxiety most intensely when they return to their day jobs.

Gradual Progress toward Asceticism
in Response to Guilt over Opulence

There is no more common feeling during the immediate post-mission immersion stage than that of guilt, a sudden conviction that there is something immoral about the quantity of material comforts that most of us enjoy most of the time in the United States in contrast with the relative material deprivation experienced by so many folks in the mission fields where we volunteer. It appears that for people who are blessed with an enduring missionary call, the initial perception of guilt matures into a conviction of responsibility and commitment. The post-immersion missionary remains a societal misfit in the USA because his or her renewed Christian values present a prophetic challenge to the consumerist and individualist values of our culture of origin. If post-immersion missionaries can become happier while becoming less consumerist, some of the missionaries' family members, neighbors, and coworkers feel morally challenged and threatened.[8]

Blaming God for the Continuing Existence of Poverty & Inequality

Such finger pointing and distrust of other people who are not missionaries, volunteers, or aid workers, is sometimes extrapolated as far as the divine dimension, particularly among young missionaries. The perennial moral conundrum of persistent poverty and acute social-political-economic inequality in combination with the belief in a justice-enamored and human-loving Deity frequently produces profound internal disorientation among missionaries. They often cycle through periods in which their conviction that God is omnipotent but, for unknown reasons, unmoved by the intense suffering of some of his children in certain geographic settings, evokes from within them bewilderment, outrage, and theological agnosticism.

Strangely enough, the majority of these spiritually undulating missionaries remain dedicated to participation in future missionary immersions even during periods when they feel most intensely alienated from God. This is because their previous moral formation and their immersion experiences have engendered in them a hu-manistic sense of solidarity with their new friends and acquaintances who are striving to survive in the midst of miserable circumstances.

---

[8] Matthew 6:24; Matthew 5:3-12; Luke 16:13; Luke 6:20-26.

Ecclesial Bureaucratic Barriers
to Future Immersions

Such cyclical spiritual estrangement is only augmented when the post-immersion missionary encounters categorical callousness and absolute dedication to self-preservation in the unlikeliest of places, a church institution. This irony abounds in a hyper-litigious context such as the United States of America due to the overreliance, at every stage of planning, upon legal counselors whose principal criterion is the preservation of the institution that provides them with employment and financial security.

It has become routine for post-immersion missionaries to encounter heartrendingly insurmountable barriers to future missionary immersions under the auspices of certain Catholic dioceses, parishes, seminaries, universities, and schools. This is an obvious tragedy and seems to contradict the gospel of Jesus Christ which exhorts us to carry his message to the ends of the earth.

Inadequate Post-Immersion Reintegration
by the Sending & Receiving Community

Numerous missionaries express regret that their mission sending and receiving communities do not adequately guide their post-immersion reintegration. They wish that their respective ecclesial missionary communities would formally concentrate on helping them to digest the memories and feelings from their immersions as well as the enthusiasm-sapping incidents of their post-immersion phase. These missionaries point specifically to: inadequate post-immersion liturgical recognition of them and their rich experiences; insufficient opportunities for them to recount salient episodes from their immersions to non-missionary sectors of their church; and the infrequency of post-immersion meetings offered by their own missionary communities, particularly in contrast to the frequency of pre-immersion meetings of those same communities. All three of these omissions contribute to the missionaries' sense of post-immersion isolation.

Overly Protective Parents

Many unmarried missionaries, those who partake in both short-term and long-term immersions, experience the phenomenon of parents who seek to protect them from all forms and degrees of discomfort and suffering. This experience is so prevalent that it appears to be an instinctive reaction to the perception that their offspring might be traumatized or even extinguished by the dangers, difficulties, and inconveniences of life and travel in materially poor countries or neighborhoods. The younger the missionary, the more intense is the perception that his or her parents are both pestering and endeavoring to dissuade or prohibit him or her from participating in any future missionary immersions.[9]

Self-Imposed Silence & Isolation
from Non-Missionaries & Non-Volunteers

Owing to the perception that no one except fellow missionaries or volunteers can comprehend what they feel as a result of their missionary immersions, many recently returned neophyte missionaries

---

[9] After ample observation and reflection, I have come to believe that it is generally unfair to categorically impugn the motives of these parents. In defense of the Cuban parents, it should not be denied that one paradigm of Catholic religious sisters and nuns that they knew in Cuba was indeed that of sisters-as-domestic-servants-of-priests. It seems that at least initially, our founders' parents did not intend to oppose God's will but rather to mitigate against gender-based exploitation. Even later, the efforts of the founders' families to convince the missionaries to choose more financially lucrative career paths was motivated by the desire that they be able to earn enough to be able to avoid geriatric pauperdom. Furthermore, the effort to cajole the missionaries to eventually abandon the travel component of their missionary commitment is an expression of their concern for the physical and psychological safety of their kin. Those parents, especially those who have emigrated under political or economic duress, by and large feel convinced that they are merely attempting to shield their children, albeit adult children, from abuse, persecution, or material indigence.

unconsciously and/or consciously isolate themselves emotionally from nearly everyone else, in an attempt to insulate themselves and their newly affirmed or newly adopted missionary values, from undue criticism and antagonism. Regrettably, many of these post-immersion missionaries do so almost as a reflex response, and thereby actually wall out some of their true supporters such as family members, co-congregants, and life-long friends.

4

ENCOURAGEMENTS TO

CONVERSION

N ow that we have delineated, surveyed, and probed the numerous obstacles to Christian missionary conversion that post-immersion missionaries must navigate, let us proceed to explore the factors that promote the advancement of missionary conversion in the post-immersion phase. In this chapter, we will categorize these testimonies that promote deeper missionary conversion according to their respective subject matter. To conclude this examination, we will identify and delve into the generative themes that arose in the narrative testimonies expressed in the focus group interviews because they are laden with conversion-producing potential.

Family, Friends, & Church

The preponderance of the missionaries whom I interviewed realized that, despite their imperfections, their cantankerousness, and their inconsistencies, their families, their church (including their parishes and missionary communities), and in some cases, their friends, provided a significant foundation of support for their respective continuing missionary conversions. This fact took some of the missionaries by surprise.

Adriano, an AeA founder, noted that despite their discouraging words, their families' actions were fundamentally encouraging:

> Our families provided the basis of our faith and they were the ones who made it possible for us to do what we did. Because despite all of the negatives influences in the society, and despite all the negative crap that our parents and family members told us, whenever we held a fundraising event, they all showed up, mothers, fathers, aunts, uncles, grandparents, friends, even the mother of the tomatoes. And they brought their money, and they would hand us a check and tell us, Here's a hundred bucks. And later, we would look at the checks and they were made out for a thousand dollars instead. And those people didn't even have enough money to buy groceries; but they gave sacrificially to us anyhow. Our families were a mystery unto themselves because their words were words of discouragement, but their actions were a tremendous support for us. That is practical theology; the rest is lip service, a smoke screen. That was what made us who we are.

One young veteran AeA missionary received unexpected post-immersion support from her pastor as well as from former missionaries in her parish:

> Especially the first time I came back from San Pedro de Macorís, that was when I felt the worst. The priest made an encouraging comment about my talk. That small, little thing made me feel better. My fellow parishioners all came up to me afterward and they responded really well to it. In fact, a couple had gone on mission themselves. They were older now, and they came up and said, I remember exactly how that feels.

Pilar, a young AeA missionary, noted the positive influence of her parents and AeA veterans during her post-immersion phase:

*For me, also AeA people that have gone on mission before, espe-
cially people my age, have been very key because, even in the middle
of the year when I'm in college, I talk to them. We don't even have
to talk about mission, but for example, about something like decid-
ing to change majors. It always has this underlying understanding
that because, like my friend said, the greater goal is to help someone
other than ourselves at some point. So, I think that affirming the
new way of life, I think that that's very much attributed to talking
to people that have experienced a similar thing. We're just lucky to
have people that we met in the group. I also think that my parents
and also people with more experience who are older that have gone
on similar experiences have been very affirming and helpful because
they helped me turn the anger and the guilt into something constructive. Instead of me just saying, I hate everybody that doesn't
go on a mission immersion, they taught me to ask, So, what can
you do about it in a positive way? How can you turn this anger
into something positive? Because so many times, people just take
the anger all the way. My parents always taught me to ask: Where
is God in that? Where is your religion in your anger? And what
are you going to do about it? I answered, It's not there! So, I think
that special people have affirmed my way of life by really questioning what I want to do. Do I just want to sit here and be angry at
everyone or do I want to do something positive about it?*

Josefina, an AeA founder, realized that her parents unwittingly
taught her the spirit of sharing that motivates all missionaries:

*And my mother and my father too encouraged my later vocation,
even though they will never know it, because we had maids who
worked in our home. And so, when Three Kings Day arrived, my
mother presented gifts for the maids' children too, and she taught
us that we were all the same. It was a great lesson in terms of sharing.*

Becky, a young AeA veteran, gave credit to her parents and colleagues for supporting her missionary career despite a comprehension gap:

If you don't know about it, then it's easier to say, I don't have to do anything about it. But once you know, then the ball's in your court. So, you're no longer ignorant and there are no longer any excuses. Now you know; so, do something. I'm trying to see why we have such different experiences when it comes to that. I want to say that age has a lot to do with it. It really does, because the majority of my friends and the people I work with were extremely interested in what I had done and were extremely interested in my pictures and wanted to know how they could help. And as much as they couldn't completely understand, because they had never been there, they were interested in understanding. And why is it that you go every summer and you sweat and have such a hard time? They wanted to know why, not necessarily for them to go, but they wanted to know. I always got a sense that they wanted to help. Maybe it's not meant for me to go on mission, but I will help you in any way I can. I've always felt that, throughout the years, from everybody that I deal with. And I've received an overwhelming amount of energy and offers of help to make this situation better. My family has always been very supportive. I think that what my missionary sister said is very similar to my situation. My parents have always been very supportive of what I've done, but at the same time, I think that a part of them is still selfish in the sense that they don't want me to go to a third world country, and they don't want me to have a hard time because I'm their daughter and they love me. And no matter what, they don't want me to have a hard time, whether it's for one day or two weeks or one year. That's the underlying sentiment. They know that what I'm doing is a good thing. I'll never forget when I went in October. I went for a funeral for one of the little boys. And I went to see his family after he had just passed away.

Before I left, because the hurricane had just passed, and everything was flooded over there, and it was just not a good time to go, my mom told me: This is the worst mistake that you've made in your life. She told me that literally before I left. I said, Okay, but I'm going to do this anyway. My mom has a huge impact on what I think and what I do. So, it was difficult to just challenge that anyways. And I went ahead, and I did it. And I remember that I came back, and I told her: You know what? I think it was the best decision that I ever made in my life. And when I explained everything to her, she kind of couldn't say anything and she said, You're right. You had to do that. But I think that no matter what, I'm always their daughter and that comes first; and my safety and my wellbeing come first. But besides that, God knows that they've always been extremely supportive. Every time I ask for something as far as donations or help packing, down to the smallest things. In that sense, they're definitely supportive.

A young AeA missionary found post-immersion support from her parents and the other young AeA missionaries with whom she had been immersed:

The first year, I felt that the only support that I got was really from the AeA group. I had the privilege of having gone with three other girls that lived in the Miami, that were my same age, that were my friends from before, pretty much. So, when I came back, I felt that actually my only sense of comfort, of any sort of comfort, was to be with them, just to be with them, even if it wasn't to talk about mission, just to be with them. Just feeling their presence brought a sense of comfort to me, and a sense of affirming everything that I had experienced, and everything that I wanted to do as a response. My parents, I could say, are active members of AeA. My dad was one of the founding members. So, talking to them about it always helped because they could relate to what I was talking about and they helped me see things that I could do and ways in which I could do it. So, they were a support also. After coming back the second year, I feel that there were certain things that affirmed my new resolutions that I didn't see before, things that before were challenges or a turn-off.

Wendy, a young AeA missionary, found post-immersion support among fellow AeA missionaries and her family for her ongoing missionary conversion:

I would say that the AeA group was the strongest support that I had both years. For the first couple of weeks after I came back from immersions, it was still mission time because I only hung out with people with whom I had gone on mission. And really, those were the only people that could really understand us because they had gone through a very similar experience. And it didn't matter how old you were, from people my age to people in their late thirties or forties; it didn't matter. The elders of the organization like Fefita, and the younger veterans like Teresita and Monica, are people that really could understand the feelings we had, that could empathize and sympathize. Maybe they didn't experience exactly what you felt, but they knew those emotions. So, definitely the organization of AeA and then really anybody that would listen, just listen to how I felt, listen to my feelings of confusion and doubt, even if they didn't understand what I had gone through. They didn't necessarily have to understand, but they tried because they loved me. They're the people that really supported me. Because people's true colors came out. I also feel that my mom was really supportive because that's the kind of person who she is. In everything that I do, she listens really well and helps me find constructive solutions without threatening my opinion. I never felt threatened by her.

Lindsay, a young veteran AeA missionary, found post-immersion support from her non-missionary friends via an innovative method:

The first year I went, my best friends kept a journal for me of what went on in Saginaw while I was gone, and I kept a journal for them of what went on during the mission immersion. So that, for me, was the most unique re-entry experience. I didn't even have to talk about it. We just kind of switched and swapped experiences. That was our way of sharing.

Becky, a young veteran AeA missionary, felt grateful that both her family and friends were supportive during her post-immersion phase, despite a gap in comprehension:

As far as relating to people, thank God, I really feel that everybody has been fully supportive as far as my family and my friends are concerned. They really always were interested in hearing what I had to say. The only difference is that they couldn't fully understand it. And it's not because they didn't want to understand it and didn't want to try to listen, but that they just couldn't, they couldn't really relate.

One young veteran AeA missionary received post-immersion support from his missionary girlfriend:

I did have somebody that I was dating at the time who went on a mission immersion. And we shared that experience, and that kind of helped because we were able to talk to each other about it.

One AeA founder realized that, from a young age, her parents had unwittingly taught her the spirit of sharing, egalitarianism, and dignity that motivates most missionaries. Several young missionaries found post-immersion support for their respective ongoing missionary conversions from their parents, family members, and other AeA missionaries with whom they had been immersed overseas.

Witnessing to & Inspiring Others to Discern
Missionary Vocations as a Measure of Fruitfulness

Numerous post-immersion missionaries have felt profoundly encouraged in terms of furthering their own respective missionary conversions by the opportunity to give witness to non-missionaries about their missionary immersion experiences, and to even inspire others to consider participating in a future missionary immersion for the first time.

Justin, a young veteran Saginaw AeA missionary, perceived the fact that he inspired others to participate in an initial mission immersion as a measure of post-immersion missionary fruitfulness. He also gave credit to his family for nurturing his missionary vocation:

My family was really interested in hearing the stories, but they didn't really grasp the fact of how much it changed me when I tried explaining it to them. They saw the change in me. And it wasn't really a conversation. We didn't have a dialogue about it. They were just able to see the change in me; and they knew that it was important to me. And it actually influenced some more of my family members to go on mission. I had two younger sisters and a cousin go on mission after I went on mission. And my father and brother also decided to go on mission. But they didn't go with AeA. They went on different missions. And I don't know if I can take credit for it, but I believe it was because of that missionary experience that I had. And so, when I came back, the storytelling that I was able to do with my family was really encouraging to me. For me, although it was different from most people, my family was very supportive. Like I said before, they were there, and they listened. They got into deeper questions with me and I saw that they were actually affected by it because they ended up going on mission.

Justin, who later served as a full-time AeA missionary, reiterated that the fact that the Holy Spirit used him to inspire others to join in initial

mission immersions, was certainly a sign of post-immersion missionary fruitfulness:

> *What helped me a lot was that I did have that outlet in a different
> way with my family and via giving the talks at my parish and to
> the youth groups. I don't know how much of my parish knew that
> I was gone or knew what I was doing. But after I did give the talk,
> I had many people come up to me who said, Good job. We'll con-
> tinue to pray for you. And then the next year, I gave another talk.
> And then the year after that, I gave another talk, and they're start-
> ing to catch on. That's another thing, my parish priest has gone on
> mission for three years now. Also, one of my missionary mentors,
> Carmen Mora, works at my parish, and she's the one who brought
> AeA to the Saginaw diocese. In my own faith community, my par-
> ish allowed me the opportunity to give a little speech about my ex-
> perience during the mass. And also, I was able to attend a youth
> group retreat for several different parishes in Saginaw, and give a
> talk, and share my experiences, and show my pictures. And I felt
> that I connected with some of the youth in those youth groups. And
> they were generally interested. And they decided to go on mission
> after that too.*

A young Saginaw AeA missionary realized that being invited to give
post-immersion witness talks encouraged his commitment to continue his missionary conversion:

> *I think that being a really close friend of someone with whom I went
> on mission helped out after returning, and I helped me keep that
> commitment and those resolutions that I decided to make for my-
> self. Also, the people who helped arrange the talks that I gave upon
> returning have helped me to maintain my missionary commit-
> ments.*

Jennifer, another young veteran Saginaw AeA missionary, realized that being invited to give post-immersion witness talks encouraged her commitment to continue her missionary conversion:

> *Diocesan support for AeA is improving in Saginaw. The nun who is the diocesan coordinator of missionary activities, Sister Corrine Weiss, gives AeA money now because she recognizes the value of what we contribute to the church. The diocese has also launched a YES (Youth Encounter Saginaw) community service and reflection retreat, and they started inviting missionaries from AeA to give talks during the retreat.*

Laura, another young veteran Saginaw AeA missionary, perceived the fact that she inspired others to inquire about her most recent mission immersion as a measure of post-immersion missionary fruitfulness:

> *I don't know if it's because I had been going for five years in a row that they were finally convinced that this is important to me, but that was the year that my godparents had me over for dinner because they wanted to hear about everything. That's how I could tell that I actually had influenced some people around me. Because all the previous years, I know I was changed, but I kind of felt that I was cheating everyone else because I had this experience that I couldn't explain, and it seemed that no one wanted to hear anyway.*

Lindsay, another young veteran Saginaw AeA missionary, agreed that the fact that she inspired others to participate in an initial mission immersion was a measure of post-immersion missionary fruitfulness:

> *When I talk about my mission immersions, I think what motivates me to talk about it is to move my listeners to want to do something like that. The only person to whom I ever felt I did that was my cousin who went on mission. It's hard because you have an experience that is so sacred to you and you want to be able to move people in a certain way.*

Vocations

During their post-immersion reflections, which of course have their roots in the immersion experiences themselves, numerous AeA missionaries discover a more permanently and profoundly fulfilling purpose and direction for their lives than the path that they had previously selected. As a result, some of them feel morally compelled to change their university programs of study toward disciplines that they believe will capacitate them to achieve a deeper and more sustained positive impact upon the lives of their newly made friends in the Caribbean countries. Such a momentous change in priorities often results in a reassessment of lifetime goals related to material acquisition for themselves. This long-term reduction in material acquisition is due to several factors that often accompany spiritual conversions, namely: the reduction in salaries due to reconsidered career choices, the regular donation of a portion of the family's income to missionary, charitable, and/or economic development causes, the increase in travel expenses, and the potential loss of ancillary business opportunities due the regular investment of time into the missionary community stateside.

A young Miami AeA missionary discovered her life's vocation and decided to change her college major in response to her missionary experiences:

> I would say that the most concrete change that I made was that, after going on mission the second year, I was a Spanish major before, and I got back and said, I need to fix this. But how can I fix it if I'm only going to know Spanish? I need to do something. I hadn't changed my major yet. But I got back to school, and I looked at my classes and said, Oh my goodness, there's nothing here regarding the poor kids. These classes are not going to help me at all. So, I started looking at the classes. So, I ended up changing my major to culture and politics with a concentration in Latin American

*economic development ... But it always goes back to the people in
the batey and the people in the Dominican Republic whose stories I
hear ... I want to change that. And I think that that's the way I've
been able to concretely make change, to follow through on a resolution.*

Margaret, another AeA missionary, discovered her life's vocation
and decided to pursue two law degrees because of her missionary
experiences:

*Neither my mother nor I ever imagined that I would become a law-
yer. But those Haitian and Dominican children, whose photos are
here on my wall, are the reason why I'm in law school. AeA has
provided me with the experiences that have converted the whole direction of my life. These experiences have pushed me further along
in terms of schooling so that I am more capable of helping them to
change things. Because as a social worker, I'm able to help just one
person at a time, one at a time, one at a time, and it just wasn't
enough when I kept seeing more and more and more and more, and
I kept going back, and I kept seeing more and more and more and
more. And I thought, If I'm just a social worker, what can I do for
these people? Maybe I can give them a bath for that day or whatever. But it's not going to change the situation. The laws have to be
changed. Diplomatic relations have to be changed. All that stuff.
That's why I'm in the craft that I am. That's how my whole conversion started. What I have always planned to do with my law
degree, at least as a part-time focus, is to go back to the bateys to
help those children of Haitian descent get their documents so that
they will be allowed to enroll in Dominican schools and get an education. Professionally speaking, I hope to practice human rights
law somewhere or maybe disaster relief or refugee work. I would
really like to do the refugee work because that's attached to my missionary experiences. And if I have trouble landing a specific job, I
can still do pro bono work and immigration law here and maintain*

my connection with the Haitian people in need. And perhaps I will restart something like the now defunct A Woman's Place. My life has been completely rocked by the missions. I have always had the spark for justice. I began studying social work and I earned my BSW. And now, with the missionary experiences under my belt, my fight against oppression has moved from down the block to across the globe. I went on to study international human rights and earned an LLM. And I am currently finishing up my JD law degree to focus on human rights and immigration. Hopefully to eventually be able to assist the Haitian immigrants in the bateys of the Dominican Republic who have changed my life. This month, I'm going to give brief lectures and short classes on the basics of immigration law to the parents at some of our schools that I work in, like the three that we have in Little Haiti. The parents have requested that; so I'm going to do it ... All these avenues for helping people were opened up to me as a result of my AeA missionary involvement. Another sign of my profound conversion was my reaction of solidarity when I saw one of the Haitian protests in progress. I just pulled my car over. It was when the Haitians were protesting because a boat full of Haitian refugees had landed, and ICE had arrested all of them, and was threatening to summarily deport them. The protest was in front of the old INS building on Biscayne Boulevard and NE 79th Street. And I was the only little white girl standing out there and singing with them because I had recently traveled to Haiti with AeA.

Alicita, a founder of AeA, discovered her life's vocation as a result of her missionary experiences:

But in the words of one of my fellow founders, we felt that we had a responsibility, such that if we failed to act, then children would not eat, and water would not get to the families in the slums. We were very clear about that. Prior to my missionary experiences, I believe that I was very skeptical, very cynical, and a person with no

129

direction and no sense of vocation. I was cynical about the world, about the United Nations, about doing good things for the world, and about the church. If I had had the chance, I would have gone church hopping and ideology hopping because I didn't see any meaning in what was going on. Our society was selfish at that time. It was the Me Decade. Nobody cared about others. And at that time, I didn't trust anybody.

A young AeA missionary discovered her life's vocation and felt powerful affirmation of her college major as a result of her missionary experiences:

I've had some more opportunities that I decided not to take because I felt that this was where God was taking me. Also, I'm going into the medical field. I'm going to become a nurse, which I had already wanted to do, but I definitely plan on doing a more long-term missionary immersion. I don't know if it'll be in the Dominican Republic, but I'd like to do at least a year-long missionary immersion. So that's one of my lifelong goals that has come out of this.

An AeA founder attributed her choices, in terms of both her studies and career path, to her missionary experiences:

I can say with absolute certainty that my choice to pursue graduate studies in theology and ministry was a direct result of my missionary experiences, without a doubt. The only reason that I started the doctorate was because I thought that if I acquired more knowledge, then I would be more useful to the evangelical mission of AeA. That is the only reason. The funny thing is that when I started, I had zero money to pay for my classes. And back then, there were no scholarships available. I registered for my first class and I said, God will provide. And God provided in the person of my sister, who had never before overtly supported me in any missionary endeavor. But I must acknowledge that she sure responded resolutely when God *motivated her to pay for my studies. And she followed through. I certainly cannot argue with that.*

Another young AeA missionary discovered her life's vocation and decided to change her college major as a result of her missionary experiences:

Now after my second immersion, college has become a positive thing for me. And especially now, because I'm way into my major. My major is international relations and economic development. I've been able to take some of the courses already and having the opportunity to deepen my understanding of the economic situations of these countries where we lend a hand as missionaries, has been very affirming for me. It's helped me to understand the deeper level. Even when going on mission this year, there were so many more things that I understood so much better than the first year, in terms of people's economic situations, their lifestyles, health, sanitation, all that kind of stuff. So, college now has become a very positive thing for me. And now, my classes are going to start, and I'm going to take lots of economics and diplomacy, and stuff like that courses. And I feel that, Oh yes! You see, now I'm going to learn more and I'm going to study, and I'm going to really be able to get into this.

Yet another young AeA missionary discovered her life's vocation and decided to change her college major as a result of her missionary experiences:

I also made some resolutions because of my missionary experiences. I did have some life-changing moments or experiences on the first mission, again not in a religious way. It wasn't that, Oh I believe so much in God now, but it was a first immersion experience of, Wow, there are people here who don't have what I have. Wow, there are people whose lifestyles are so different than mine. Also, I made the resolution and I realized what a selfish person I was. I realized how I never wanted to step out of my comfort zone, how I loved just being comfortable all the time, how I loved just being happy. And I was afraid almost of stepping out of my comfort zone. I never wanted to feel unhappy. I never wanted to do anything that would take away my comfort, my happiness. And I realized that I needed to stop being that way. I realized on the first mission immersion that I needed to stretch my comfort zone, and that I needed to step out of that because there were people that had needs. And I couldn't just sit around and be comfortable while there were people that had needs that I needed to help meet. My second year, like I said, was a much more religious experience. I felt God all around and I felt even a little mad at myself for having not believed before. I felt, girl, what's wrong with you? You were wasting so much time. How could you have not believed? How could you have doubted so much? Also, as result of my first mission, I decided on my career path. I'm currently studying international relations and economics, hoping to go into economic development. I hadn't been sure of what I wanted to study. And after I went on mission, it just all of a sudden became so clear that this was my mission; this is what I wanted to do. My desire in terms of my career, my future, still has not wavered. I'm still studying the same thing with the same intention. I also plan to continue my involvement in AeA. I'm also more open in terms of other spiritual avenues. Like when my friend here was saying that when she came back the first year, she felt that she didn't want to be in anything else but AeA, I feel that, in some ways, this year, there are certain things that I don't want to belong to anymore because they're not conducive to my cause or my new lifestyle. There are things that are taking away from that or that are deviating me or distracting me. But I'm also more open to really anything that has to do with our faith, and with reaching out to other people, to other kinds of service work. I never even had a major because I was just entering college. So, I didn't even have one. But that's why I picked it, because of that.

One AeA founder began to discover her missionary vocation during a discernment immersion with religious sisters:

At the time, a group of us were considering the religious life. So, we were going to a month-long mission immersion experience of living with the Sisters of the Apostolate in their novitiate. It was a very powerful experience that answered some of my questions, but not others. The experience ruined my life, ruined me for life in the good sense. I've never been the same again. It was a very life-transforming experience. It was a very difficult experience because we were very much left alone. The mistress of novices, their formation director, was not there because she had gone to the general chapter meeting of their order, and the sisters that were left behind with us were all nervous and bent out of shape because the mistress of novices was planning to stay in España for a while. So, everything was in chaos and nobody really paid attention to us. So, the four of us, each twenty-one years of age, lived through the experience with no preparation, none of what we in AeA do today. We were very cold. We went hungry. We dealt with fleas and lice and you name it. I came home with the certainty and the knowledge that I was a different person, but not knowing or understanding really what had happened. I did my own process of discernment and became convinced that although I could not live with those people and that I could not lead that kind of a life, nevertheless, something had happened inside of me.

Michaela, an AeA immersion leader, affirmed that numerous students discovered their lives' vocations and discerned their college majors as a result of their missionary experiences:

I definitely would say, Yes, especially when you take into account the adolescents that we take on mission immersion trips. Often, they come back with more focus in terms of making some kind of long-term career commitment to poor people. For example, before she went, one of my students had already decided to study nursing.

But after the immersion, she decided that she wanted to be a nurse who would focus on the care of indigents in this country. Another girl pledged that, after she graduated from nursing school, she would return to the Dominican Republic as a volunteer nurse during her annual vacation time. So, no matter which career field that they select, they always keep the concern for the Haitian or Dominican people in the back of their minds and in their hearts. So, I would say, Definitely. Even a girl who prepared to go on a mission immersion with us to the Dominican Republic but never went, has already made arrangements to go to Mali this summer in order to work as a volunteer in microfinance projects for women. So, the missionary formation that she learned from AeA, at the preparation meetings at Saint Dominic's parish, has inspired and prepared her to help expand a microcredit program in Africa. Another boy who traveled with AeA wrote his college admissions essays about his mission immersion experience. Whenever I ask my Catholic high school students about what they plan to do with their lives in terms of careers, they all express some sort of social justice concern which reflects the impact that the immersion made upon them. Whether they plan to become physicians, nurses, or lawyers, their immersion experiences influence what kind of foci they plan to have in their chosen career fields, or what type of pro bono work they plan to do, or how they plan to spend their vacation time after they graduate. First of all, even before they go, I perceive that someone or something is already drawing them toward the missions. And then, once they experience an immersion, they can no longer ignore their respective vocations. Once they go, it stays in their blood forever.

Becky, an AeA immersion leader, spoke of how she found that her vocation is to become an advocate for poor Caribbean children:

I think that every year I'm moved differently. There's this song that we like to sing during immersions that asks: Looking all around me and with all of this, how can I not be moved? That's really how I see it. We're moved by the people there in that city whom I really believe are angels walking on this earth. How can I not be moved? And how can I not think, Oh, my gosh, God is good. There are some amazing people in this world. So, I think that every year, I am moved in that way. I am inspired in that way. More specifically last year, because we were introduced to a project that Sor Angelina Lebrón of the Franciscan Sisters was starting, and that she wanted us to help her launch, I did find a purpose in life. Putting my career aside, I always said that my purpose was to be a voice for kids that didn't have a voice. Now I can say that I have another purpose as well, and that's to build a school for these kids so they can get an education, kids who wouldn't otherwise receive a formal education. It's not a short-term goal, and it's not something that I'll accomplish in two years. No, I think that this is going to be my lifelong purpose, and it's my lifelong mission to accomplish this, and to make sure that these kids can go to school and get an appropriate education. So, definitely spiritually, it's moved me to a deeper level of faith. And at the same time, I've been able to find another purpose for my life.

Lourdes, an AeA founder, explained that each time she engages in a post-immersion reflection, she feels compelled toward a deeper missionary conversion and to continue to respond compassionately to the distress of her materially destitute Caribbean friends:

My first missionary immersion experience was working in a slum in Santa Fe de Bogotá, adjacent to a prison. And there I saw things that I had no idea existed other than on television and in National Geographic magazine, things that I thought that I would never experience firsthand. For example, I saw a child pick up a bone that a dog had just abandoned and start to chew on it. The knowledge that a new world had been unveiled to me, and that somehow something had snapped inside me, that internal change that the immersion had provoked within me, combined with the ending of a relationship that I had with a man that perhaps was on its way toward a deeper commitment. All of that went to pieces because now nothing made sense anymore in that world. And I had a hunger for a more spiritually focused life, which a few years later blossomed into AeA. And regarding post-immersion resolutions, since I have been a member of AeA, I have always believed that I have got to do something about what I'm seeing and what I'm experiencing, and regarding how the people we meet and visit are forced to live. And I have felt exhausted, and wanted to give up, and to say, To hell with all of this. But then I think of the faces of the people who are waiting and hoping to find something to eat tomorrow. So I get up out of bed, and I go back to work, and I do whatever I can do for them, like selling the doughnuts, and preparing for the dinner-dances, and preaching at the masses, and attending planning meetings, and coming here to this interview so that our missionary brother can finish this dissertation and graduate, and so that people can read it, and be further inspired to act in solidarity and keep doing generous things on behalf of materially poor people. Sometimes I participate in all these things because I truly want to, and at other times, I have to force myself. I have the sense that I own the responsibility. I wouldn't be able to sleep tranquilly if I were to give it all up and drop my commitment to AeA. I get angry every other day about it, but then I am driven by what I have witnessed to answer the call of God and the cry of the poor.

Alicita, an AeA founder, shared that when she partakes in post-immersion reflections, she feels emotionally overwhelmed, motivated to become more Christlike, and more responsible for alleviating the suffering of materially poor children:

My first missionary immersion experience was in the Andes Mountains on the outskirts of Santa Fe de Bogotá. And it was my first experience face-to-face with extreme poverty. And to this day, I can remember being overwhelmed with sadness and crying profusely at the scene of little girls in dirty rags, barefoot, barely dressed in very cold weather, searching for food in trash piles. I was moved to the point where I couldn't handle the realization that I was warm inside the convent at night while they were so cold outside in their flimsy shanties. And I was disturbed by the image of very young women whose job it was, from sunrise to sundown, to make bricks by hand all day long, like the Israelite slaves in Egypt. Those scenes hit me very hard. And the final hit came at the end of my immersion when a young man prayed that there would be more people like us who would give their love to others. And for me, I always say that, upon reflection, this was the sacrament of confirmation for me, because through those words, I realized that I could love, that I had received so much, that I had been given so much in life, so much that I had to share. So my reaction was one of I don't know exactly what. I just know that I cried with tremendous sentiment. And then, upon my return, I kept thinking about all these things that happened to me, that I experienced and witnessed. And I knew I wanted more. I had to discern how I was going to live after this experience. I was highly disoriented and angry. I knew what I did not want. I ended up searching for another experience of a year in length in the Dominican Republic. So my feelings then were of inadequacy, of not belonging, of sadness and anger, and of a need to do more, a need to do, a need to become someone who could make a difference in those children's world particularly. I know for a fact, that unless someone has lived this experience, it's nearly impossible to relate to, and that despite whatever people want to do to soothe you, sometimes it's counterproductive. My family gave me a watch for Three Kings Day that I believe did not cost more than a hundred dollars, because my parents could not afford anything extravagant. But to me, it was too expensive. I insisted that they take it back to the store. So my feelings were very troublesome. That Columbian experience only led me to a great sense of a call to do more and be more Christlike. So I went to the Dominican Republic because I

received a letter inviting me to spend a year in los Guandules, and
I said, Yes. That was many years ago, back in 1973. So, when I hear
of people celebrating anniversaries of religious life or of weddings,
I realize that they are celebrations, but they also make me feel a hor-
rible sense of responsibility and of commitment, both then and now.
I say horrible because it's insurmountable. It's mind-blowing. And
it's exhausting most of the time.

Focus on People more than Poverty

The majority of AeA missionaries mention that after their initial immersions, their ability to sustain their newly established friendships with folks in the Caribbean countries, as well as the spiritual and emotional fortitude needed to commit to participating in the next immersion season, are very well served by the emphasis that AeA formation places on striving to focus on people and human relationships, instead of allowing ourselves to be overwhelmed by the glaring material disparities between the opulence of the USA and the beachside tourist resorts, in contrast to the poor neighborhoods of the Caribbean countries.

Pilar, a young AeA missionary, emphasized how her AeA missionary training taught her to focus on people more than on their material deficiencies:

AeA teaches us to be missionaries and not just activists, aid work-
ers, or social workers. We are taught to focus on the people, not the
poverty.

Another AeA veteran missionary accentuated the fact that her AeA missionary training taught her to focus on human relationships more than on injustices:

Some people say that there is a big difference between being a mis-
sionary and being a seeker of social justice. They're not mutually
exclusive by any means, but they are different. We're both in the

social justice realm, but we missionaries focus on the relationships and the sharing. And we do care totally about the social justice aspects ... But we approach crises and poverty through relationships instead of through denunciations.

One veteran missionary highlighted how her AeA missionary training taught her to value friendships over tangible material accomplishments:

It's a relationship, especially with AeA. We're building relationships. It's not like we just go visit once and never see the people again.

Another veteran AeA missionary likewise emphasized the priority of friendships over tangible material accomplishments:

It's not like going to build a house and then leaving for good. Those people can say, Well, I built a house. But I say, Look, that's my family. That's a picture of my family in the batey up there, seriously. Up there on my family wall in my living room, that's my family. I have photos of the batey kids up on the wall in my daughter's nursery.

Still another young AeA missionary stressed the fact that his AeA missionary training taught him to focus on spirituality more than on social justice:

In reference to our AeA sister's run-in with that negative longterm missionary, I'm sure that she was coming from more of a social justice perspective. It's one thing to have your own perspective, but it's another thing to tell somebody else that her perspective is wrong by accusing her of romanticizing poverty. I think that being a missioner means being somebody who's in the social justice sphere. But somebody who's exclusively a social justice seeker is missing out on the spirituality of missionaries.

Simplicity of Lifestyle in Response to Materialism

It is common for missionaries after each successive immersion to feel increasingly motivated to consume less materially in order to achieve two goals: one, to be able to share more with others; and two, to make more room in their souls for God.

One AeA founder praised God for liberating her from selfish materialistic cravings:

> *I think that we have acquired the sense and habit of sharing whatever we have. I've had a good life. And I've made a good living from the job that I have had. And I have been able to do things for others with the money that God has blessed me with and allowed me to earn. And I have been able to share that. Everybody is always asking me: With your salary, why don't you have a BMW or a Mercedes Benz or a house at the beach? Why, if a Honda takes me every place that I want to go, would I ever buy a BMW or a Mercedes Benz? That would be completely foolish to me. And I have lived well. I have not lived poorly or humbly. I do not want to create any false pretenses here. I have lived well. But there are a lot of things that I cannot do because they are just against my principles, for example, the buying of the Mercedes Benz or the jewelry or the constant purchasing of clothing. I think that I crossed out all of that kind of selfish consumption years ago. There's not a longing in me to acquire those things. I'm not being self-sacrificial here. I don't feel that I'm depriving myself of something. I really don't long to amass material prizes. I just don't need them. And I thank God every day for that because if I had not come face-to-face with the child chewing on the bone that the mongrel had eschewed, then maybe I would be in that fast lane of insatiable consumption because I have the economic capacity to be there. And I have been blessed not to have that nagging desire to surround myself with luxuries. God is very wise. I am very content with a two hundred*

forty-eight-dollar television set instead of one that is the size of a
swimming pool. I didn't buy a VCR until they were almost being
discontinued and the DVD players were already replacing the
VCRs. So, I had a VCR with no way to connect it to the television
set because they were incompatible. I'll tell you again that I have
had a very comfortable life. I have indulged myself numerous times.
But God has liberated me from those desires, from the illusion that
I need to endlessly acquire new possessions. Thanks be to God.

Another AeA founder described how God has led her, via her post-immersion reflections, toward ever more committed asceticism. She even praised God for denying her sufficient income to indulge her selfish materialistic cravings:

For me, the religious conversion happened before my missionary
involvement. The religious vocation, the spiritual change, hap-
pened before the time of my first missionary immersion. That's why
I decided to enter the convent. And when I did travel on my first
couple of AeA mission immersions, then that godly vocation which
was very clear since the beginning found its purpose, its cause, its
match, because that call was directed toward the poor by my early
AeA missionary immersions. Then it was no longer just a simple,
generic religious vocation. Now it was transformed by these im-
mersion experiences into a call to serve the poor. And over the
years, it has been an evolutionary process of increasing intensity.
In terms of resolutions, the only message that is constantly rein-
forced is that I need to live a simple life. I need to simplify, simplify,
simplify, to the point that that has just become part of who I am.
And so it has been a process, each time more profound, each time a
deeper understanding of Jesus and of why. Even my whole entire
life makes more sense with each immersion and return. Things
come full circle. It's just amazing what I have been able to under-
stand about myself in the process of my long-term response to my
missionary vocation. I consider the fact that I have not had that

same economic earning potential as many of my contemporaries, has been God's way of saving me from that shallow, empty rat race because I am a lot weaker than some of my missionary companions. And I have thought about that a lot; and upon reflection, I am very happy that I have had such limited earning potential in my career as an educator. Everything has to do with the vocation from God. Everything has to do with the vocation because my vocation has been a religious vocation. And every time that I reflect upon it, I realize that it goes further and further back. I am not trying to be pretentious, but I have realized that God has been calling and guiding me for a long time. I am blessed that I do not have a job that could afford me these material temptations because I would not have been able to resist them for all these years.

Community Service in the USA

Numerous missionaries report that community service volunteering in the USA between overseas missionary immersions not only helps them to keep their missionary fires lit, but for many of them, serves as the ramp up toward their initial missionary vocations.

A young missionary noted that office and logistical work for AeA in the USA helped her maintain her missionary fervor during her post-immersion phase:

The AeA directors give you work to do when you come back, especially if you feel you need it, especially if you come back feeling oh my God, nothing that I do is enough. And what can I do to help? Sometimes they'll call you and ask you: Can you do this for me? And you say, Oh, sure, because it makes you feel useful and better, and I think it kind of helps to quench that guilt that you feel right when you come back, guilt over not doing anything to make life better for your new Caribbean friends or not doing enough. And when they give you opportunities to work, to do things for AeA, then it helps you feel better. When they sense that we're feeling down, they call and say, Oh, come to the office because we need you to pack these boxes. It makes you at least feel that you're doing something, and something for AeA. AeA helps us in the sense that they give us the opportunity to do things and be proactive, to do things when we're feeling that we haven't done enough or that we don't do enough for others in the daily course of our own lives.

Another young missionary concurred that community service work in the USA helped her maintain her missionary fervor during her post-immersion phase:

Another thing that has helped me affirm my resolutions is doing other types of service activities. When I went on mission and went back to school and didn't have direct contact with other vulnerable populations, I believed that I might forget what I learned very easily. I first thought, Well if it's not mission, then it's not good enough. If you don't go for two weeks, if you don't go for forever, then this service thing is stupid. But I think that trying out different service things at school, working with other types of populations, and having different experiences, that also reinforces our resolutions because, whether you're working with kids, adults, inmates, whomever, you still get that reinforcement. It's humanity that you're working with. So, I think that that's kind of a way that I've tried to bring mission back to wherever I am.

One veteran AeA missionary gave credit to her community service work in the USA for starting her down the path toward becoming a missionary:

Personal choices made me pursue my resolutions for conversion. But, of course, no decision is made in a vacuum. So, I guess the people who have influenced me the most would be the cofounder of AeA, who was my college professor, and my college roommate and lifelong friend, as well as all the other people along the way. Those are the people who have influenced me. Well, regarding my

143

personal choices and my conversion, I entered college thinking that I would be an advertising major. But two weeks before school started, during the preseason for soccer, we had to go do community service and teach soccer to little kids, and nobody else beside me seemed to care about it. I got all involved in it. My teammates were all business, marketing, and advertising majors. I said to myself, I just don't fit in with these people. So, I switched my major to social work right then, and I think my conversion kind of started right there. And right after my first year of college, I went on a mission trip, and that in turn deepened the transition that I was making toward serving others. And each successive immersion made a stronger and stronger impact on me. Then I went on to earn my master's degree in international human rights law. So, I'm now deep into this commitment to serving others, and that's my lifelong choice now. That's it. That's the road that I'm on. There's no turning back. I'm ruined for life. As I mentioned before, my conversion began with community service volunteering. And working with homeless people contributed greatly to my conversion as well. I know that it doesn't have anything directly to do with overseas missions, but while studying at a local Catholic university, I did an internship with homeless people at a social advocacy agency called A Woman's Place ... We made a great impact on their lives and the lives of their children, so much so that it blew me away ... It was a beautiful little place. It was perfect. It was welcoming. All of our clients were homeless, and the majority of them had a mental illness ... We helped make them feel like they belonged somewhere and that they were part of a group, just like AeA does. We didn't treat them as if they were different from anyone else. It was as if we were on a mission trip, when we treat everyone like brothers and sisters, which is what they really are. We offered them every opportunity within our possibilities. We offered them outlets for their pains and frustrations that resulted from being homeless. We displayed that outlook that I'm stuck with, what I would call a missionary outlook.

Spiritual Guides/Advocates

Throughout AeA's prehistory and history, wise spiritual guides or advocates have selflessly offered their time, expertise, and love to guide the formation of the AeA community. These advocates have included a plethora of ordained, formally consecrated, and lay missionary guides, including the exiled leaders of the Cuban apostolic movements.

An AeA founder signaled the crucial role that ordained and consecrated spiritual guides and other missionaries have played in the formation and continuation of AeA:

> *Because of the missionary fervor that we had, and because we had a structure, a great Cuban Christian brother, Brother Alfredo Morales, would come over from Santo Domingo two or three times a year. Our primary Haitian friend and guide, a wonderful Monfortian priest, Father Boniface Fils-Aimé, would come over two or three times a year. Other nuns, priests, and brothers would come over two or three times a year. Missionaries from Ecuador that we had never met before, but whom we knew were in our line of work, would come and we would host all-day-long days of reflection with them on Saturdays at different people's houses. It was a period of great spiritual growth for all of us. And we would all go take courses offered at SEPI, the Southeastern Pastoral Institute. We were blessed at a particular time in history with the friendship of Jesuit priests, particularly Father Eduardo Álvarez, and Cuban priests working in other Caribbean countries like the Dominican Republic, and the Haitian and Canadian Monfortian priests later. They can only be compared to the apostles; they were titanic ... The Piarist priest who directed SEPI, Father Mario Vizcaíno, taught us how to discern among the many projects that were offered to us, by employing criteria, such as: the probability of eventual success, the*

avoidance of paternalism, continuity, the probability of self-perpet-
uation, and so forth.

Another AeA founder signaled the crucial role that clerical spiritual guides have played in the formation and continuation of AeA as well as the wise and steady direction of its trajectory:

Since our inception, we have studied constantly and always sought
out ongoing educational opportunities. God sent us very special
people to serve as our spiritual guides during our forty-year trajec-
tory, extraordinary missionary Jesuit priests above all, as well as
extraordinary missionary nuns, extraordinary Monfortian fathers
and brothers such as Gilbert Petitpas, Fracilius Petit-homme, Wil-
ner Donecia, and Ronel Charelus, extraordinary Salesians, and ex-
traordinary bishops. We should compile a list, and write about each
of them, and honor them. Missionary life has helped us and myself
personally to value life, and that which is essential in life, and it
has helped me to understand that everything else is secondary. Seek
first the Reign of God and his justice and everything else will be
added. So, our preoccupations changed. I have never worried
whether or not my purse matched my shoes. Do I notice that certain
material things are pretty? Yes. Do I like them? Yes. And would I
like them if I could acquire them? Yes. And have I at times enjoyed
such material things? Yes. But is obtaining material possessions
my priority? No, that is not my priority ... Over the years, God has
sent us marvelous, marvelous guides to inspire us with delicious
messages and challenges. We can also look back and trace the
sources of goodness and generosity in our lives, particularly our
families ... But I was skeptical before I met the Apostolinas and our
Cuban exile bishop, Bishop Agustín Román, and attended those
marvelous three-day-long Ignatian retreats with the Jesuits. Those
were the retreats that converted and transformed me. They were
what really spoke to me, those tremendous and powerful retreats

directed by the Jesuit fathers like Amando Llorente and Bishop Agustín Román.

One AeA founder gave credit to the apostolic movements that came from Cuba for recognizing the need to promote missionary outreach from Miami and for encouraging the birth and growth of AeA:

All of these Cursillistas were special people who had a calling to service way out there beyond most Christians, like I have not witnessed in a long time. And they had such strategic intelligence. But it was not what you see today. The problem now is that people focus so much on frivolities. There is no longer social action. They pray and they read the encyclicals, which is good; but it is not the whole thing. They had such an extraordinary capacity for love. And these people saw in us the answer to their prayers, because a lot of these people, when they were younger, when they were our age, had lived through a very traumatic experience in Cuba. Fidel Castro arrived right in the middle of when they were doing a lot of social work in the church, helping out a lot of people. Prior to that, most of them had belonged to la Acción Católica. They were educated and committed laity. La Acción Católica was an extraordinary organization. La Acción Católica was a youth movement in Cuba which had sound and advanced theological foundations, and at the same time, a lot of labor with the people. These people lived out the three integral pillars of Christianity: piety, study, and action. These people were very pious; they received communion and practiced daily adoration of the Blessed Sacrament. They were very theologically oriented, and at the same time, they were working in the worst places in Cuba, and doing a lot of stuff for the church at all levels. When Fidel arrived, many of them were imprisoned, many were abused and tortured, and there was a serious, targeted dismantling of their projects. So, fourteen years later, they met us in Miami, and they saw, in the second generation, the same aspirations. But they saw that we needed guidance and that we needed a helping hand to get

established in the right way. You should have seen them ... My
uncle stood up and said: This is a bigger project than any single
parish can handle. This is something that must be extended
throughout the whole archdiocese.

Divine Initiative

Despite numerous adversities, missionaries credit God for guiding
us, both as individual missionaries and as a missionary community
over the long haul. We perceive divine influence in both our initial
missionary vocation and our long-term path.

Josefina, an AeA founder, explained how living through forced emi-
gration from Cuba and its incumbent adversity, motivated her to act
with compassion and in solidarity. Nevertheless, she attributed the
arc of her missionary conversion to divine guidance:

> *So, for me, coming face-to-face with obvious injustices spurs me to*
> *think that this is my life happening all over again, just to someone*
> *else. But now, I am in a position where I can do something about*
> *it; whereas, before, I was young and powerless. I think that all of*
> *that becomes part of God's plan for me. I think that God is very*
> *wise, and really, He is at the helm of my life and I know it. And*
> *now at my age, I can look back and see that there has been a direc-*
> *tion, a flow, and that God has guided the flow of my life, and that*
> *things make sense. So, certainly, I have developed a desire to sim-*
> *plify my life and to do as much as I can to alleviate the injustices*
> *that I witness.*

Adriano, an AeA founder, attributed the convergent missionary trajectories of AeA's founders to divine guidance:

> *I was thinking that even if I had never become a part of AeA, Alicita*
> *would have been able to do this well anyway. But you know what?*
> *God did not want it to happen like that. And do I know why God*
> *wanted it that way? I don't know why. I was the worst person*

available to accomplish these things because I was the person who possessed the least intellectual capacity for these things. I could barely speak English. And when I was an adolescent, I was a very insecure person, very insecure. I didn't let it show; but I was. And insecurity does not produce good results. By using me, God used an instrument that was very inadequate to the task. And I believe that if God decided to use me, then it was to demonstrate that AeA was his doing and not mine or the founders' or anybody else's. In other words, he would have had to have chosen someone very capable of organizing and launching projects like Carlos Cueto, who was the Saint Paul of AeA and Alicia Marill, who was the founding mother or the Virgin Mary of AeA. But I was like Saint Peter. We never knew that we were founding a missionary community that was going to last for over forty years, and have a major purpose and role, and all that. We were basically trying to fulfill a need. We had to do something for the poor and something for God, to work for the Reign of God. That was the need at hand and that was what we were doing. We would have done anything to be able to fulfill that need. We felt compelled by our love for God to strive to help peace and justice flourish in the Caribbean.

Another AeA founder attributed the longevity and efficacy of AeA to divine guidance:

At times, we go off in the wrong direction, precisely because we are searching and testing, because we are not content to sleep spiritually. However, that which always maintained us was the love of Christ, because all of us were very much in love with Jesus Christ. Each of us expressed that love the best way that he or she could at the time. The common denominator that filled all of us was our love for Christ. It was a personal experience of seeing Christ who was calling us to enter his kingdom, and all of us desired to be a part of that kingdom. And some of us were more humanistic, and some of us were more spiritual, and some of us were more pastoral,

149

and some of us were more whatever; but all of us worked for the common good. I must say that meeting Alicita, the person who started AeA with me, was definitely an outrageous experience because I found a mirror of myself in somebody who was dynamic and explosive, somebody who could move, motivate, and push all the zeal, all the energy to serve God, all the energy to seek justice, to fruition. God definitely saw to it that I found the support I needed in the person of my cofounder. And then a community of people who were just a community of Christians joined us. They found us and we found them. Being a member of our AeA community in Miami was really like living in the primitive church as recorded in the Acts of the Apostles. We all desired to contribute to the Reign of God, which is the mission of our savior Jesus Christ.

Partnership in Divinely Inspired Urgency

AeA's founders were united by a shared sense of urgency to respond to God's self-sacrificial love for them through striving together to alleviate a measure of the suffering and to extend dignity-inducing conditions for God's other children in the Caribbean is-lands. If the founders had opted not to respond to God's call with such intensity and exigency, then the flame of AeA may have been extinguished decades ago.

One AeA founder spoke of how, from the outset, the founders shared a voracious, divinely induced appetite for accomplishments that would advance the Reign of God on earth:

We are insatiable in terms of the things that we want to accomplish for the Reign of God because everything is not enough. And everything is the result of our love for Jesus Christ. We can never do enough for Him. The three of us have that as a common denominator, that whatever it is that we are doing now, it is never enough; and we are impatient, always wanting to do more.

Adriano, an AeA founder, echoed the divinely inspired sense of urgency that united the founders:

We were unstoppable. It was beyond us. It was bigger than us. We didn't even know what was happening. We realized that we needed to do this or that and off we went. We were too serious for our parents and they were highly concerned that we were involved way too much in the church. Do you know why the Navy Seals are so good? Because they train, they act, and then they train some more. AeA was exactly like that. We went on the mission immersions, acted, and returned to the missions, and then acted, and then went back to the missions. And that is a method that is unstoppable. The only weeks we took off were to go on the immersions. We were committed to each other and to God. Anything or anybody who would get in the way of what we were doing, got the boot. We kicked them out. You could not disrupt our inner circle. If you tried, you were done. You could not interrupt our mission. We were dedicated to our mission. Anybody who criticized what we were doing, was out. I should also mention that our relationships with the archdiocese were always primordial for us. To be in communication with the archbishop was always very important to us. And Archbishop McCarthy gave us the wings to be a group, to live out our lay vocation to the fullest. He told us: I wish that there were more groups like yourselves.

Carlos, an AeA founder, described the divinely inspired sense of urgency that the founders shared. He is also convinced that, due to the overwhelming misery that they encountered in the slums of Santo Domingo, he would have felt hopeless without the support of his fellow AeA members:

In my spiritual journey, my first trip to the missions was sandwiched in between the big conversion events for me, which were participating in a Cursillo retreat and then attending my first Ignatian retreat later in that same year. And in the midst of all that, came AeA. I went to one of those slide presentations also, after they had already been working for about six months. I just saw the slides, and I said, I gotta go there. The first slide showed a bridge with a pile of trash that spanned the ravine on the main highway in front of the school of Saint Domingo Savio. And the smoke filled the air, but I couldn't smell it. And I saw that, and our eventual cofounder, Alicita, was sitting there with her little bandana, and I saw that, and I said: I've got to go there. It was two or three slides into the presentation; and I said: I gotta go there. I don't know why I reacted so immediately, but I ended up going there. The highest height and the lowest depth of the mission immersion experience to me was actually walking through the slum of los Guandules, because the trip was seven days long, but the visit to los Guandules lasted only about a day and a half. The most impactful experience was walking through los Guandules. I was a young professional and a career-oriented guy, and I looked around, and all of a sudden, I realized that even if I had fifty million dollars, I couldn't make a dent in terms of what this place needs. And I started crying. I had already met the other founders of AeA, Alicita and Adriano. I had already met the Cuban Jesuit priest, Father Eduardo Álvarez. I had bought a beautiful camera that cost six hundred dollars. But I had all these guilt trips and misgivings while I debated inside myself regarding whether or not it was right to spend this much money on a camera while so many people were dying from lack of medication, clean water, and food. I was worried about the morality of this expenditure, despite the fact that I hadn't even arrived there for the first time yet. Well, the priest blessed my camera. He said: You go ahead and buy your camera and enjoy it. I promised him that I would put it to good use; and sure enough I did. I think that most of the first thousand slides of AeA were taken with that camera. I remember walking through los Guandules, camera in hand, and meeting all the personalities that I had heard about so many times during the slide presentations in Miami that we staged to collect

funds. I'll never forget saying, If I had fifty million dollars, If I had
fifty million dollars, I could not begin to make a difference. Where
would you start? Building schools? No, that would take a genera-
tion. Building hospitals? You would need clean water and a reliable
source of electricity, and we don't have that either. It was like the
wall of death. No matter which way you turned, there was abso-
lutely no hope. Where do you start? Fifty million dollars would not
even make a dent. But I was blessed because I had already started
working with AeA before going on my first trip and I had AeA
already in place as my safety net and as my place where I could
empty myself, and upon which I could throw myself with all of
these apostolic and missionary ambitions. I had an outlet, an ave-
nue, somewhere, a release, a place where I could channel all of these
anxieties. The world would have been terrible for me if I had not
had AeA to which to come back. By the way, when you participate
in a Cursillo experience, they try to get you rooted into one of these
Cursillo communities. And I never went back to a parish Cursillo
group because I had AeA, despite the fact that the Cursillo had been
a life-turning experience for me. I was doing AeA presentations
with these guys before I even went on my first trip. We would do
two to three presentations a week. We were studying at the time.
By hook and by crook, whenever we had a day off from school. I
don't know how we did it. We maintained full-time jobs, we studied
full time, and we did presentations. We were busy with AeA until
1 or 2 AM every night, every night. We did AeA work from 6 PM
to 2 AM every week night, plus all day Saturday and all-day Sun-
day. AeA was a full-time job. I mean it was literally, not figura-
tively, a full-time job. We would do two or three presentations a
week. We made presentations to church and civic organizations as
well as to homeowners' associations and condominium associations
in Hialeah. We would show them our slides, narrate them, and so-
licit contributions. Back in those days, AeA did not have the struc-
ture or the patience or the acumen or the insight or the fortitude to

be able to take somebody who was not an independent thinker or who could not contribute his or her own ideas, to be able to say, If you want to help us, then this is what you can do. You either got it and immediately jumped on this already-moving train and started doing stuff or we would just thank you for your monetary contribution and continue what we were doing and that was it. It was neither good nor bad; that's just the way it was. AeA at that stage was an organization for born leaders. There is no value statement in that. That's just how it was. We were like the twelve apostles, selected by God, and empowered by the Holy Spirit. We had something that was very important. We, the three of us, had a love of Christ, a missionary zeal. We had a lot of energy, endless energy, endless energy. And we still had a social life. We still partied every weekend. None of us was in a committed relationship or engaged to be married or recently married or had kids or anything like that. We had concentric circles of participation. But there was that core group that was committed to the whole thing and kept it going.

Alicita, an AeA founder, spoke of the divinely inspired sense of urgency that bound the founders together. Furthermore, she emphasized the significance of the communal aspects of AeA to her ongoing conversion and commitment:

It was such that the task at hand required oomph; it required self-starters. The first three or four years of AeA were unreal, according to anyone's standards. It was such that if we wanted to repeat it right now, we would not be able to. Our main Haitian mentor, the Monfortian priest Pè Bo, made the following comment, You guys are obsessive about Amor en Acción. He would tell us that frequently: You are obsessed, obsession. I answered him: You're right. But if we are not obsessive about what we do, then the children in Haiti don't eat. And that's exactly what we believed; that the livelihood and survival of these people and these children depends on us. He said: You breakfast Amor en Acción, lunch Amor en Acción, dinner Amor en Acción. He was just being honest. Pè Bo became our friend. He is balanced. He is our missionary guide, our super wisdom source. But he realized that we did not rest. He would listen to classical music; we didn't. We didn't take time for anything else. We felt that we had a responsibility, such that if we failed to act, then children would not eat, and water would not get to the families in the slums. We were very clear about that. Prior to my missionary experiences, I believe that I was very skeptical, very cynical, and a person with no direction and no sense of vocation. I was cynical about the world, about the United Nations, about doing good things for the world, and about the church. If I had had the chance, I would have gone church hopping and ideology hopping because I didn't see any meaning in what was going on. Our society was selfish at that time. It was the Me Decade. Nobody cared about others. And at that time, I didn't trust anybody. By way of my post-immersion reflections I have noticed that I do not exactly experience God mystically via the poor. I do believe that the encounter with the poor, from a spiritual perspective, brings us to a realization of who we are. And I don't disassociate the human from the divine. I think that God is present in our lives, period. And therefore, I realized that I would be a better human being if I were in contact with God and the perspective of God in the world. So, to me, it's very important to focus, not just on Christ, but on Christ's mission and on Christ's mission to bring about the Reign of God and if we believe in Christ, then we need to follow the mission of Christ. We are not missionaries by choice; we are missionaries by divine call, commissioned to bring the Reign of God. And we help bring that Reign of God completely by fixing God's problems on Earth. The problems that exist today are somehow up to us to address. It's up to us to feed the hungry, to give water to the thirsty, to visit the imprisoned, to welcome the stranger, to nurture the sick, not just to visit the sick, if you study it, the scripture says to bring the sick back to life. Life from the experience of real life. What drives

155

me is a spiritual energy that I find in community, living Christ's mission of the Reign of God. And that produces an energy within me. I cannot live it alone. To be tranquil and alone for a while is very good; it sharpens my ability to discern better; it helps me to compose my thoughts; but this sharing gives me life, this community is nurturing for me, for me it is Eucharistic. But then where do I go from here? Yes, Christ loves me, and I love him; He suffered, and I suffer. Yes, and meanwhile the world still sleeps, doesn't it? What do I need to do to wake up the world? Whatever I do as an educator, via my work with youth, in my academic work, whenever I am asked to preach, is about bringing about the Reign of God. The Reign of God is goodness; it's how I can bring love and goodness, concretely. If you don't have a sheet of paper, I give you my paper. If you don't have water, I try to bring you water. If you need a hug today, I give you a hug. If you are my student, then I do the best that I can do, so that you can fulfill your mission.

Community Fostered by Frequency

The founders and members of AeA derived energy and enthusiasm from God and from each other. They are wholeheartedly convinced that the regularity and frequency of their meetings created the conditions for the formation of a truly Christian community according to the model exhibited in chapters two and four of the Acts of the Apostles. Not surprisingly, they are convinced that AeA will become stronger and endure longer, to the extent that we reestablish a similar rhythm of gathering.

One AeA veteran attested that the frequent and regular meetings of the community were a principal factor that contributed to the vitality of AeA:

While there were no specific re-entry meetings, there was a community to which to come back that met every week. And that is why AeA was so vibrant, because we were a real community. So, some people would travel and then come back. But the community was constantly meeting together. We met every Friday for years and years and years.

Another AeA founder agreed that the frequency and regularity of the meetings were essential factors that facilitated the growth and vigor of AeA:

But when there was an active community, what happened was, apart from a community that shared, the nurturing and mentoring occurred. Frequency is that which makes a community function.

One AeA founder concurred that meeting together every weekend was an indispensable element in forging the founders of AeA into a real community:

What made it work was, regardless of whatever level at which some-one wanted to participate, there was always the weekly meeting, and they could enter and leave according to the degree that they wished to participate. The only Friday that we took off literally was Christmas Eve. Other than that, every Friday there was an AeA meeting. By the way, we became a community, literally. And people would flow in and out at will. But we always knew that on Friday, at somebody's house, between 8 and 11 o'clock at night, there was going be an AeA meeting and after that we would go to Versailles restaurant. Saturday we would go out, and probably some of us would have some social event together, and on Sunday we would meet at Saint Raymond and go to church together, and after that we would go to dinner, and then we would go to the movies to-gether. If you do that once or twice, it's nice. But if you do that every week, year-after-year, then it becomes a pattern of living. You establish a community. Maybe we weren't registered at the Vati-can; but who cares? But it was definitely a community. However, we had a lot of fun because whether we were eating out or dancing, we were either planning our next trip or reminiscing about our last

trip. Or we were selling tickets to finance our next project. We se-
lected Versailles because it was the perfect place to sell tickets for
our fundraising events. Don't assume that we went there with the
intention of wasting time. We were focused on our goals.

Another AeA founder affirmed that meeting together every weekend
helped AeA develop into a genuine community:

I had the desire to continue growing in the faith through some
weekly encounter process. ... I figured out that we could do several
things. I could provide some structure. We could begin to have
weekly structured meetings where we could do some prayer, some
biblical study with our Jesuit mentor, and it would be a perfect set-
ting for us to create an organizing committee to plan whichever big
dance event that we were going to have. ... And then the other
thing was, we had a community that was already organized, and
we found that meeting every Friday was so good that we just de-
cided to perpetuate that pattern of meeting every Friday evening
throughout the year. All the way through 1983, we would meet,
rain or shine, with the exclusion of Christmas Eve, even on Thanks-
giving Day weekend. On New Year's Eve, we would celebrate to-
gether and ring in the New Year together. It was constant.

One veteran AeA immersion leader, who does not reside close to
most of the other AeA members, has found it more feasible to continue to foment her missionary conversion between AeA immersions
by participating in a JustFaith community that meets regularly within
her local parish.

Since I live up North in Broward County, my parish JustFaith
group has served as my post-immersion base community. After
coming home from AeA mission immersions, I know that the
JustFaith community that I am a part of has helped. It has helped
me also to come home from AeA mission immersions by helping me
to reintegrate, by helping me to get involved in my own

community, and by helping me not feel afraid to protest or march with the Immokalee farm workers. That was the first protest in which I participated. I wasn't worried anymore. Did I get arrested? No. And although I was afraid, I didn't care anymore. Participation in that group has given me more courage. They have been a very good support group for me because we all share the same philosophy that you can be Christian and not necessarily a liberal. Involvement in terms of opposing injustices is not question of being a liberal. It's a component of being Christian. It's a question of living out the faith. They are very supportive. Just like AeA, it's a community of faith which is involved in social justice. So if you need somebody to understand you after a missionary immersion or somebody to go somewhere with you for moral support, then they are the people that support you and upon whom you can call. It is an ongoing community. This is the third year that I have been a JustFaith member.

Re-Entry Debriefing Meetings

Since the primitive AeA community met nearly every weekend of the year, the founders and members did not feel the necessity to schedule a specific meeting or series of meetings in order to ease the cross-cultural re-entry transition and to deepen the respective missionary conversions of the post-immersion missionaries. However, in light of the fact that AeA now includes missionaries who reside in the Saginaw, Michigan diocese, as well as young folks who study out of town, specific attention to post-immersion and cross-cultural transition issues have gained much more significance. The predictably painful feelings of post-immersion estrangement are only magnified by such geographical separation.

One veteran AeA immersion leader spoke of the affirmation that she has felt during post-immersion re-entry meetings:

I think that the post-immersion re-entry meetings are good because oftentimes we have not seen each other since we traveled together, and the meeting helps me to feel reaffirmed about the choice that I had made months earlier to commit myself to dedicating all the effort that is inherent in preparing for a mission immersion, especially in my case, where I am responsible for my students in addition to myself. I feel affirmed when I am able to reunite with them. I hear myself internally saying, Yes, this is why I went. This is my missionary community. We all believe in the same thing. It reaffirms what happened during the immersion. It gives me that little boost that I need to continue on in the world. For me, the re-entry meetings serve as a reaffirmation that choosing to undertake all the effort inherent in preparing an immersion group is the right thing to do. And they serve to encourage me that we can go on to apply its lessons to our daily lives here in the USA.

Another veteran AeA missionary indicated that there are distinct ways to conduct post-immersion re-entry meetings, some of which are beneficial and others that are futile:

Re-entry meetings can be helpful, if there are others that have had experiences of comparable impact and if the meetings are led correctly. Sometimes those meetings can devolve into picture swapping sessions, but other times I remember sharing some of my most vivid images and memories while trying to make the formation leaders understand my gratitude. I have attended a couple of them where the dominating sentiment could be summarized by statements such as: Look at this! Remember this? Yeah, I had so much fun, fun, fun! Let's remember all the nice stuff! Whoopee! But I've been to some other meetings in which one of our formation leaders has slowed us all down and has told us to transition into a prayerful mode. Then, she always asks us to describe the most vivid image that is locked in our heads and hearts from the immersion trip. There is always something from each trip that my heart holds onto.

Eucharistic Liturgies

The founders of AeA believe that God fortified and inspired them via the sacrament of the Eucharist. Therefore, together they sought out frequent opportunities to celebrate it in a variety of settings. Today, they yearn for a revival of this potent tradition among AeA's successive generations. Some of the young missionaries have personally experienced the power of the Eucharistic liturgy to unify friends spiritually across great geographical divides.

Lindsay, a young Saginaw AeA veteran, discovered the unifying power of the Eucharistic liturgy:

> *I grew close to two of the girls from Miami. And in the midst of my spiritual awakening, I thought, Oh my gosh. This is what the presence of God feels like. I was talking to people my age especially. I remember her asking: What is your favorite part of the mass? I answered, Well, I know it by heart, but I don't really know. The exit-signs? And so I thought about it, and I thought about it, and I thought about it, and I answered, It's the part when we say, Lord, I am not worthy that You should enter under my roof; but only say the word and my soul shall be healed. And I wondered: What is the word? That's my favorite part, but I don't even understand it. And after I talked to her about my favorite part of the mass, and after realizing that I even had one, it has become something that now every Sunday at every mass, I look forward to that part. To answer the question, for me, it was my peers on my mission immersion trip that affirmed my values and actually made me think about what was the most important part of mass to me, which is a very simple thing about which I had never thought before. My peers did indeed continue to affirm my values after the immersion because it was something that I took away from mission that didn't necessarily have to do with the immersion experience. It was just a result of a conversation that I had with a fellow missionary, and it was*

affirmed because I still, to this day, when I hear that part, I think about that conversation we had. And it was really the first conversation that I ever had with someone my age about mass or my beliefs. And it is affirmed every Sunday when I get to say it again and think about it. And I still get chills.

Margaret, a young AeA veteran, asserted the unifying power of the Eucharistic liturgy:

But somehow by the act of sharing my faith with the people I met there, and participating in masses together, mass became a unifying symbol for me. I mean when I would come back to the USA and attend mass, I would feel like I was connected with them because I knew that my Dominican friends were sharing in the same readings. You know how universal the Catholic church is. That became a reason why I enjoy being Catholic, because the mass connected all of us somehow. Every Sunday when I'm at mass, I'm thinking they're going to be reading the same readings.

An AeA veteran signaled the unifying effect of liturgical music for missionaries:

I notice that many of the missionaries assembled during the post-immersion community masses close their eyes and recall singing those songs during evening prayer sessions during their immersions. The singing seems to transport the people's souls back to their respective mission immersions. The singing reignites their memories. It serves as a bridge between Miami and Quisqueya.

One AeA founder affirmed the unifying effect of liturgical music for missionaries:

The music, the singing is a bonding experience because it takes us back to the immersions and back to those people who so love to sing, like the Dominican people, who love to sing.

One founder pointed out the centrality of Eucharistic liturgies among the founding generation of AeA:

Celebrating the liturgy together is a very profound experience for us. Eucharist is definitely at the core of our missionary spirituality. And communal Eucharistic celebrations are especially meaningful to us.

Another AeA founder echoed the central role that the Eucharist has played among the founding generation of AeA:

I believe that the Eucharist has been a very strong, unifying, spiritual force in the life of AeA. It's a sacrament, a concrete path that God uses to send us grace and power.

Another AeA founder called attention to the centrality of Eucharistic liturgies among the founding generation of AeA:

We used to celebrate the Eucharist in our community four or five times per year. Whenever a priest friend would join us, we would sit down and celebrate the Eucharist, right there in our houses. A group of twenty or thirty of us would meet for a two- or three-hour-long mass and that was our meeting. It was very similar to what the apostles did in the beginning. They would meet to dine together, and they would celebrate the Eucharist.

Another AeA founder contrasted the intensity of the role that the Eucharist has played among the distinct generations of AeA:

Particularly in the early years of AeA, we lived the Eucharist very intensely, with Eucharistic celebrations in our homes. In contrast, the younger AeA generation expects to participate in the Eucharist only in a church building or chapel or retreat house or on a special occasion.

Another AeA founder signaled a resurgence in the degree of significance ascribed to the Eucharist among many of our young veteran missionaries:

Many of our young veteran leaders are extremely profound in terms of prayer and the Eucharist, and I respect them a great deal for that, because I know that they do it due to an internal motivation. And I believe that, right there is a marvelous seed for a rebirth of many other things that are happening in AeA. During mass at our parish the other Sunday evening, I was meditating on the Act of Contrition and when I when I lifted my eyes, I saw one of our young veterans serving as an extraordinary minister of the Eucharist. And when we saw each other and she said to me, The Body of Christ, tears came to the eyes of both of us. It affected me because I saw someone from AeA who was giving me the Eucharist. It was very powerful. It was a sign of the presence of God. That's the Eucharist, right? To share Christ in reality, in people. That is very profound. And so, how did the Eucharist become important to AeA? We always, for whatever important cause or issue, would celebrate the Eucharist together and we would receive communion while sitting on a living room floor. The next generation of AeA is doing it too. This is not something that we can create or invent. This is the work of the Spirit of God.

Conversion-Promoting Generative Themes

Because they are indispensable to the shared praxis method of practical theology, it is vital to pause here to ascertain the generative themes revealed by the narratives in the foregoing segment on post-immersion encouragements to conversion.

Moral Support from Family, Friends, & Church

It appears that every missionary who remains committed to the missions, encounters someone who supports him or her by listening repeatedly to his or her immersion stories and by not contradicting his or her post-immersion conversion resolutions. These supportive people often include close family members, friends, teachers, clergy, other religious ministers, and fellow missionaries. Conversely, it is common for neophyte post-immersion missionaries to opt to maintain their distance from friends who openly contradict their newly appropriated missionary values, such as, more frequent prayer, advocacy for and aid to weak and poor people, and the eschewing of self-indulgent behaviors.

Witnessing to & Inspiring Others to Discern Missionary Vocations

Being invited to give witness talks to stateside church groups encourages growth, commitment, and spiritual stamina among post-immersion missionaries. It is common for neophyte post-immersion missionaries to view themselves as mission recruiters who feel compelled to inspire non-missionaries to actively discern whether or not God is calling them to mission.

Vocations

There may be no more visible evidence of missionary conversion than a radical change in career path or university program of study, as is frequently seen among post-immersion missionaries. These transformations tend to show a shift away from self-reliance and materialism and toward increased reliance on God and the missionary community, personal asceticism, and dedication to the active promotion of the integral self-elevation of politically-economically-socially shunned people.

Focus on People Instead of Poverty

Missionaries who learn to focus on people more than on their material poverty grow more readily in wisdom and enjoy longer missionary careers than those post-immersion missionaries who allow themselves to feel overwhelmed by the needs that they observe in the mission fields.[10]

Community Service in the USA

Participation in local community service projects helps countless post-immersion missionaries to further their missionary formation because, as when immersed overseas, they are able to interact with marginalized people and other religiously motivated volunteers. Not surprisingly, many missionary vocations are discerned by religious people when they reflect upon their own domestic community service.

Spiritual Guides/Advocates

Beyond the indispensable aforementioned supporters, spiritual advocates or guides play crucial roles as motivators and stimulators of reflection, conscience, and action. These inspirational advocates are particularly vital during the nascent and formative years of a missionary community.

Partnership in Divinely Inspired Urgency

As the lives of numerous saints indicate, a divinely inspired sense of urgency is essential when founding a new religious congregation or missionary institute. Such urgency is indispensable because, in every age and place, an abundance of naysayers emerges. This is why those who prove successful at launching and sustaining their new endeavors do so by joining with a handful of inspired and like-minded pioneers.

---

[10] Janet Ruffing, "Socially Engaged Contemplation: Living Contemplatively in Chaotic Times," *Handbook of Spirituality for Ministers: Perspectives for the 21st Century*, no. 2 (Mahwah, NJ: Paulist, 2000), 418-419; Robert J. Wicks, *Self-Ministry Through Self-Understanding: A Guide to Christian Introspection* (Chicago, IL: Loyola University, 1983), 86-87; Putnam, *Bowling Alone*, 67.

Unifying Power of Eucharistic Liturgies

Many contemporary Catholic missionaries find that post-immersion Eucharistic liturgies unite them spiritually and cognitively with their fellow missionaries and their friends in foreign lands. The uniformity of the calendar of the lectionary-guided biblical readings and the constancy of the order of the mass consistently contribute to this experience of cross-border and overseas solidarity. Some missionaries express genuine surprise and delight when struck with this epiphany.

Conclusion

Now that we have heard, examined, and categorized the raw material of the testimony of the missionaries regarding the factors that discourage and encourage post-immersion missionary conversion, in the following chapter, we will proceed with a sociological and philosophical critique of the generative themes derived from this scrutiny.

5

SOCIOLOGICAL-PHILOSOPHICAL

REFLECTION

N ow that we have carefully documented our current praxis, Groome's method guides us to reflect critically on that praxis and to connect our praxis to the wider Christian praxis and vision. This chapter critically analyzes the conflict between US culture and the missionary vision of AeA as revealed in the testimonies of the returned missionaries. To this end, I employ the sociological and philosophical resources of Robert Bellah et al. and John Kavanaugh SJ.

We begin this chapter with an interdisciplinary examination of AeA's early and current praxes through the lenses of sociological and philosophical literature that critically analyzes contemporary US culture. We then proceed to identify clashes between American culture and the post-immersion Christian missionary values of AeA as revealed in the testimonies given during the focus group interviews.

Robert Neelly Bellah et al.

Robert Neelly Bellah, a sociologist in the tradition of Emile Durkheim, collaborated with his research and writing team, comprised of Richard Madsen, William Sullivan, Ann Swidler, and Steven Tipton, to compose *Habits of the Heart: Individualism and Commitment in American Life*. Bellah et al. stand out among the scholarly commentators on the topic of United States culture thanks to the attention that they give to the historical, philosophical, and religious roots of our society.

Going back to the colonial era, they provide appreciable context for grasping the sources of our current social reality. In order to orient their readers regarding the emergence of the culture which has enshrined individualism in the USA, Bellah et al. begin with a nod to political philosopher John Locke, governor John Winthrop, republican architect and president Thomas Jefferson, ambassador Benjamin Franklin, and president George Washington. Bellah et al. then proceed to add to this historical-philosophical baseline the observations of two French sojourners to the USA, Alexis-Charles-Henri Clérel de Tocqueville (in the early nineteenth century), and to a lesser degree, Michel Guillaume Jean de Crèvecoeur (in the late eighteenth century). Bellah et al. examine the effects of the various strands of individualism (biblical, republican, utilitarian, and expressive), as well the cultures of managerialism and psychotherapy, upon the development and maintenance of communities in the USA. They note that as true communities weaken, enclaves often emerge as a response to the human need for genuine community.[1]

---

[1] Political scientist Robert David Putnam also leans on de Tocqueville in his historical-statistical analysis of "social capital" in the USA. In *Bowling Alone*, Putnam traces the nearly steady rise of American social capital from the colonial era through its marked decline which commenced in 1960. Putnam repeatedly asserts the fact that the churches are and have always been the principal source of social capital in the USA, as evidenced by the fact that many of them serve to motivate their members to practice philanthropy and volunteer service while acting as incubators of the civic skills (such as public speaking and human resource management) that buttress the building and maintenance of human communities and participatory citizenship. Robert Putnam, *Bowling Alone: The Collapse and Revival of American Community* (New York, NY: Simon and Schuster, 2000), 29ff. Bellah repeatedly salutes Putnam's coining and elaboration of the concept of social capital. Robert Bellah et al., "Individualism and the Crisis of Civic Membership," *The Christian Century* (Chicago, IL: The Christian Century, March 20-27, 1996): 260. Robert Bellah, "Comments on the Position Papers," *Ethical Perspectives* 5, no. 2 (Leuven, Belgium: Centre for Ethics, Katholieke Universiteit Leuven, 1998):

John Francis Kavanaugh SJ

Jesuit Father John Francis Kavanaugh was a Christian social philosopher who identified the depersonalizing system that colonizes perception, feeling, motivation, and behavior in hyper-materialistic societies, while proposing an alternative system that antithetically strives to humanize these same societies.[2]

In *Still Following Christ in a Consumer Society: the Spirituality of Cultural Resistance*, Kavanaugh observes that this vicious objectifying "Commodity Form" (Pope Saint John Paul II labeled it the "Culture of Death")[3] has been produced by both communist and capitalist superstructures. Kavanaugh has dubbed the virtuous alternative system the "Personal Form" (Pope Saint John Paul II branded it the "Gospel of Life").[4] On the topic of consumerism, Kavanaugh, whom I consider to be a modern-day prophet in the biblical tradition, is not timid about pointing the finger regarding the consequences, the causes, or the culprits.

Kavanaugh begins with the widely attested observation that "our ability to relate to other persons has atrophied,"[5] because our philosophical priorities have become inverted in contemporary US society. Possessions have become ends or "ultimates," and "the final judge of our merit."[6] He further asserts that "buying and consuming have become vehicles for experiencing the sacred."[7] Kavanaugh then proceeds to indicate the practical results of such extreme ontological

---

158ff. Robert Bellah, "Shingaku and Twenty-First Century Japan," *Symposium on the 270th Anniversary of the Founding of Shingaku* (Kyoto, Nippon: RobertBellah.com, October 15, 2000).

[2] Kavanaugh, *Still Following Christ*, 54; John Kavanaugh, *Who Count as Persons? Human Identity and the Ethics of Killing* (Washington, DC: Georgetown University, 2001), 48ff.

[3] Pope John Paul II, *Evangelium Vitae*, 74.

[4] Pope John Paul II, *Evangelium Vitae*, 12.

[5] Kavanaugh, *Still Following Christ*, 10.

[6] Kavanaugh, *Still Following Christ*, 55-56.

[7] Kavanaugh, *Still Following Christ*, 12.

materialism. "Once self-worth is defined in terms of appropriation, the cultural myth will relentlessly be one of materialism, property, consumption, buying-power, competition, and greater economic exploitation."[8]

Kavanaugh takes pains to repeatedly blame the modern marketing industry for inventing "false needs," and for striving to convince people at every stratum of society that the acquisition of objects is more spiritually satisfying over the long term than committing oneself to other human persons covenantally:

> *Aldous Huxley described advertising as the organized effort to magnify and intensify our craving in such a way as to stimulate the principal causes of our suffering and wrong-doing: it is the highest barrier between our personhood and our fulfillment .... Jules Henry condemned advertising as the brutalization of human desires and the degrading of our humanness.*[9]

Kavanaugh unveils the meta-message lurking behind the gloss of advertisements: the fraudulent pledge that the joy dispensed by commodities outlasts any subjective affective benefits that divine or human relationships can offer, be they familial, amorous, or charitable:

> *The Thing is not woundable. It is invulnerable. And the culture that enthrones things, products, objects as its most cherished realities, is ultimately a culture in flight from the vulnerability of the human person. It is the unguardedness of personal existence, which is fled when we escape from interiority, or evade committed intimacy, or harden our hearts to the unjust degradation of people.*[10]

---

[8] Kavanaugh, *Still Following Christ*, 46; See also Kavanaugh, *Who Count as Persons?* 22ff.

[9] Kavanaugh, *Still Following Christ*, 51.

[10] Kavanaugh, *Still Following Christ*, 17.

In fact, Kavanaugh insists that we employ creature comforts to shield ourselves from "wounded" people who might frighten us profoundly by reminding us of our own vulnerability.[11]

As mentioned, Kavanaugh proposes the Personal Form as the best response to counteract the dominant Commodity Form. He asserts that in order to metaphysically face reality in the USA, people must realize that our culture has grown deeply idolatrous. "One form of life, one gospel, reveals men and women as replaceable and marketable commodities; another gospel, inalterably opposed to the first, reveals persons as irreplaceable and uniquely free beings."[12]

Kavanaugh counsels any person or group of persons who experience the spiritual-existential inadequacy of a super-materialistic culture to contemplate the Christian or Jewish[13] worldview as a robust and valid alternative:

> The Gospel of Christ is the most countercultural and the most significantly revolutionary document one could ever hope to find. It reveals the meaning and purpose of human life in terms which are close to being absolutely contradictory to the form of perceiving and valuing human persons in our culture. The gospel presents an image of God which shatters most categories that both atheists and believers employ; and it offers a model of humanity which is wholeheartedly personalistic, liberating, and ultimately exalting of human life.[14]

---

[11] Kavanaugh, *Still Following Christ*, 16.

[12] Kavanaugh, *Still Following Christ*, 21; See Pope John Paul II, *Evangelium Vitae*, 2.

[13] Kavanaugh asserts that both Judaism and Christianity (both of which emanate from the God of Yisrael who is fundamentally revealed in the Tanakh or Old Testament) feature values rooted in God's understanding of personhood, and therefore, either is capable of providing a sufficient framework and bulwark for sustaining the countercultural commitment needed to live via the Personal Form. Kavanaugh, *Still Following Christ*, 76.

[14] Kavanaugh, *Still Following Christ*, 83.

This Gospel of Life or Personal Form emanates from the self-sacrificial love of the Deity.

While Kavanaugh is strident in his critique of capitalism without limits, he steers clear of advocating for a communist alternative. Although he employs some of Marx's terminology, especially the "fetishism of the commodity" (which Kavanaugh believes Marx derived from the biblical Psalm 115), Kavanaugh delineates what he views as socialism's fatal flaws:

> At the center of Marxism is a gaping hole. It is absence of spirit. There is little of compassion and hope. There is a lack of faith in the resilience and freedom of men and women. And most damaging of all, there are ultimately no good reasons provided for persons to be free and alive. People are expendable.[15]

Kavanaugh, Pope Saint John Paul II, and Pope Benedict XVI emphatically decry both extreme capitalism and extreme socialism as dehumanizing.[16] Both extremes are overly materialistic in their worldviews and both have generated Commodity Forms.

Clashes Evident in the Testimonies

Employing the nomenclature of both Kavanaugh and Bellah et al. with the goal of encapsulating the heartfelt longing of post-immersion missionaries, it could be said that post-immersion missionaries strive to reconstitute at least an enclave of the Personal Land within the gigantic US Commodity Land after returning from the mobile missionary Personal Land enclave.

To this end, we seek simplicity within our hyper-consumerist culture; we choose to favor people over things; we seek community within

---

[15] Kavanaugh, *Still Following Christ*, 166.

[16] Pope John Paul II, *Sollicitudo Rei Socialis*, 21; Pope Benedict XVI, "Letter of his Holiness Benedict XVI to the Bishops of Latin America & the Caribbean," *Aparecida*, 6-9.

our individualistic culture; we seek sacramental nourishment; we seek to maintain direct contact and relationships with materially poor people in our own native land; we strive to continue to hear God's voice clearly amidst our advertising-saturated culture; and we seek to inspire our coreligionists to discern their own potential missionary vocations.[17]

Culture Shock

AeA missionaries report that upon our return to the USA, we have struggled with: consumerism; alienation; individualism; backsliding from integral Christian living by succumbing to temptation; and uneven reintegration processes among diocesan AeA communities.[18] The principal contrast perceived by missionaries upon re-entry to our US homeland is the disparity between material wealth and material poverty, opulence versus subsistence.

Emotionally, we often feel repulsed by the luxurious lifestyles that we have observed and enjoyed for the duration of our lives up until our most recent missionary immersion. We judge the expenditures of resources as wasteful. We admonish those around us to reduce their consumption levels, particularly regarding water, food, electricity, clothing, and fuel. We feel compelled to shun deluxe venues, including pricey restaurants, hotels, cruise ships, and even shopping malls.

One ironic yet frequent phenomenon that many of us exhibit in our initial post-immersion stage is a proclivity to isolate ourselves physically, emotionally, and spiritually from our non-missionary and non-volunteer family members, friends, coworkers, schoolmates, and neighbors due to a conviction that owing to their submersion in our super-materialistic American culture, they are incapable of comprehending anything about the overseas missionary immersion

---

[17] See Putnam, *Bowling Alone*, 66-68, 79, 116-119.

[18] Pope John Paul II, *Evangelium Vitae*, 23.

reality. At least temporarily, it is common for missionaries to believe that we belong to the austere culture in which we were momentarily immersed and not to the lavish culture of our native USA.

Two young AeA veterans have felt so detached from the possessions in their own bedroom closets upon returning from mission immersions that they report that they have stood before these armoires and gawked incredulously at the sheer quantity and cost of their contents. One of these thoughtful young women was unsure whether her family was on vacation because she perceived her family's house to be a luxurious hotel for several hours post immersion. An even more acute manifestation of this estrangement phenomenon is the fact that immediately upon re-entry, our founders (all of whom are Cuban exiles to the USA) testify that they perceive themselves as extraterrestrial visitors to Planet Earth.

Kavanaugh affirms this extreme sense of estrangement experienced by spiritually alert Christians with regard to their own US culture:

> *A follower of Jesus might find himself or herself to be an outsider in a culture dominated by the commodity. It should be no shame to feel different, even to feel a bit disjointed and out of place, in a civilization which divinizes the thing ... Christianity at rock bottom radically conflicts with American culture, even subverts it. The last thing that Christians need is to become more secularized .... In a culture of lived atheism and the enthroned commodity, ... the practicing Christian should look like a Martian. He or she will never feel fully at home in the commodity kingdom. If the Christian does feel at home, something is drastically wrong ... We Christians [risk] compromise with the powers that be, with wealth, hedonism, nationalism, and economic ideology. We [risk] becom[ing] too comfortable with Caesar.[19]*

---

[19] Kavanaugh, *Still Following Christ*, 113-128; See Pope John Paul II, *Evangelium Vitae*, 23, 32.

In fact, primarily due to the harsh ethical nature of her nine-to-five work environment, one of our founders feels so personally traumatized by the cross-cultural transition of post-immersion re-entry that she likens it to undergoing open heart surgery without anesthesia. Another of our founders was subjected to a most outrageous verbal assault of a eugenic genocidal nature when his boss told him that by virtue of spearheading a nutritional program for Haitian children, he was a hindrance to Nature because he was "interrupting the natural process of Nature's attempt to eliminate all of those people."

Innumerable missionaries have found that the highest-ranking officials of Christian educational institutions have overtly failed to embrace fully the missionary callings and commitments of their students and faculty. While at one Christian high school, the principal gives permission and tolerates the short-term immersions, some administrators and faculty members intentionally opt out of attending the succinct post-immersion slide show presentations.

Bellah et al. present an insightful historical overview of how the culture of the United States of America became so individualistic, while simultaneously pointing out the key ameliorating moral and religious aspects of US culture that originally served as an effective counterbalance to the extreme consequences of market capitalism:

> *Modern individualism emerged out of the struggle against monarchical and aristocratic authority that seemed arbitrary and oppressive to citizens prepared to assert the right to govern themselves. In that struggle, classical political philosophy and biblical religions were important cultural resources ... Yet both these traditions placed individual autonomy in a context of moral and religious obligation that in some contexts justified obedience as well as freedom."*[20]

---

[20] Bellah et al., *Habits*, 142-143; See also Bellah et al., "Individualism and the Crisis of Civic Membership," 263; See also Putnam, *Bowling Alone*, 66-68, 79, 116-119.

In fact, Bellah et al. remind us that the British Puritan pilgrims who colonized Massachusetts envisioned a society guided by the principles of both biblical and republican individualism. Bellah et al. assert that:

> From its early days, some Americans have seen the purpose and goal of the American nation as the effort to realize the ancient biblical hope of a just and compassionate society ... Their fundamental criterion of success was not material wealth but the creation of community in which a genuinely ethical and spiritual life could be lived .... The Puritan settlements ... can be seen as the first of many efforts to create utopian communities in America ... For Winthrop, success was much more explicitly tied to the creation of a certain kind of ethical community than it is for most Americans today ... John Winthrop decried what he called "natural liberty," which is the freedom to do whatever one wants, evil as well as good. True freedom, what Winthrop called "moral" freedom, "in reference to the covenant between God and man," is a liberty "to do only that which is good, just, and honest."[21]

Lamentably, we as a society have strayed widely from the original, balanced intent of our founding fathers. We seem to be trapped in an Ivan Boesky, Michael Milken, Jeffrey Skilling, Andrew Fastow, Jordan Belfort, Bernard Madoff, Gordon Gekko spiral of avarice.[22] Even many of the infamous "robber barons" or "captains of industry" of the "gilded age" or the "industrial revolution" eventually manifested the enduring momentum of the original ideals of the founders of our country, as their abundant philanthropic legacies attest. For example, Andrew Carnegie argued in 1889 that "surplus wealth is a sacred

---

[21] Bellah et al., *Habits*, 27-29.

[22] Kavanaugh, *Still Following Christ*, xxii-xxiii; Gordon Gekko is the hyper-greedy financial mentor and antagonist in the films *Wall Street* (1987) and *Wall Street 2: Money Never Sleeps* (2010).

trust which its possessor is bound to administer ... for the good of the community."[23]

Bellah et al. underscore the fact that Winthrop, Jefferson, Washington, and de Tocqueville all identified the Christian religion as the indispensable bulwark against unbridled greed. Jefferson appropriated biblical language when counseling his fellow Americans: "Love your neighbor as yourself, and your country more than yourself."[24] Washington, in his farewell address, labeled religion and morality the "indispensable supports of political prosperity," the "great pillars of public happiness," and the "firmest props of the duties of men and citizens."[25] De Tocqueville observed that, "the main business of religion is to purify, control, and restrain that excessive and exclusive taste for well-being."[26] He went on to note that "Christianity teaches that we must do good to our fellows for love of God."[27]

Nevertheless, Bellah et al. emphasize the ever-evident point that, "individualism lies at the very core of American culture."[28] They go so far as to employ religious language to drive home their argument:

> *We believe in the dignity, indeed the sacredness, of the individual. Anything that would violate our right to think for ourselves, make our own decisions, live our lives as we see fit, is not only morally wrong, it is sacrilegious.*[29]

---

[23] See Putnam, *Bowling*, 117.

[24] See Bellah et al., *Habits*, 31.

[25] See Bellah et al., *Habits*, 222; See also Robert Bellah, "Civil Religion in America," *Dædalus: Journal of the American Academy of Arts and Sciences* 96, no. 1 (Cambridge, MA: American Academy of Arts and Sciences, Winter 1967): 7.

[26] See Bellah et al., *Habits*, 223.

[27] See Bellah et al., *Habits*, 223; See also Bellah, "Civil Religion in America," 12.

[28] Bellah et al., *Habits*, 142.

[29] Bellah et al., *Habits*, 142.

They credit John Locke for profoundly influencing our emerging eighteenth-century nation with regard to individualism and the social contract:

> *The essence of the Lockean position is an almost ontological individualism. The individual is prior to society, which comes into existence only through the voluntary contract of individuals trying to maximize their own self-interest."*[30]

Bellah et al. also recognize the powerful role that contemporary psychology plays in terms of buttressing and augmenting American individualism. As Robert Coles declares, "For psychology, ... the self is the only or main form of reality."[31] Moreover, unlike counselors in many other societies, psychotherapists in the USA tend to treat their clients' emotional wounds by alienating them from their family, friends, neighbors, and hereditary values. Bellah et al. poignantly describe this North American therapeutic bias:

> *The work of therapy is often aimed at so distancing us from our parents so that we may choose, or seem to choose, freely, which aspects of them we will resemble and which not. Leaving home in a sense involves a kind of second birth in which we give birth to ourselves. And if that is the case with respect to families, it is even more so with our ultimate defining beliefs.*[32]

In other words, true personal freedom, as defined by psychology, begins with the rejection of one's familial and societal philosophical inheritance and the simultaneous enshrinement of absolute postmodern, self-generated tastes. Bellah et al. are adamant that the contemporary US psychotherapy industry insists that:

---

[30] Bellah et al., *Habits*, 143.

[31] See Bellah et al., *Habits*, 143.

[32] Bellah et al., *Habits*, 65.

The self must be maintained as the intuitive center of the wants and impulses that define right action, and as the unimpeachable evaluator of the good or bad feelings by which the utility of our acts can be calculated and the depth of our self-expression intuited ... Separated from family, religion, and calling as sources of authority, duty, and moral example, the self first seeks to work out its own form of action by autonomously pursuing happiness and satisfying its wants.[33]

The hedonistic leisure culture of late US adolescence perennially surfaces as both a violent shock to the consciousness of recently returned missionaries as well as a blatant obstacle to further missionary conversion. The testimony of one young veteran serves as a representative sample of this phenomenon. She attests that "the college party scene was something that did impede my sense of mission and my pursuit of my resolutions." The starkness of the contrast between a Christian missionary lifestyle and an ambiance of bacchanal US collegiate weekend revelry is such that it is not uncommon for post-immersion missionaries to eschew the company of their pre-immersion friends whom the missionaries perceive either as spiritually shallow or stagnant, inextricably immersed in materialism, or as outright contradictory influences upon their newly minted post-immersion conversion goals.

Interspersed throughout the history of AeA, there have been periods of inadequate post-immersion reintegration procedures. Especially for a first-time missionary, a fumbled re-entry process can leave him or her feeling disoriented, angry, intensely lonely, abandoned, and even disgusted. Inadequate debriefing by the receiving community or church can serve to magnify the pain of culture shock. In Miami, this experience was more common in AeA's early years when the founders, without the benefit of models, were just figuring out how

---

[33] Bellah et al., *Habits*, 78.

to establish and manage a missionary community that featured short-term immersions and long-term commitments. More recently, Saginaw AeA missionaries have described the inadequacy and shallowness of what they refer to as "picture parties," which they lament lack sufficient "spiritual component[s]." While immersed together in a materially sparse setting, missionaries intentionally set aside time each evening to pray and to discuss their experiences. Thereby, they all solicit and obtain regular support from God and each other. Since the lay missionaries no longer reside together upon re-entry, they suddenly are left without the nightly prayers and shared reflections. This sudden rupture of the mutually supportive missionary immersion routine is aggravated by our excessively materialistic culture which is replete with a myriad of versions of the false promise that happiness is literally for sale.

Seeking Simplicity in a Culture of Consumerist Idolatry to make Room for Relationships with Self, Others, & God

Kavanaugh maintains that the central philosophical error in the contemporary USA is idolatry, which he defines as the "dispossession of our humanity in the name of our artifacts."[34] He makes the case that this idolatry has the effect of radically dehumanizing our society:

> *The unified theme is that persons do not count, unless they are certain kinds of persons. If they are not endowed with value by power, affluence, productivity, or national interest, they may be sacrificed on the altar of our way of life. What is ours, what we possess, what we own and consume has become the ultimate criterion against which we measure all other values. As an ultimate, this criterion has become our functional god.*[35]

---

[34] Kavanaugh, *Still Following Christ*, 58; See also Kavanaugh, *Who Count as Persons?* 59.

[35] Kavanaugh, *Still Following Christ*, 26; See also Pope John Paul II, *Evangelium Vitae*, 64.

Kavanaugh's social critique was foreshadowed by Hellenic philosopher Socrates who bragged, "I love to walk through the marketplace and look at all the things that I do not need."[36] Even more tellingly, he declared that "He who is not contented with what he has, would not be contented with what he would like to have."[37] This talk of contentment calls to mind the insights of de Tocqueville who contends that Americans exhibit "restlessness in the midst of prosperity"[38] and "sadness" even in the midst of our pleasures because we "never stop thinking of the good things [we] have not got."[39] Marra James mirrors de Tocqueville's observations on American anxiety in the midst of prosperity:

> Many people feel empty and don't know why they feel empty. The reason is we are all social animals and we must live and interact and work together in community to become fulfilled ... Most people have been sold a bill of goods by our system. I call it the Three Cs: cash, convenience, consumerism. It's getting worse. The reason you don't feel a part of it is that nobody is a part of it. Loneliness is a national feeling."[40]

Kavanaugh takes pains to articulate the causes of our national sense of emptiness and isolation:

> Our lack of intimacy, community, personally enduring relationships, our sense of competition and lack of solidarity nudge us into possessing and accumulating things in order to fill up the lack we experience by missing persons in our lives. Our sense of powerlessness in changing the social system and its disordered priorities only serves to confirm and support our economic way of life. Our

---

[36] Diogenes Laertius, *The Lives and Opinions of Eminent Philosophers*, (c. 250; repr., Whitefish, MT: Kessinger, 2010), 69.

[37] Diogenes Laertius, *Lives and Opinions*, 69.

[38] See Bellah et al., *Habits*, 117.

[39] See Bellah et al., *Habits*, 117.

[40] See Bellah et al., *Habits*, 158.

inability to live simply, to enjoy life without a continual sense of
craving and dissatisfaction is good news for economic growth.[41]

Kavanaugh concurs with economist and political philosopher Myron Magnet (who is echoed in the comments of Marra James) regarding the spiritual-philosophical hollowness of our consumer culture: Magnet posits that "the money society has expanded to fill the vacuum left after the institutions that embodied and nourished those values – community, religion, school, university, and especially family – sagged or collapsed or sometimes even self-destructed."[42] Kavanaugh notes that:

> *Persons relate to things as if they were persons; they relate to persons, including themselves, as if they were things. Having patterned ourselves after the image of our commodities, we become disenfranchised of our very humanness … Those who make idols and put their trust in them become like them.*[43]

Similarly, Kavanaugh follows psychologist Michael Yapko, who points out that, as a result of the dearth of profound relationships with the self, others, and God, "people are having substitute relationships with their cars, computers, … and bank accounts."[44]

Kavanaugh concludes that people of faith as well as people with humanitarian motives need to adopt a comprehensive lifestyle of cultural resistance that he calls the Personal Form:

> *We are called by [Jesus Christ] to a life of simplicity, a life without racism or vengeance, a life of compassion and trust, a sharing of our goods, a consciousness of and attention to the world's poor, and*

---

[41] Kavanaugh, *Still Following Christ*, 60; See also Pope John Paul II, *Evangelium Vitae*, 26.

[42] See Kavanaugh, *Still Following Christ*, 11; See also Robert Bellah, "Taming the Savage Market" (Chicago, IL: *The Christian Century*, September 18-25, 1991): 845.

[43] Kavanaugh, *Still Following Christ*, 58; See also Pope John Paul II, *Evangelium Vitae*, 36.

[44] See Kavanaugh, *Still Following Christ*, 8.

a committed covenant in faith, hope, and love. In a culture increas-
ingly demanding the thingification of human life, we are called to
struggle for the personalization of the universe. In a world made
ever more mechanical, threatening, and alien to personhood, we are
called to render reality benevolent.[45]

Missionaries emerge from both camps that Kavanaugh addresses, those who long to serve God intensely and those who long to serve humanity intensely. Miraculously, by way of our conversion experiences during our immersions and our post-immersion reflections, both groups tend to move closer toward each other and increasingly appreciate each other's perspectives.

The most natural and common post-immersion impulse among missionaries is to struggle against the waste of material resources by themselves and others. Furthermore, and with each additional immersion, the commitment to personal asceticism deepens. What motivates this desire? Missionaries report a trio of stimuli, namely, a revulsion toward selfishness, a perceived need to depend more directly and intensely upon God and thereby less upon matter, and a recognition of the degree to which creature comforts serve to buffer us from empathizing with marginalized people.[46] One young missionary attested to this third phenomenon:

> *Things like, being in the air conditioning all the time; not ever be-*
> *ing without food; not ever experiencing the heat. Miami is just as*
> *hot as the Dominican Republic, but yet I have been here the whole*
> *summer and I have never once said, I am so hot, because I get in the*
> *car, and I turn on the air conditioner here. I am living in the same*
> *city as someone in Overtown and I am experiencing something*
> *completely different because I have air conditioning and he or she*

---

[45] Kavanaugh, *Still Following Christ*, 126.

[46] See Pope John Paul II, *Evangelium Vitae*, 23.

might not. So, I think that just the comforts that I have make me forget.

While luxuries tend to erase our missionary memories and numb our consciences, ongoing contact and communication with other missionaries, volunteers, and weak and materially poor people have the opposite effect; maintenance of these relationships tends to sharpen our consciences and reverse our moral amnesia.

Numerous missionaries point out what they perceive as a principal difference among missionaries and activists or single-minded seekers of social justice. Our missionaries report that they have noticed that the latter often miss out on the benefits of missionary spirituality. As we see it, the central disparity is that missionaries learn to focus more on relationships with people than on their poverty.

We have found that this marked shift in focus affords us longevity as missionaries as well as the myriad benefits of true friendship because we discover that we are free to feel the full range of emotions that characterize genuine mutuality. Conversely, many activists grow exhausted because they concentrate almost exclusively on material conditions and therefore become locked into a non-reciprocal giver-to-receiver pattern of interaction with those whom they serve.

Sadly, such lopsided affiliations tend to preclude the joy that frequently arises out of authentic egalitarian companionship. Moreover, as missionaries, we never fail to acknowledge that our habit of invoking God's guidance always serves to boost our spirits. This divine liaison gives us the durable advantage of a hopeful outlook regarding the present and the future. By choosing to give priority to human and supernatural relationships, we find that with vigorous and lasting values, we are able to replenish the spiritual vacuum left by the intentional paucity of objects and merchandise.[47]

---

[47] See Ruffing, "Socially Engaged Contemplation," 418-419; See also Wicks, *Self-Ministry Through Self-Understanding*, 86-87; See also Putnam, *Bowling Alone*, 67.

Seeking Community
amidst a Culture of Individualism

Bellah et al. share with us the insights of many thoughtful Americans such as Episcopal Father Morrison who observes that contemporary American life "places enormous pressures on people to marginalize and isolate them and force them away from community."[48] Kavanaugh elaborates on the consequences of such social disintegration:

> *The fragmentation of relatedness and intimacy is the hidden termite eating at the foundations of commitment to others. It is manifested in the breakdown of family life, in the increasing rate of divorce, in the abandonment of our children to the streets and the airwaves, in the decline of civic and neighborly community, in the growing popularity of prenuptial contracts made fashionable by the rich and famous, in the new malady called time famine.[49]*

Why prenuptial agreements? Because we are living under postmodern circumstances that make it treacherous to presume that the mores of our grandparents' generation still hold true in the minds and hearts of our beloved. Nowadays in the USA, the vows of matrimony do not mean the same thing to everyone. Many people believe that the bond should be dissolved whenever it feels confining. Bellah et al. stress that:

> *It is the moral content of relationships that allows marriages, families, and communities to persist with some certainty that there are agreed-upon standards of right and wrong that one can count on and that are not subject to incessant renegotiation."[50]*

---

[48] See Bellah et al., *Habits*, 240.

[49] Kavanaugh, *Still Following Christ*, 10; See also Bellah et al., "Individualism and the Crisis of Civic Membership," 262.

[50] Bellah et al., *Habits*, 139-140.

Conversely, they explain that, "in the absence of any objectifiable criteria of right and wrong, good or evil, the self and its feelings become our only moral guide."[51] They warn us that "radical individualism … tends to elevate the self to a cosmic principle."[52]

Bellah et al. cite American transcendentalist Ralph Waldo Emerson, who emphasized the imperative that each individual forge intellectually and religiously independent ideals: "A man should learn to detect and watch that gleam of light which flashes across his mind from within, more than the luster of the firmament of bards and sages."[53]

As previously indicated, Bellah and friends insist that, in the USA, our therapeutic culture insists that in order to become complete respectable adults, we must 'cut the umbilical cord' of dependence upon our families of origin by moving out of our parents' houses and 'making it' on our own fiscally, emotionally, and philosophically.[54] Bellah et al. lament this core aspect that makes American-style psychotherapy so unique and so influential:

> *Psychoanalysis and psychiatry is the only form of psychic healing that attempts to cure people by detaching them from society and relationships. All other forms, shamanism, faith healing, prayer, bring the community into the healing process, indeed use the interdependence of patient and others as the central mechanism in the healing process.*[55]

Moreover, Americans are encouraged to analyze our relational commitments from a "contractual" perspective.[56] In other words, our

---

51 Bellah et al., *Habits*, 76.

52 Bellah et al., *Habits*, 236; See also Putnam, *Bowling Alone*, 24.

53 Bellah et al., *Habits*, 63.

54 Bellah et al., *Habits*, 65.

55 Bellah et al., *Habits*, 121.

56 Bellah et al., *Habits*, 130.

society teaches us to ask if we are receiving as much as we are giving, as if our interpersonal and communal relationships were essentially mathematical equations. The implication is that we ought to abandon those relationships that do not at least balance out. As a more humanizing alternative, Bellah et al. instead propose the Aristotelian vision of "civic friendship:"[57]

> The traditional idea of friendship had three essential components. Friends must enjoy one another's company, they must be useful to one another, and they must share a common commitment to the good. Today we tend to define friendship mostly in terms of the first component: friends are those we take pleasure in being with. What we least understand is the third component, shared commitment to the good, which seems to us quite extraneous to the idea of friendship. We have difficulty seeing the point of considering friendship in terms of common moral commitments. For Aristotle and his successors, it was precisely the moral component of friendship that made it the indispensable basis of a good society. For it is one of the main duties of friends to help one another to be better persons ... Traditionally, the opposite of a friend is a flatterer, who tells one what one wants to hear and fails to tell the truth ... The "unconditional acceptance" that was supposed to go with true love and friendship did not mean the abandonment of moral standards, even in the most intimate relationship.[58]

Bellah et al. astutely identify the US cultural phenomenon of "mythic individualism," whose protagonists are "cowboys" and "hard-boiled private detectives."[59] By virtue of their unique and pure "sense of justice," the cinematic cowboys arrive episode after episode in order to save a society into which they can never completely fit. Bellah et al. inform us that "the hard-boiled detective, who may long for love and success, for a place in society, is finally driven to stand alone, resisting

---

[57] Bellah et al., *Habits,* 133; Bellah, "Taming the Savage Market," 846.

[58] Bellah et al., *Habits,* 115.

[59] Bellah et al., *Habits,* 144-146.

the blandishments of society, to pursue a lonely crusade for justice."[60] The message of this cultural myth is that:

> *To serve society, one must be able to stand alone, not needing others, not depending on their judgment, and not submitting to their wishes. Yet this individualism is not selfishness. Indeed, it is a kind of heroic selflessness. One accepts the necessity of remaining alone in order to serve the values of the group. And this obligation to aloneness is an important key to the American moral imagination."[61]*

Concisely stated, "the myth says you can be a truly good person, worthy of admiration and love, only if you resist fully joining the group."[62] Bellah et al. punctuate their argument by pointing to our universally beloved president:

> *Abraham Lincoln conforms perfectly to the archetype of the lonely, individualistic hero ... In the face of almost universal mistrust, he nonetheless completed his self-appointed task of bringing the nation through its most devastating war, preaching reconciliation as he did so ... What saved Lincoln from nihilism was the larger whole for which he felt it was important to live and worthwhile to die.[63]*

Notwithstanding the centuries-old American ideal of the radical independence of the individual, Bellah et al. remind us that we still long for interpersonal human affirmation:

> *We find ourselves not independently of other people and institutions but through them. We never get to the bottom of ourselves on our own. We discover who we are face to face and side by side with others in work, love, and learning ... However much Americans extol the autonomy and self-reliance of the individual, they do not*

---

[60] Bellah et al., *Habits*, 145.

[61] Bellah et al., *Habits*, 146.

[62] Bellah et al., *Habits*, 145; See also Putnam, *Bowling Alone*, 24.

[63] Bellah et al., *Habits*, 146-147.

imagine that a good life can be lived alone. Connectedness to others in work, love, and community is essential to happiness, self-esteem, and moral worth.[64]

As is natural among human persons in every culture, the aspirations of Americans eventually turn toward our children, grandchildren, and the future of our society. Therefore, even adults who consciously admire the value of self-reliance discover that "they have difficulty transmitting their own sense of moral integrity to their children in the absence of such a community."[65]

Missionaries find the community of fellow missionaries and volunteers to be an indispensable buttress to our values and sense of purpose. When we are isolated from such likeminded agents for too long, we grow weary, sad, and bewildered. AeA's historical experience reveals two particular facets of missionary communities that have proven vital to the birth and burgeoning of AeA, namely, a divinely motivated sense of urgency and the pivotal formative role of consecrated, professed missionary priests, sisters, and brothers. As mentioned in chapter four, one of our founders vividly encapsulated the former aspect by describing the founders in the early years as being as collectively unstoppable as the Navy Seals because they trained, acted, and then trained some more.

Need for Sacramental
(especially Eucharistic) Nourishment

Each generation of AeA missionaries has felt a need for sacramental sustenance with a particular emphasis on Eucharistic nourishment. While our founding generation began as an innately sacramental community who reveled in domestic celebrations of the Lord's Supper, many members of our younger generations have suddenly

---

[64] Bellah et al., *Habits*, 84.

[65] Bellah et al., *Habits*, 247; See also Putnam, *Bowling Alone*, 404.

discovered its power to unite us internationally and cross-culturally during or immediately after our respective immersions.

For AeA, the Eucharistic sacrament is both spiritual food and a bridge across the Caribbean Sea. Kavanaugh and Bellah et al. affirm the value and potency of Jewish and Christian rituals, both in terms of generating group cohesion and forging a collective moral conscience.

Bellah et al. insist that both group and individual identities are distilled in the crucible of rituals which they dub "practices of commitment." They argue that, "We cannot know who we are without some practical ritual and moral structure that orders our freedom and binds our choices into something like habits of the heart."[66] They go on to assert that:

> People growing up in communities of memory not only hear the stories that tell how the community came to be, what its hopes and fears are, and how its ideals are exemplified in outstanding men and women; they also participate in the practices, ritual, aesthetic, ethical, that define the community as a way of life. We call these 'practices of commitment' for they define the patterns of loyalty and obligation that keep the community alive.[67]

In addition to their role as constitutive rites, Bellah et al. claim that these Jewish and Christian ceremonies fortify and shape the members of these "communities of memory" into positive moral agents in the wider society:

> Worship calls to mind the story of the relationship of the community with God: how God brought his chosen people out of Egypt or gave his only begotten son for the salvation of humankind. Worship also reiterates the obligations that the community has undertaken, including the biblical insistence on justice and righteousness, and

---

[66] Bellah et al., *Habits*, 137.

[67] Bellah et al., *Habits*, 154.

on love of God and neighbor, as well as the promises God has made
that make it possible for the community to hope for the future ...
Through reminding the people of their relationship to God, it estab-
lishes patterns of character and virtue that should operate in eco-
nomic and political life as well as in the context of worship. The
community maintains itself as a community of memory.[68]

Kavanaugh concurs with Bellah et al. in viewing the ritual traditions of Judaism and Christianity as indispensable in terms of maintaining vestiges of values that are genuinely human and divine as opposed to commodified. Kavanaugh states that "the values rooted in person-hood are apparently on the decline ... Their last defense resides in the traditions and lived practice of Judaism and Christianity."[69] Kavanaugh reiterates the affirmative, transformative, and barrier-transcending properties of the sacraments:

Sacramentalization is an elevation, an exalting and celebration of
the most intimately human aspects of our lives. Sacraments re-
trieve and make holy the critical moments of growth and human
development ... The sacraments are personal and corporate affir-
mations of the Personal Form ... A sacrament re-members us, puts
us back together, heals our individual and corporate fragmentation
... Sacraments are crucial ... for our effort to embody the univer-
sality of our personhood in a way that transcends culture, coun-
tries, class, society, and temporal history.[70]

From a missionary perspective, the capacity of the sacraments to achieve border-transcending universality renders them exceedingly vital. Of course, this has been AeA's precise experience.

---

[68] Bellah et al., *Habits*, 227.

[69] Kavanaugh, *Still Following Christ*, 76.

[70] Kavanaugh, *Still Following Christ*, 139-140.

[71] Kavanaugh, *Still Following Christ*, 144.

Kavanaugh's message dovetails with the praxis-derived wisdom of AeA in that both assign preeminence to the sacrament of the Eucharist. He emphasizes that "the Eucharist ... is the sacrament most fully embodying the Christian life, the Personal Form, our ways of communal resistance, and the act of remembering."[71] Kavanaugh again agrees with Bellah et al. that formal Christian and Jewish worship services both unify us with God and convey the imperative to love, share with, and advocate for justice for weak and materially poor people:

> Seeing the face of our God in food that sustains us in our poverty, we are sent forth to minister to our brothers and sisters in poverty, through whose faces, again, we will encounter the living God. The sacrament of the poor reminds us of the poor.[72]

As Kavanaugh insightfully indicates, according to Matthew's gospel, Jesus admonishes us in his final discourse, intentionally situated for emphasis immediately before his arrest, torture, and execution, that how we treat society's rejects is how we treat God. Kavanaugh prophetically states that:

> The last text before the Passion narrative is one that clearly delineates the conditions of salvation, the expression of faith, and the intimacy of God's presence in our lives. Note that it is not tithing, not sacrifice, not church-going, not even the most meticulous fidelity to sobriety, continence, or obedience, that Christ insists upon: it is our response to the least of human persons, to the poor, the sick, the old and abandoned, the hungry and thirsty, the naked, the imprisoned and unattended .... If Christians turn away from the "least of these," ... they are turning away from none other than the

---

[72] Kavanaugh, *Still Following Christ*, 145.

Christ they profess to believe in. They are turning away from the
greatest commandment. They are turning away from God.[73]

Because of the mystical union with both God and neighbors that is
attained via the Eucharistic liturgy, AeA has always made it a point
to send off and receive its missionaries with a mass.

Need for Continued Direct Contact with
& Service to Materially Poor People

Missionaries report that direct relationships with and service to materially poor and marginalized people in the USA has contributed
mightily to the intensity of our respective missionary vocations both
before our initial and between our successive overseas immersions.
With this in mind, Kavanaugh warns us that:

> *The Commodity Form of existence makes claims upon our lives*
> *through the systemic interpenetration of every area of our experi-*
> *ence: the loss of solitude and personal identity, the dissolution of*
> *community and commitment, the insensitivity to the multifaceted*
> *occurrences of injustice, the insinuation of consumerism into our*
> *very manner of living, and the repression of our consciousness of*
> *the poor.*[74]

He cautions us regarding the deleterious effect that the Culture of
Death or Commodity Form can have on our awareness of and solidarity with our weak and materially poor neighbors. This Commodity Form system, driven by advertisers, seeks to fragment human society, discourage sharing, and promote egotism, because such perceptions and behaviors foment spending and profit margins.[75] Kavanaugh astutely depicts this demoralizing scenario:

---

[73] Kavanaugh, *Still Following Christ*, 97-98.

[74] Kavanaugh, *Still Following Christ*, 163.

[75] Kavanaugh, *Still Following Christ*, 59-61; See also Pope John Paul II, *Evangelium Vi-tae*, 19.

> *Christian men and women today are huddled together in their sense of sinful searching for false power and the security of idols .... They feel oppressed by the present Roman Empire, the lived atheism of the Commodity Form, in which life, human sexuality, labor, love, and human dignity itself are subject to alienation. The new forms of relativism, skepticism, and selfishness are bewilderingly omnipresent.*[76]

Kavanaugh posits that because we are subjected to the propaganda of the commodified culture, we become convinced that recognition of the presence of at-risk and marginalized neighbors can only serve to threaten our own existence and therefore they must be hidden and avoided. He contends that wounded people frighten us because they "remind us of our own vulnerability" and mortality.[77] Kavanaugh resolutely advocates a bold, countercultural solution:

> *Our antidote ... is what we most fear; the letting go of the armor which has become our cage; the opening of our eyes to the wounded whose existence we deny; the touching of our hearts by those for whom the consumer dream is at best a false promise, at worst, a proven nightmare. The marginal. The sick. The dying. The poor. The old. They might teach us. But we deny our need for learning ... A return ... to our human personhood will demand not only a rediscovered interior life, a renewal of interpersonal relationships, a reawakening to the joys of simplicity, and a rediscovery of our passion for justice. It will also require a reopening of our hearts to the marginal people of our world.*[78]

Bellah et al. are of the same mind as Kavanaugh in terms of what is required to encourage the emergence of philosophically and spiritually satisfying persons and communities: "A self-worth having only comes into existence through participation with others in the effort

---

[76] Kavanaugh, *Still Following Christ*, 128.

[77] Kavanaugh, *Still Following Christ*, 16.

[78] Kavanaugh, *Still Following Christ*, 18-19.

to create a just and loving society.[79] Many post-immersion missionaries express recurring feelings of guilt and melancholy in between seasonal foreign immersions owing to that irrevocable transformation of our moral sensibilities that the comprehensive immersion experience elicits. We feel impelled to act in favor of our debilitated neighbors to assuage our agitated consciences.

Kavanaugh explains that: "the affective drive to do something - human willing - is revealed not as appropriation and competition, but as the inherent human exigency to give one's self away in love, in service, and in the joys of covenant."[80] Kavanaugh reminds us that our Judeo-Christian faith teaches us that we have an ethical duty to ameliorate the suffering of all persons who are denied their God-given dignity: "Social action is not the preserve of some special-interest group. It is an imperative of faith."[81]

Need to Continue Hearing God's Call & Inspire Others to Discern New Missionary Vocations

Like all faith-filled people, post-immersion missionaries feel the need to maintain momentum regarding their respective Christian conversions. Perhaps the most significant fruit of discerning a post-immersion missionary call from God is the radical change in university programs of study and subsequent career paths, including the discernment of formal religious vocations. These transformations evidence a shift away from reliance on material wealth and toward increased reliance on God. Having opportunities to give witness talks to stateside church groups encourages growth, commitment, and spiritual stamina among post-immersion missionaries. Numerous post-immersion missionaries have felt profoundly encouraged about the trajectories

---

[79] Bellah et al., *Habits*, 83.

[80] Kavanaugh, *Still Following Christ*, 107-108.

[81] Kavanaugh, *Still Following Christ*, 120.

of their own respective missionary conversions when they have been successful at inspiring others to participate in a missionary immersion for the first time.

Bellah et al. take pains to point out significant differences among jobs, careers, and callings:

> *In the sense of a job, work is a way of making money and making a living. It supports a self defined by economic success, security, and all that money can buy. In the sense of a career, work traces one's progress through life by achievement and advancement in an occupation. It yields a self defined by a broader sort of success, which takes in social standing and prestige, and by a sense of expanding power and competency that renders work itself a source of self-esteem. In the strongest sense of a calling, work constitutes a practical ideal of activity and character that makes a person's work morally inseparable from his or her life. It subsumes the self into a community of disciplined practice and sound judgment whose activity has meaning and value in itself, not just in the output or profit that results from it ... A calling links a person to the larger community, a whole in which the calling of each is a contribution to the good of all.*[82]

Bellah et al. assert the crucial moral and metaphysical importance inherent in attending to God's vocation. They argue that "the absence of a sense of calling means an absence of a sense of moral meaning."[83] The preponderance of missionaries consulted echo the emphasis of Bellah et al. on the sense of meaning that is imparted when we respond positively to the calls of God and of the poor.

Kavanaugh likewise gives priority to the ethical content of Judeo-Christian religious vocations. Kavanaugh stresses the fact that the biblical prophets "call for a covenant [with God] that must be

---

[82] Bellah et al., *Habits*, 66.

[83] Bellah et al., *Habits*, 71.

expressed in fidelity to human dignity."[84] As Kavanaugh indicates, missionaries readily declare that the communal bonds that they establish both with friends in the missionary fields and within their missionary communities, serve as a marvelous amplifier of God's voice:

> A communitarian life demands a commitment of time, energy, and sacrifice … A community of this kind must be consciously choice-ful; explicitly committed to and willing to be called to the life of the Gospels; open to change through the authentic living-out of its principles, and willing to be challenged to fuller Christian praxis; and prepared to confront the patterns of the Commodity Form – injustice, manipulation, domination, dishonesty, escape – not only as they appear in the culture at large but also as they surface within the group itself.[85]

Hearing God's voice within a missionary context alters our perceptions irreversibly. The more connected we remain to our overseas friends and to our missionary community, the more intensely we believe that we can never do enough to respond to our ever-just Creator and to the gaping necessities of our overseas and over-the-borderline friends.

Many missionaries have discovered that our Christian missionary vocations consist of three stages, the pre-immersion ascendency stage, the post-immersion reflection-commitment-maintenance stage, and the compulsion to motivate non-missionary Christians to probe their own potential missionary vocations. We view this recruitment effort as part and parcel of striving to expand the Reign of God on earth.

Regardless of our respective degrees of missionary involvement, the nearly omnipresent Commodity Form exerts influence upon all

---

[84] Kavanaugh, *Still Following Christ*, 79.
[85] Kavanaugh, *Still Following Christ*, 133.

families within the USA. Young missionaries have found that the Culture of Death also regularly makes use of politicians, public relations officers, journalists, secularized schoolteachers and university professors as its spokespersons. Tellingly, envoys exhibit passionate determination to squelch the voices of God and debilitated people. One young AeA missionary valiantly exposed this pervasive and pernicious phenomenon:

> *A lot of the classes that I had were detrimental too; they worsened my faith. I had a lot of professors who would talk badly about the church, badly about Catholicism, who would confuse me, who would talk badly about religion in general. A lot of people with some very, very liberal mentalities. But it was particularly bad for me at that moment, bad because it was feeding me all these negative things, and things that were contrary to what was going to help me fulfill my commitments. So, college for me, the first year, was very bad.*

Concluding Reflections on the Clashes of Values

Post-immersion missionaries pine for a worldwide culture that is closer to the heart of the God of the covenant and the incarnation. We yearn to share the genuine community of the Personal Form or the Gospel of Life. Our hearts and minds are permanently branded with that vision of the Reign of God of which we caught several glimpses during our immersions and our pre-immersion preparation sessions. But after we return, we are forced to realize that major components of our native culture are vehemently antagonistic to our newfound Personal Form missionary values. Nevertheless, we remain convinced that God wants us to, and that our friends in the mission lands need us to, pursue the further expansion of God's Reign on earth. Therefore, we seek material simplicity, genuine community, sacramental nourishment, and ongoing direct relationships with materially poor people back home in the USA.

Now that we have explored sociological and philosophical critiques of our American culture as well as their implications for the post-immersion reintegration of our missionaries, we turn to the Christian perspective as presented by conversion theologians and the magisterium in search of additional wisdom that might assist post-immersion missionaries in this crucial endeavor.

6

CONVERSION THEOLOGY REFLECTION

T he previous chapter analyzes the conflict between US culture and the missionary vision of AeA. This sixth chapter critically correlates our post-mission immersion experiences with theologies of conversion that specifically inform the post-immersion phase of the mission cycle. To this end, I draw upon the conversion theologies elaborated by Lewis Ray Rambo, Donald Louis Gelpi SJ, David Jacobus Bosch, and official Roman Catholic Social Doctrine.

This chapter addresses Groome's third and fourth movements by catalyzing a dialectical hermeneutic between the Christian story and vision and AeA's story and vision. The assertions of the aforementioned theologians of conversion offer the wisdom harvested from the macrocosm of centuries of Christian missionary endeavors to the microcosm of one lay missionary community at the dawn of the third Christian millennium.

Notwithstanding the obvious weight of two millennia of Christian missionary tradition, the experiences of one missionary community (Amor en Acción) do indeed serve as a source worthy of reflection, a communal text that can validly contribute to a vital and fruitful dialogue with the wider church regarding the viability of present and future missionary propositions, particularly the emerging model that features repeated short-term immersions combined with long-term commitment.

I contend that we can more effectively facilitate the long-term conversion of missionaries in the post-immersion stage by improving the consistency of our post-immersion reintegration methods in light of the insights offered by these conversion theologians.

Lewis Ray Rambo's Approach to Conversion

Sequential Stages of Conversion

Lewis Ray Rambo, the preeminent synthesizer in the field of conversion theology, offers a comprehensive look at theological conversion by skillfully integrating a myriad of perspectives on religious conversion from psychology, sociology, anthropology, history, missiology, and theology. To this end, Rambo has devised his sequential stage model of the conversion process.

Via this inclusive model, Rambo is able to identify and scrutinize the indispensable roles played by the contexts, crises, quests, encounters with advocates, interactions with religious communities, commitments, and consequences.[1] Notwithstanding the rigid insistence of many missionaries and missiological theorists that religious conversion follows a linear progression, Rambo demonstrates that the various aforementioned factors which comprise the conversion process can more accurately be characterized as interactive and cumulative,[2] particularly because both the advocates and the potential converts have leverage that they exercise in a back-and-forth dynamic.[3]

---

[1] Rambo, *Understanding Religious Conversion*, 17; Lewis Rambo, "Conversion: Toward a Holistic Model of Religious Change," *Pastoral Psychology* 38 (New York, NY: Springer, 1989): 38, 47-63.

[2] Rambo, *Understanding Religious Conversion*, 5.

[3] Rambo, *Understanding Religious Conversion*, 52, 66, 167.

Intensification

"Intensification" is the principal type of conversion (in contrast with the other types of conversion, namely, apostasy or defection, affiliation, institutional transition, and tradition transition)[4] identified by Rambo that accurately describes the post-immersion conversion phenomenon of missionaries. Rambo informs us that:

> *Intensification is the process of personal renewal and the deepening of conviction within one's religious community. Hence, it is assumed that the person is already, to some minimal degree, involved in the community of faith, but that his or her spiritual experience becomes more profound.*[5]

Contexts as Impediments

Rambo also reminds us that the dynamics of conversion occur within a context, and at times, within multiple contexts. Specifically, Rambo identifies two categories of contexts, the macrocontext and the microcontext, which are often in opposition to each other.[6]

For AeA missionaries, who usually participate in short-term overseas immersions, their principle macrocontext is the aforementioned Commodity Form of the USA. Furthermore, for these same AeA missionaries, their corresponding microcontext consists of the AeA missionary community, guides, and collaborators, whose values dovetail with those of the Personal Form while contravening those of the Commodity Form.

---

[4] Rambo, *Understanding Religious Conversion*, 12-14; Lewis Rambo, "Current Research on Religious Conversion," *Religious Studies Review* 13 (Hoboken, NJ: Wiley-Blackwell, 1982): 149-159.

[5] Rambo, *Understanding Religious Conversion*, 173.

[6] Rambo, *Understanding Religious Conversion*, 21-23.

Rambo's extensive research has led him to conclude that our multiple contexts generate more inertia than impetus to change in the religious sense:

> *Forces of resistance and attraction fill the intellectual, spiritual, and cultural climate of society. Religious organizations, as well as other cultural media (whether books, magazines, television, or movies) convey messages to people every day that changing one's life is either desirable or undesirable. Reading a book, talking with a friend, attending a lecture, or participating in a synagogue, church, ..., or meditation center puts us all within the contextual sphere that is the ecology of conversion. Although people are aware of these influences, they usually avoid change. Resistance is pervasive.*[7]

Rambo attributes this inertia to the psycho-social phenomenon known as enmeshment. Rambo reports that: "enmeshment with old systems of religions, family, society, and politics seldom encourages movement to a new religious option. Personal and social conditions rarely facilitate change."[8] The grip of these socio-familial entanglements can prove to be a real impediment to spiritual progress.

Conversion is painful for many because it uproots converts from their past and throws them into a new future. However exciting the new option may be, the convert may not want to give up past relationships and modes of living that are still in many ways a part of his or her core identity.[9]

This brand of resistance to dramatic spiritual growth is most intensely felt by missionaries who are still below thirty years of age, that is, those who feel most deeply embedded in their friendship networks.

---

[7] Rambo, *Understanding Religious Conversion*, 165-166.

[8] Rambo, *Understanding Religious Conversion*, 87. Lewis Rambo, "Conversion," *Encyclopedia of Religion* (New York, NY: MacMillan, 1987): 76.

[9] Rambo, *Understanding Religious Conversion*, 53-54.

With the pervasive stagnating influence of this macrocontext in mind, what explains the potency of post-missionary immersion reflections to instigate conversions? Rambo illuminates the importance of the role of crises in sparking religious conversions. He cred-its William James and other early social psychologists with signaling "the way in which conversion is often preceded by anguish, turmoil, despair, conflict, guilt, and other such difficulties."[10] Rambo explains how the discomfort and disorientation precipitated by a crisis (such as the culture shock experienced when a missionary re-enters US society) can provoke conversions:

> *Crisis provides an opportunity for a new option. Crises force individuals and groups to confront their limitations and can stimulate a quest to resolve conflict, fill a void, adjust to new circumstances, or find avenues of transformation ... Disorientation in life sometimes triggers the search for new options ... The crisis may be the major force for change, or it may be simply the catalytic incident that crystallizes the person's situation.*[11]

Since conversion means change, the contact with marginalized people can be said to provoke a crisis significant enough to prompt the neophyte post-immersion missionaries to feel compelled to respond with a greater degree of commitment in addressing the reality of deprivation in which their newly minted overseas friends subsist.[12] Likewise, in the post-immersion stage, these missionaries speak of a need to dedicate more time and effort to cultivating the depth of their own respective relationships with God. The disorientation or culture shock that confronts post-immersion missionaries motivates them to

---

[10] Rambo, *Understanding Religious Conversion*, 9.

[11] Rambo, *Understanding Religious Conversion*, 166.

[12] Rambo, *Understanding Religious Conversion*, 44-48.

seek options that better satisfy their suddenly discovered interior spiritual-existential vacuums.[13]

Guilt

As previously indicated, a crucial variety of post-immersion crisis that confronts new missionaries is an intense perception of guilt, that is, guilt over our material opulence concurrent with the material deprivation that our friends overseas must negotiate day in and day out.[14] Rambo informs us that many converts express a "sense of guilt [that is] primarily a keen realization that their actions had harmed other people and hence somehow violated their relationship to God."[15] Consequentially, Rambo reports that "conversion [is] an experience that enable[s] them to experience a lifting of the burden of sin and [to] feel a sense of liberation from the pain of their actions."[16]

Post-Conversion Depression

Another key type of crisis acknowledged by Rambo is the "inevitable tapering off from the emotional peak of decisive commitment" that he has labeled "postconversion depression."[17] Numerous post-immersion missionaries affirm Rambo's insight. Rambo explains that:

> *The human reality seems to be that the power of the conversion experience will eventually dissipate for most people, and thus maintenance procedures become important to protect a person either from*

---

[13] Rambo, *Understanding Religious Conversion*, 166; Lewis Rambo, "Psychology of Conversion," *Handbook of Religious Conversion* (Birmingham, AL: Religious Education, 1992), 165.

[14] Rambo, *Understanding Religious Conversion*, 83-84, 160-162.

[15] Rambo, *Understanding Religious Conversion*, 161; Lewis Rambo, Raymond Paloutzian, and James Richardson, "Religious Conversion and Personality Change," *Journal of Personality* 67, no. 6 (Maulden, MA: Blackwell, December, 1999): 1050.

[16] Rambo, *Understanding Religious Conversion*, 161.

[17] Rambo, *Understanding Religious Conversion*, 136; Rambo, Paloutzian, and Richardson, "Religious Conversion and Personality Change," 1055.

severe depression or from abandoning the new religious commit-
ment altogether.[18]

The Bible refers to such abandonment of religious commitment as apostasy or backsliding. In fact, in the biblical view, this is the diametric opposite of conversion.[19]

Quest for Fulfillment

Rambo builds upon the foundation of Seymour Epstein's "four basic human motivations" in his formulation of the factors that prompt people to pursue the goal of religious conversion:[20]

Most converts are actively engaged in seeking fulfillment ... The poten-
tial convert, like all other people, is motivated by the desire to experience
pleasure and avoid pain, maintain a conceptual system, enhance self-
esteem, establish gratifying relationships, and attain a sense of power
and transcendence.[21]

Rambo delineates five specific categories of benefits that converts can derive from the religious communities to which they commit: "(1) a system of meaning (cognitive); (2) emotional gratification (affective); (3) techniques for living (volitional); (4) charisma (leadership); and (5) power."[22]

Dimensions of Interaction

Drawing upon the work of psychologists of religious phenomenology Robert Ziller, Theodore Sarbin, and Nathan Adler, Rambo

---

[18] Rambo, *Understanding Religious Conversion*, 136.

[19] 2 Kings 21:22; Proverb 14:12; Jeremiah 14:7; Hosea 11:7; Matthew 5:13; Matthew 24:12; Luke 8:13; Luke 9:62; John 15:6; Galatians 4:9; 1Timothy 6:10; Revelation 3:16.

[20] Rambo, *Understanding Religious Conversion*, 63-64.

[21] Rambo, *Understanding Religious Conversion*, 166-167.

[22] Rambo, *Understanding Religious Conversion*, 81; Lewis Rambo, "Charisma and Conversion," *Pastoral Psychology* 31 (New York, NY: Springer, 1982): 96ff.

formulates "four dimensions of interaction" within the "matrix of transformation" that serve to effectively facilitate legitimate religious conversion. He identifies relationships, rituals, rhetoric, and roles as key factors in solidifying long-term spiritual transformation, and asserts that:

> Conversion takes place (1) when a person or group is connected to relationships in a religious community; (2) when rituals are enacted that foster experience and action consonant with religious mandates and goals; (3) when the rhetoric or system of interpretation of life is transformed into a religious frame of reference; and (4) when a person's role or sense of place and purpose is enacted and guided by religious sensibilities and structures.[23]

Rambo proceeds to explicate succinctly how these four elements function within the mind of each convert:

> Relationships create and consolidate emotional bonds to the group and establish the day-by-day reality of the new perspective. Rituals provide integrative modes of identifying with and connecting to the new way of life. Rhetoric provides an interpretative system, offering guidance and meaning to the convert. Roles consolidate a person's involvement by giving him or her a special mission to fulfill ... These four elements interact and reinforce one another in the conversion process.[24]

Rituals

Because Rambo believes that rituals are so vital to the progression of religious transformation, he probes the various nuances of their positive influence upon potential converts and the established congregations of believers that receive the converts. Rambo observes that

---

[23] Rambo, *Understanding Religious Conversion*, 34.

[24] Rambo, *Understanding Religious Conversion*, 107-108; Lewis Rambo and Lawrence Reh, "Phenomenology of Conversion," *Handbook of Religious Conversion* (Birmingham, AL: Religious Education, 1992), 231.

"ritual actions consolidate the community" because they "instill a deeper sense of belonging."[25] He further notes that rituals are methods that religious groups use to inform and invite outsiders to participate.[26]

Rambo points to the potentially mystical nature of rituals; he asserts that believers perceive rituals as "a dance with God."[27] He even mentions that Victor Turner's three-step "ritual process" of "separation, transition, and consolidation," requires some measure of normally painful apostasy from, or rejection of, the believer's current faith commitment.[28] Rambo is so convinced that rituals contribute significantly to the conversion process that he promotes their increased and sustained employment by conversion advocates:

> It is clear that ritual may have an important effect on the conversion process. It is my view that religious action – regularized, sustained, and intentional – is fundamental to the conversion experience. Ritual fosters the necessary orientation, the readiness of mind and soul to have a conversion experience, and it consolidates conversion after the initial experience.[29]

Rambo's emphasis on the transformative power of rituals echoes Catholic magisterial teaching. In order that catechumens or converts "will be joined to Christ their teacher," the bishops of Vatican II, in *Ad Gentes Divinitus*, instruct Catholic catechetical formation leaders to engage them in rituals:

---

[25] Rambo, *Understanding Religious Conversion*, 115. Rambo, "Charisma and Conversion," 102.

[26] Rambo, *Understanding Religious Conversion*, 115.

[27] Rambo, *Understanding Religious Conversion*, 115.

[28] See Rambo, *Understanding Religious Conversion*, 113-118; See also Lewis Rambo, "Theories of Conversion: Understanding and Interpreting Religious Change," *Social Compass* 46, no. 3 (Thousand Oaks, CA: Sage, 1999): 259.

[29] Rambo, *Understanding Religious Conversion*, 114.

The catechumens [converts] should be properly initiated into the mystery of salvation and the practice of the evangelical virtues, and they should be introduced into the life of faith, liturgy, and charity of the people of God by successive rites.[30]

Common Good

Rambo lauds Jesuit Father Donald Gelpi's emphasis on the imperative nature of the social-political component for Christian religious conversion to be authentic. He dubs this component as the acquisition of "a sense of mission and a reason for living."[31] This imperative propels genuine converts to widen their affective horizons beyond themselves and their families.

The classic case of Saul the persecutor is a good illustration of this element of conversion. He became Paul [the super missionary] not for the sake of his own soul merely; he was turned around to share the good news with the gentile world. Many people experience a profound new awareness that their life is not theirs to be spent in selfish indulgence; they have gained a purpose, whether it be sharing the good news of salvation or simply being a loving person who serves others for the sake of God.[32]

Donald Louis Gelpi SJ's Perspective on Conversion

Rambo enthusiastically introduces us to the multifaceted and erudite contributions of Jesuit theologian Donald Louis Gelpi to the field of normative Christian conversion theology. Gelpi explains his conception of the term "conversion" in this way:

I use the word conversion ... to mean the decision to assume responsibility for a distinguishable area of experienced growth and

---

[30] Vatican Council II, *Ad Gentes Divinitus*, 14.

[31] Rambo, *Understanding Religious Conversion*, 161.

[32] Rambo, *Understanding Religious Conversion*, 161.

development. Converts turn from irresponsible to responsible liv-
ing ... Responsibility means accountability. Responsible people
measure the motives and consequences of their actions against
norms and ideals they recognize as personally binding. They also
recognize that they must answer to others for their motives and for
the consequences of their decisions.[33]

In a later treatment of the same topic, Gelpi adds that:

Those who live responsibly recognize that they must give an ac-
count of their personal choices to themselves, to other people, and,
in the case of a theistic religious conversion, ultimately to God.[34]

Five Dimensions

Rambo offers an overview of Gelpi's reflections regarding a normative understanding of Christian conversion which reveal the influence of fellow Jesuit Father Bernard Lonergan:

Gelpi proposes five dimensions of conversion: affective, intellectual,
ethical, religious, and social. Affective conversion means taking re-
sponsibility for one's emotional life, with its passions, feelings, and
intentions ... Moving from selfishness to the love of others de-
mands a fundamental shift in emotional valence. Intellectual con-
version requires the person to confront all forms of false ideology
and consciousness that distort understanding and interpretation.
Logic and rigor are required of the intellectual convert. Ethical or
moral conversion challenges the person to move from mere gratifi-
cation of immediate personal needs to living by consistent princi-
ples of justice. Moving from a personal hedonistic calculus to other-
directed living by and for justice is mandatory in this type of

---

[33] Donald Gelpi, "The Converting Jesuit," *Studies in the Spirituality of Jesuits* 18(Saint Louis, MO: Seminar on Jesuit Spirituality, 1986): 4-5.

[34] Gelpi, *Conversion Experience*, 261; Donald Gelpi, *Experiencing God: A Theology of Human Emergence* (New York: Paulist, 1978), 180.

conversion. Religious conversion challenges the person to live for the one true God and not mere idols. Religions that foster self-indulgence and oppression of others are corrupt. True religion challenges an individual to transcend personal gratification and the creation of permissive gods in our own image ... Gelpi has ... advocated sociopolitical conversion as mandatory. Genuine conversion requires that the person move and grow beyond mere personal conversion. Engaging the social institutions and systems of the wider world requires yet another level of conversion, and entails acknowledging accountability and taking responsibility, to the fullest degree possible, for the quality of life produced by these institutions. While the substance of other forms of conversion is important, the core evaluation of social conversion is justice for all. For Christian converts, then, challenging institutions to live according to the ethics of Jesus Christ would be a consistent, logical goal.[35]

Gelpi succinctly identifies the respective goal of each of the dimensions of conversion:

Each form of conversion deals with a different kind of problem. Affective conversion cultivates emotional and imaginative health. Intellectual conversion strives for truth. Religious conversion deals with the demands of faith. Socio-political conversion strives to realize the common good. Personal moral conversion defends personal rights and duties.[36]

Dynamics & Counter-dynamics

Gelpi emphasizes the interdependence of each of the five dimensions of conversion upon each other, labeling their interrelated effects as dynamics and counter-dynamics. He labels the ways in which the different forms of conversion mutually reinforce one another as the

---

[35] Rambo, *Understanding Religious Conversion*, 146-147.

[36] Gelpi, *Conversion Experience*, 49.

dynamics of conversion, and the way in which the absence of conversion in one realm of experience undermines conversion in other realms as the counter-dynamics of conversion.[37] Beginning with affective conversion, Gelpi tells us that people need to learn to consciously redirect negative emotions toward life-engendering resistance to the forces of evil and injustice.[38] Conversely, the lack of affective conversion "produces the stubborn refusal to repent and to respond to the in-breaking of God."[39]

As a result, the absence of affective conversion "inhibits and subverts authentic religious conversion."[40] Turning from affect to intellect, Gelpi explains that intellectual conversion capacitates people to see through ideologies and thereby overcome the pitfalls of fundamentalism which seeks to convince people that social injustice is simply a component of the natural order.[41] Gelpi warns that the absence of intellectual conversion perverts the other types of conversion with a "shallow fundamentalism that rationalizes emotional pathology, personal and public immorality, and the grossest forms of religious hypocrisy."[42]

Moving from cognition to religion, Gelpi reminds us that religious conversion offers indispensable norms for the promotion of a just social order. On the other hand, he cautions that from the perspective of Christian faith, societies should only be considered just if they incarnate a divinely willed social order.[43] Shifting from religion to personal morality, Gelpi asserts that while

---

[37] Gelpi, *Conversion Experience*, 42-43; Donald Gelpi, *Committed Worship: A Sacramental Theology for Converting Christians* (Collegeville, MN: Liturgical, 1993), 1:56ff.

[38] Gelpi, *Conversion Experience*, 37.

[39] Gelpi, *Conversion Experience*, 47.

[40] Gelpi, *Conversion Experience*, 47.

[41] Gelpi, *Conversion Experience*, 52.

[42] Gelpi, *Conversion Experience*, 48.

[43] Gelpi, *Conversion Experience*, 53.

personal moral conversion does not create great art or solve scientific and scholarly problems, ... it does demand that art, literature, science, and scholarship all develop in ways that foster rather than violate fundamental human rights.[44]

On the contrary, Gelpi points out that when the affective, intellectual, social-political, and religious tiers of development are tainted with personal immorality, they "embody a practical hypocrisy that distorts and subverts their authentic growth."[45]

The overwhelming vision and imperative that Jesus calls the Reign of God compels Gelpi to stress the dynamics and counter-dynamics surrounding the social-political dimension of conversion above all others. While Christian social thinkers believe that the dynamic force behind social-political conversion is God,[46]

Gelpi converges with Bellah et al.[47] and Kavanaugh[48] by suggesting that the opposing counter-dynamic impulse is generated by individualistic consumer societies and their "ideologies of isolation."[49] Such ideologies enslave human energy to the service of the narrow interests of the self, whereas this aspect of conversion liberates people to transcend that individualistic focus. He ardently emphasizes the deprivatizing effect of social-political conversion:

Socio-political conversion deprivatizes the other forms of conversion. We privatize our consciences when we refuse to concern ourselves with issues of public morality. We privatize affective

---

[44] Gelpi, *Conversion Experience*, 50.

[45] Gelpi, *Conversion Experience*, 51; Donald Gelpi, "The Converting Catechumen," *Lumen Vitae* 42 (Brussels, Belgium: International Centre for Studies in Religious Education, 1987): 409.

[46] J. Philip Wogaman, *Christian Ethics: A Historical Introduction* (Louisville, KY: Westminster/John Knox, 1993), 1ff.

[47] Bellah et al., *Habits*, viii.

[48] Kavanaugh, *Still Following Christ*, 4.

[49] Gelpi, *Conversion Experience*, 52-53.

development by focusing narrowly on issues of personal growth and on the emotional dimensions of interpersonal relationships. We privatize intellectual development when we ignore the public, institutional consequences of human beliefs and prejudices. We privatize religion by sentimentalizing it. Privatized Christianity cultivates a shallow pietism, which distorts the religious faith by muting or ignoring the radical social, economic, and political demands of the kingdom of God.[50]

Gelpi points out that, as it deepens, this facet of conversion radically transforms religious faith by placing believers in "prophetic opposition to the forces of unbelief, immorality, and injustice."[51] Conversely, Christians who manage to ignore the "prophetic demands of the radical gospel subvert authentic faith with hypocrisy."[52] It almost goes without saying that Christian missionaries, the majority of whom work among and on behalf of materially poor, infirm, and socially marginalized people, do indeed risk duplicity if we do not support the legitimate social-economic-political aspirations of those whom we serve.

David Jacobus Bosch's Understanding of Conversion

In his treatment of the theology of conversion as it pertains to missiology, preeminent South African missiologist David Jacobus Bosch leans heavily on the Gospel according to Luke and its companion document, the Acts of the Apostles.[53] Luke-Acts is central to Bosch's understanding of conversion in relation to Christian mission. Bosch emphasizes the high stakes nature of repentance and conversion. Bosch explains that according to Luke-Acts "to turn one's back on

---

[50] Gelpi, *Conversion Experience*, 54; Gelpi, *Committed Worship*, 1:35.

[51] Gelpi, *Conversion Experience*, 55.

[52] Gelpi, *Conversion Experience*, 57.

[53] Bosch, *Transforming Mission*, 117-118.

one's past is tantamount to turning from 'darkness to light.'"[54] As a result, missionaries "cannot possibly be indifferent about the destiny of others."[55]

Bosch ironically insists that according to Luke-Acts, "personal conversion is not a goal in itself;" conversely, the conception that the "winning of souls" for Christ is a worthy missionary objective "flatly contradicts Luke's understanding of the purpose of mission."[56] Rather, Bosch argues that Luke-Acts reveals that "conversion does not pertain merely to an individual's act of conviction and commitment;"[57] instead, conversion moves the individual believer into the community of believers and involves a real, even a radical, change in the life of the believer, which carries with it moral responsibilities that distinguish Christians from 'outsiders,' while at the same time stressing their obligation to those 'outsiders.'[58]

Bosch declares that "a major element in Luke's missionary paradigm" is the proclamation of a "new relationship between rich and poor," with a particular emphasis on "economic justice."[59] Bosch asserts that these "moral responsibilities" inherent in Christian conversion consist of striving to evangelize non-Christians as a manifestation of brotherly love while concurrently striving to restructure social relationships with an eye toward economic justice. By virtue of their "encounter with Jesus," the disciples "could not remain barren or idle;" rather, they "strove to bear fruit."[60] Thus, Bosch states:

---

[54] Bosch, *Transforming Mission*, 117; Acts 22:18.

[55] Bosch, *Transforming Mission*, 117; David Bosch, "Mission in Jesus' Way: A Perspective from Luke's Gospel," *Missionalia* 17 (Menlo Park, South Africa: Southern African Missiological Society, 1989): 3ff.

[56] Bosch, *Transforming Mission*, 117.

[57] Bosch, *Transforming Mission*, 117.

[58] Bosch, *Transforming Mission*, 117; See also David Bosch, *Witness to the World: The Christian Mission in Theological Perspective* (Eugene, OR: Wipf & Stock, 1980), 15ff.

[59] Bosch, *Transforming Mission*, 117.

[60] Bosch, *Transforming Mission*, 118.

In Nazareth, Jesus did not soar off into the heavenly heights but drew his listeners' attention to the altogether real conditions of the poor, the blind, the captives, and the oppressed. He championed 'God's preferential option for the poor.' He announced the Jubilee, which would inaugurate a reversal of the dismal fate of the dispossessed, the oppressed, and the sick, by calling on the wealthy and healthy to share with those who are victims of exploitation and tragic circumstances.[61]

In a way reminiscent of James in Chapter 2 of his epistle,[62] Bosch ardently punctuates his reflection on conversion: "Where self-centered sentiments reign supreme, the rich cannot claim to be involved in mission and cannot be in continuity with the Lukan Jesus and church."[63] He insists that the sharing of material goods with the poorest people is an essential manifestation and sign of genuine conversion for all Christians and for missionaries in particular.

Bosch's Epistemological Break

To the plethora of insights on Christian conversion offered by Rambo and Gelpi, Bosch adds the concept of an "epistemological break." Epistemology deals with the acquisition and veracity of knowledge. The term, "epistemological break," might more accurately be labeled an "epistemological rupture" or "epistemological breakthrough" because it means shattering or overcoming an obstacle to the advancement of thought. Another synonym that accurately describes this phenomenon is "paradigm shift."

Bosch asserts that today's Christian missionaries who are focused on issues of conversion must assimilate the epistemological breakthroughs indicated by Liberation Theology. Bosch points out that instead of the educated, unbelieving philosophers of olden days, the

---

[61] Bosch, *Transforming Mission*, 118.

[62] James 2:14-26.

[63] Bosch, *Transforming Mission*, 118; See also Bosch, "Mission in Jesus' Way," 7.

principal interlocutors of the theologians of today are materially poor and culturally marginalized people.[64] Then Bosch tells us that "equally important in the new epistemology is the emphasis on the priority of praxis."[65] Bosch goes on to distill six features from this new epistemology.

First, theologians such as Jesuit Father Juan Luís Segundo point out the presence of a profound suspicion that not only Western science and Western philosophy, but also Western theology ... were actually designed to serve the interests of the West ... [and to produce] a rationale for imperialistic domination.[66]

Second, "the new epistemology refuses to endorse the idea of the world as a static object which only has to be *explained*"[67] by philosophers. Rather, as Karl Marx suggests, the new philosopher should endeavor to change the world.

Third, as Sergio Torres and Virginia Fabella insist, commitment to the poor and marginalized is "the first act of theology."[68] Father Matthew Lamb admonishes us that:

> *Orthopraxis aims at transforming human history, redeeming it through a knowledge born of subject-empowering, life-giving love ... Vox victimarum, vox Dei. The cries of the victims are the voice of God.*[69]

Fourth, theologians now "can only theologize credibly if it is done *with* those who suffer."[70]

---

[64] Bosch, *Transforming Mission*, 423.

[65] Bosch, *Transforming Mission*, 423; See also David Bosch, "The Church in Dialogue," *Missiology* 16, no. 2 (Eugene, Oregon: American Society of Missiology, April 1988): 142.

[66] See Bosch, *Transforming Mission*, 424.

[67] Bosch, *Transforming Mission*, 424.

[68] See Bosch, *Transforming Mission*, 424.

[69] See Bosch, *Transforming Mission*, 424.

[70] Bosch, *Transforming Mission*, 424; Bosch, "The Church in Dialogue," 133.

Fifth, as José Míguez Bonino informs us, "doing is more important than knowing or speaking."[71]

Sixth, missionary theology is best achieved by means of a "hermeneutical circulation," in which we proceed from praxis to reflection.[72] Bosch argues that, "ideally, there should be a dialectic relationship between theory and praxis."[73] Dominican Father Gustavo Gutiérrez punctuates the issue eloquently by stating that "orthopraxis and orthodoxy need one another, and each is adversely affected when sight is lost of the other."[74]

This paradigm-shift of which Bosch writes, challenges Christian missionaries to reevaluate our conceptions of conversion. Primarily, Bosch and the liberation theologians challenge us to redefine true spiritual transformation in terms of the extent to which we are impelled to reach out to materially deprived and socially marginalized people in order to express God's loving care for them via our non-paternalistic actions that demonstrate solidarity while we accompany them in their ongoing efforts to overcome intractable socio-economic-political injustices.[75] This outward focus stands in stark contrast to conceptions of spiritual conversion that concentrate on the salvation of one's own soul.[76] Bosch argues that the goal of conversion for missionaries and other Christians is neither primarily to generate the

---

[71] See Bosch, *Transforming Mission*, 425.

[72] Bosch, *Transforming Mission*, 425.

[73] Bosch, *Transforming Mission*, 425; See also David Bosch, "Evangelism: Theological Currents and Cross-Currents Today," *International Bulletin of Missionary Research* 11, no. 3 (New Haven, CT: Overseas Missionary Study Center, July 1987): 99.

[74] See Bosch, *Transforming Mission*, 425.

[75] David Bosch, "The Scope of Mission," *International Review of Mission* 73, no. 289, (New Haven, CT: Overseas Missionary Study Center, January 1984): 29.

[76] An internally focused concept of conversion is exemplified by Saint Thomas à Kempis, *The Imitation of Christ* (1418; repr., Mineola, NY: Dover, 2003), 1ff and Saint Teresa de Jesús de Ávila, *Interior Castle* or *The Mansions* (1577; repr., Radford, VA: Wilder, 2011), 1ff.

capacity to achieve internal serenity in the face of adversity and destitution nor to recruit quantities of human souls for Christ.[77]

Kavanaugh's approach to this epistemological breakthrough reveals that missionaries and other Christians need the grace of God to break free of the shackles of the Commodity Form to thrive and support others who strive to thrive amidst the true Christian community offered by the Personal Form.[78]

This implies that our previous uncritical, selfish, materialistic pre-immersion values, that were laid bare in chapters three and four and critically analyzed in chapter five, must be called into question. We must solicit divine courage in order to be able to let go of our excessive material crutches which we had taken for granted for a lifetime and which serve to shield us from the emotional-philosophical-spiritual vulnerability that we inevitably feel when we shift our focus in the immersion and post-immersion phases to the world's disposable people and their precipitating contexts.

In order to undergo conversion, Christian missionaries need to hear and respond to the voices of society's victims which are simultaneously the voice of God. In order to grow religiously, we North Americans need to learn to heed these divine and deprived voices in spite of the din of our hyper-commercial culture. As indicated above, Bosch beckons us to heed the Jesus as revealed in Luke's gospel who wants us to follow his lead in establishing a "new relationship between rich and poor" which evidences a particular emphasis on "economic justice."[79]

---

[77] Bosch, *Transforming Mission*, 117; See also Bosch, *Witness to the World*, 71.

[78] Kavanaugh, *Still Following Christ*, 131.

[79] Bosch, *Transforming Mission*, 117.

Synthesis of Conversion Theologies
with Regard to Missionaries

Christian missionaries implicitly believe in the value of conversion, as well as in the genuine human capacity to be converted, ultimately by God, albeit through some measure of human mediation. This is evidenced by both their efforts to first deepen themselves spiritually, and subsequently to offer themselves to God as means of achieving the goal of changing the hearts, minds, and habits of others.

More specifically, this study addresses the issue of the ongoing conversion of missionaries after our hearts and minds have been opened, stretched, informed, and challenged by our immersion experiences. Precisely since the post-immersion phase normally lasts longer than the other stages, it can provide multiple opportunities for targeted stimulation toward further conversion.

Bellah et al. teach us that commitment to communal life is the most effective counterbalance to the pitfalls and isolating consequences of unadulterated individualism.

Kavanaugh challenges people of faith to support each other in an intentional struggle against the false promise that joy and satisfaction are commodities that can be literally acquired in the economic marketplace. Moreover, Kavanaugh calls us to imitate Jesus and his disciples by facing and embracing frail and materially destitute people who possess the ability to frighten us because they can reveal and foreshadow for us our own potential and eventual vulnerabilities.

Rambo defines conversion for us as taking responsibility for growth. Rambo shows us that conversion is multidimensional and interactive. Rambo identifies the proven components of profound and ongoing conversion: relationships, rituals, rhetoric, and roles.

Gelpi warns us of the necessity of a comprehensive approach to conversion in order to prevent a lack of conversion in any one dimension (affective, intellectual, religious, personal-moral, or social-political) from undoing the conversion achieved in any other adjoining dimension. Gelpi exhorts us not to permit a narrowly focused conception of conversion to privatize and stifle full, authentic conversion as called for by the Reign of God.

In a similar vein, Bosch challenges us via his insistence that genuine theology must be developed in collaboration with marginalized people, and likewise, by way of his assertion that true Christian conversion always benefits others, particularly the weakest and most neglected.

Catholic Social Doctrine

The entire corpus of Catholic Social Doctrine or Teaching, which has been summarized recently by the Pontifical Council for Justice and Peace in the *Compendium of the Social Doctrine of the Church*,[80] certainly impinges in a plethora of ways upon the missionary endeavors of the Christian churches. Within that framework, three facets most profoundly inform the discipline of missiology, namely: human dignity and rights; the common good or the universal destination of goods; and solidarity.

Since all human beings are equal according to the divine perspective because God created humans in God's own image,[81] all, regardless of status, innately possess the same dignity, and therefore are entitled to the whole spectrum of human rights that are economic, cultural, political, and social.[82] In his social encyclical *Sollicitudo Rei Socialis,* Pope Saint John Paul II confirmed the inextricable link among these three social facets:

---

[80] Pontifical Council for Justice and Peace, *Compendium*, 1ff.

[81] Genesis 1:27.

[82] James B. McGinnis, *Bread and Justice: Toward a New International Economic Order* (Mahwah, NJ: Paulist, 1979), 9-20.

The exercise of solidarity within each society is valid when its members recognize one another as persons ... By virtue of her own evangelical duty, the Church feels called to take her stand beside the poor, to discern the justice of their requests, and to help satisfy them, without losing sight of the good of groups in the context of the common good.[83]

Pope Pius XI, in *Quadragesimo Anno*, prophetically denounced the most pervasive consequence of economic exploitation that results from the failure by people and structures to honor that divinely imbued dignity:

The distribution of created goods, which, as every discerning person knows, is laboring today under the gravest evils due to the huge disparity between the few exceedingly rich and the unnumbered propertyless, must be effectively ... brought into conformity with the norms of the common good, that is, social justice.[84]

Pope Saint John Paul II, in *Centesimus Annus*, echoed Popes Leo XIII and Pius XI with these words, "God gave the earth to the whole human race for the sustenance of all its members, without excluding or favoring anyone."[85] Pope Pius XII, in his Radio Message to commemorate the fiftieth anniversary of *Rerum Novarum*, asserted that:

The human person cannot do without the material goods that correspond to his primary needs and constitute the basic conditions for his existence; these goods are absolutely indispensable if he is to

---

[83] Pope John Paul II, *Sollicitudo Rei Socialis: On the Social Concerns of the Church on the 20th Anniversary of Populorum Progressio* (Città del Vaticano: Libreria Editrice Vaticana, 1987), 39.

[84] Pope Pius XI, *Quadragesimo Anno: On the Reconstruction of the Social Order on the 40th Anniversary of Rerum Novarum* (Città del Vaticano: Libreria Editrice Vaticana, 1931), 58.

[85] Pope John Paul II, *Centesimus Annus: On the 100th Anniversary of Rerum Novarum* (Città del Vaticano: Libreria Editrice Vaticana, 1991), 31.

feed himself, grow, communicate, associate with others, and attain the highest purposes to which he is called.[86]

When missionaries witness widespread deprivation, they typically feel compassion and respond with resolute solidarity. Pope Saint John Paul II ardently affirms that the virtue of solidarity with those who suffer is precisely the appropriate fruit of the conversion that opening our hearts to extremely poor people elicits from Christians.

In this affirmation, he concurs with preeminent missiologists David Bosch, Claude Marie Barbour, and Anthony Gittins by linking inextricably Christian conversion with outreach to those who are materially poor, those who are chronically infirm, those who are imprisoned, and those who have immigrated.

Because Saint John Paul II's logic and insight are so profound on this score, and because this study aspires to examine the influence of friendship with the least of society upon the conversion of Christians, his instruction is inval-uable:

> For Christians, as for all who recognize the precise theological meaning of the word "sin," a change of behavior or mentality or mode of existence is called "conversion" ... This conversion specifically entails a relationship to God, to the sin committed, to its consequences and hence to one's neighbor, either an individual or a community. It is God, in "whose hands are the hearts of the powerful" and the hearts of all, who according his own promise and by the power of his Spirit can transform "hearts of stone" into "hearts of flesh" (cf. Ezekiel 36:26). On the path toward the desired conversion, toward the overcoming of the moral obstacles to development, it is already possible to point to the positive and moral value of the growing awareness of interdependence among individuals and nations. The fact that men and women in various parts of the world feel personally affected by the injustices and violations of

---

[86] Pontifical Council for Justice and Peace, *Compendium*, 171.

human rights committed in distant countries, countries which per-
haps they will never visit, is a further sign of a reality transformed
into awareness, thus acquiring a moral connotation. It is above all
a question of interdependence, sensed as a system determining re-
lationships in the contemporary world, in its economic, cultural,
political, and religious elements, and accepted as a moral category.
When interdependence becomes recognized in this way, the correl-
ative response as a moral and social attitude, as a "virtue," is soli-
darity. This then is not a feeling of vague compassion or shallow
distress at the misfortunes of so many people, both near and far. On
the contrary, it is a firm and persevering determination to commit
oneself to the common good; that is to say to the good of all and of
each individual, because we are all really responsible for all. This
determination is based on the solid conviction that what is hinder-
ing full development is that desire for profit and that thirst for
power already mentioned. These attitudes and "structures of sin"
are only conquered — presupposing the help of divine grace — by a
diametrically opposed attitude: a commitment to the good of one's
neighbor with the readiness, in the gospel sense, to "lose oneself"
for the sake of the other instead of exploiting him, and to "serve
him" instead of oppressing him for one's own advantage (cf. Matt
10:40-42; 20:25; Mark 10:42-45; Luke 22:25-27).[87]

Pope Saint John Paul brilliantly underscores the biblical mandate to embrace our role as our brothers' and sisters' keepers, in spite of the temptation of selfishness, the inertia occasioned by structural sin, and the impediment of distance.

Catholic Social Doctrine & Conversion

As mentioned above, a unifying principal of Christian conversion among such scholars of conversion theology as Kavanaugh, Rambo,

---

[87] Pope John Paul II, *Sollicitudo Rei Socialis*, 38.

Gelpi, and Bosch is that authentic conversion must motivate the convert to reach beyond his or her comfort zone in order contribute to the improvement of the lives of suffering people. In other words, true conversion manifests itself via the promotion of the common good.

The scriptural revelation and the church's magisterial teaching emphasize the centrality of the common good to the Reign of God. Isaiah's portrait of God's mountain in the post-messianic age,[88] the Beatitudes delineated in the gospels,[89] the exhortation in the Letter to the Romans,[90] as well as Vatican II's *Gaudium et Spes*[91] and *Lumen Gentium*,[92] all affirm that God's Reign prominently features the common good of humanity on earth as a constitutive element.

The arrival, realization, and expansion of the Reign of God together comprise the essential goal or mission of the Christian church. The comprehensive body of CSD, whose roots are firmly imbedded in the Bible, presents a holistic vision of the Reign of God on Earth. CSD offers a reflection on the realities of our world in light of revelation. As the *Compendium of the Social Doctrine of the Church* proclaims, CSD strives to articulate "God's plan of love for humanity."[93]

Its hallmarks are: life and dignity of the human person; pursuit of the common good; solidarity with people who suffer and are vulnerable; a well ordered society; a just and participatory government; subsidiarity; preferential treatment for families and poor people; protection of workers; care of creation; and opposition to violence and offensive warfare.

---

[88] Isaiah 11:1-9.

[89] Luke 6:20.

[90] Romans 14:17.

[91] Vatican II, *Gaudium et Spes*,1ff.

[92] Vatican II, *Lumen Gentium: Dogmatic Constitution on the Church* (Città del Vaticano: Libreria Editrice Vaticana, 1964), 9ff.

[93] Pontifical Council for Justice and Peace, *Compendium*, 11.

In CSD, we find guidance and practical norms for social conversion. CSD lays out a coherent social philosophy for Christians and others. CSD offers guidance on how Christians and Christian missionaries ought to approach and negotiate the market, the state, and the culture. More specifically, it is CSD that teaches us to engage our frenetic and troubled society via the See-Judge-Act method.[94]

Gelpi vigorously points students of conversion toward CSD, which has its origins in, and continues to prod our consciences under the guidance of, the Holy Spirit, right into our era, in order to awaken in us that indispensable "prophetic opposition to the forces of unbelief, immorality, and injustice."[95] Gelpi exhorts us to realize that:

> *Religious conversion ... provides norms all ... political activists need in promoting a just social order... From the standpoint of Christian faith, no society counts as just which fails to incarnate that kind of social order willed by God. Since divine revelation yields a privileged insight into the way in which God wants human society ordered, it too helps authenticate the human search for a just social order.*[96]

Gelpi highlights that for Christians, faith requires "discipleship," which means we are obligated to follow or imitate Christ obediently. In other words, "conversion to Jesus Christ makes very specific moral demands" of his disciples and "demands of converts that they see, in

---

[94] Cardinal Joseph Cardijn, *Laypeople into Action* (Adelaide, Australia: ATF, 1964); Pope John XXIII, *Mater et Magistra: Mother and Teacher: On Christianity and Social Progress* (Città del Vaticano: Libreria Editrice Vaticana, 1961), 236; Pope Paul VI, *Octagesima Adveniens: On the 80th anniversary of Rerum Novarum: Call to Action* (Città del Vaticano: Libreria Editrice Vaticana, 1971), 4; Pontifical Council for Justice and Peace, *Compendium*, 11; Episcopal Conference of Latin America & the Caribbean, *Aparecida*, 19.

[95] Gelpi, *Conversion Experience*, 55; Donald Gelpi, *Charism and Sacrament: A Theology of Christian Conversion* (Mahwah, NJ: Paulist, 1976), 32.

[96] Gelpi, *Conversion Experience*, 53.

Jesus' proclamation of the Reign of God, the human embodiment of God's saving will for humanity."[97]

It is fitting here to survey the corpus of CSD in order that post-immersion missionaries might apprehend a panoramic view of what the Reign of God on Earth ought to encompass. Although Popes Gregory X[98] (1272), Paul III[99] (1537), and Gregory XVI[100] (1839) boldly asserted the full humanity and right to liberty of Jews, Native Americans, and Africans respectively, Pope Leo XIII's *Rerum Novarum*[101] (1891) effectively inaugurated the Catholic Church's concerted consideration, critique, and counsel regarding the socio-economic, political, and cultural forces that shape the modern industrialized and urbanized world.

Rerum Novarum asserted the rights of laborers within the context of the myriad of abuses that emerged during the Industrial Revolution. Nevertheless, Pope Leo rejected class struggle and socialism as appropriate remedies. This seminal document affirmed the dignity of work, the right to private property, and the right of workers to establish professional associations.

In the midst of the Great Depression, Leo XIII's successor, Pope Pius XI promulgated *Quadragesimo Anno*[102] (1931) in order to recommend that modern societies reorder themselves according to the principle of subsidiarity in order to counteract the increasing concentration of property and political power in the hands of a few.

---

[97] Gelpi, *Conversion Experience*, 105.

[98] Pope Gregory X, *Protection of the Jews* (http://www.papalencyclicals.net/Greg10/g10jprot.htm, 1272), 1.

[99] Pope Paul III, *Sublimus Dei: On the Enslavement and Evangelization of Indians in the New World* (http://www.papalencyclicals.net/Paul03/p3subli.htm, 1537), 1.

[100] Pope Gregory XVI, *In Supremo Apostolatus: At the Summit of Apostolic Power: On Slavery* (http://www.papalencyclicals.net/Greg16/g16sup.htm, 1839), 1.

[101] Pope Leo XIII, *Rerum Novarum*, 1ff.

[102] Pope Pius XI, *Quadragesimo Anno*, 80.

Pope Saint John XXIII, when faced with an international context that included technologically advanced nations juxtaposed against poor, non-industrialized countries, published *Mater et Magistra*[103] (1961) in the hopes of encouraging closer transnational cooperation on behalf of indigent people. In this document, Pope Saint John formally endorsed the See-Judge-Act method for responding to suffering and injustice.

As in *Mater et Magistra*, Pope Saint John XXIII, in *Pacem in Terris*[104] (1963), cajoled political leaders to abandon the perilous global arms race, particularly its nuclear component, and instead dedicate their intellectual and material resources to the further development of economies so that they would be able to offer dignified work and standards of living to all people. Pope Saint John united two major traditions of human rights theory, Natural Law and the Enlightenment. Pope Saint John offered his encyclical in the wake of the erection of the Berlin Wall and the Cuban Missile Crisis of 1962.

During Vatican II, the Catholic bishops of the world, in union with Pope Saint Paul VI, reaffirmed the messages of Pope Saint John XXIII via *Gaudium et Spes*[105] (1965). Turning its attention to the state of the church's ongoing missionary efforts, Vatican II also produced *Ad Gentes Divinitus*[106] (1965) which declared that mission is the "nature" and first priority of the church. Furthermore, the spiritual transformation that is sought by missionaries must be accompanied by social action which leads to justice, peace, and economic improvement for poor and afflicted people. Genuine conversion needs to bring about

---

[103] Pope John XXIII, *Mater et Magistra*, 1ff.

[104] Pope John XXIII, *Pacem in Terris: Peace on Earth* (Città del Vaticano: Libreria Editrice Vaticana, 1963), 1ff.

[105] Vatican Council II, *Gaudium et Spes*, 1ff.

[106] Vatican Council II, *Ad Gentes Divinitus*, 1ff.

a "progressive change of outlook and morals, [and] must become evident with its social consequences."[107]

In the context of multiple African wars of independence from European colonial empires and the war in Vietnam, Pope Saint Paul VI composed *Populorum Progressio*[108] (1967) in which he advocated for increased solidarity among all peoples of the Earth and called upon materially rich nations to assist the poor nations in terms of promoting integral human development since the goods of the Earth really belong to all of humanity. This development comprises the fostering of full human potential in all aspects, including the social, cultural, and spiritual senses, as well as the economic and technological spheres. Pope Saint Paul identified development as the new name for peace and argued that mounting disparity tempts the poor to choose violence and revolution as viable solutions.

Several years later, in the wake of the African-American civil rights movement in the USA and the continuing women's rights movements throughout Western societies, Pope Saint Paul VI wrote *Octogesima Adveniens*[109] (1971) in order to denounce discrimination based on ethnicity, gender, and religious creeds, and in order to advocate for action to be taken worldwide by individual Christians and local churches on behalf of the new urban poor, such as elderly and disabled people. In this call to action, Pope Saint Paul VI echoed Pope Saint John XXIII's counsel that the faithful employ the See-Judge-Act method in pursuit of the biblically inspired notions of justice.[110]

In the context of widespread anti-colonial movements and calls for liberation and justice issued by Ibero-American, African, and Asian church leaders, the 1971 Synod of Bishops reaffirmed Pope Saint Paul

---

[107] Vatican Council II, *Ad Gentes Divinitus*, 13.

[108] Pope Paul VI, *Populorum Progressio*, 1ff.

[109] Pope Paul VI, *Octagesima Adveniens*, 1ff.

[110] Pope Paul VI, *Octagesima Adveniens*, 4.

VI's exhortations and added the need for concerted advocacy on behalf of "voiceless" people such as unborn children, migrants, refugees, political prisoners, and torture victims, in their document entitled *Justitia in Mundo*[111] (1971). The bishops declared that "action on behalf of justice and participation in the transformation of the world fully appear to us as a constitutive dimension of preaching the Gospel."[112]

Again, in *Evangelii Nuntiandi*[113] (1975), his apostolic exhortation on the topic of missionary endeavors, Pope Saint Paul VI insisted that evangelization and the proclamation of the Christian gospel are inextricably intertwined with the promotion of justice and liberation of God's children from all forms of oppression. Pope Saint Paul VI ascribed to "a true atheistic secularism" the primary responsibility for generating the multiple temptations that in turn produce oppression, namely, the spread of "consumer societies," the "pursuit of pleasure as the supreme value," and a "desire for power and domination."[114]

In the context of widespread unemployment, underemployment, and migration of workers, in *Laborem Exercens*[115] (1981), Pope Saint John Paul II invoked Pope Leo XIII's *Rerum Novarum*, specifically on behalf of these laborers, both industrial and agricultural, including migrants or economic refugees. Pope Saint John Paul proclaimed the dignity of both work and laborers and elaborated a spirituality of work. The Polish pontiff criticized both capitalism and Marxism which tend to treat human beings as mere instruments of production. He condemned collectivism and affirmed the right to private property, albeit subordinate to the priority of the common good.

---

[111] Synod of Bishops, *Justitia in Mundo: Justice in the World* (Città del Vaticano: Libreria Editrice Vaticana, 1971), 20.

[112] Synod of Bishops, *Justitia in Mundo*, 6.

[113] Pope Paul VI, *Evangelii Nuntiandi*, 29.

[114] Pope Paul VI, *Evangelii Nuntiandi*, 55.

[115] Pope John Paul II, *Laborem Exercens*, 1ff.

In the context of the enduring Cold War between the communist and capitalist blocs, Pope Saint John Paul II promulgated *Sollicitudo Rei Socialis*[116] (1987) assigning blame for the widespread underdevel-opment and deprivation to both sides which incline toward imperialism, neo-colonialism, militarism, and proxy wars. The foreign debts of materially destitute countries force them to export more of their capital to the already wealthy financier nations, thereby causing even greater misery.

While the Eastern socialists are callous to the moral imperative to respect the gamut of human rights of their denizens, the Western capitalists are likewise culpable for the near-ubiquitous suffering in the Southern hemisphere due to their self-indulgence and wastefulness coupled with their unwillingness to prioritize the needs of the many over the wants of the privileged few. Pope Saint John Paul asserted that God's natural creation also needs preservation even as crucial economic development projects advance to improve the lives of marginalized people. He reiterated the centrality of the concepts of solidarity, structural sin, and the preferential option for the poor.

In the wake of the collapse of communism in Eastern Europe and the Soviet Union, Pope Saint John Paul offered *Centesimus Annus*[117] (1991) to orient his audience amidst this period of great upheaval and euphoria for some. Pope Saint John Paul declared that socialism's "fundamental error" is its atheism which denies the innate God-given dignity and responsibility of each human person. While admonishing his audience not to embrace unbridled capitalism as an all-encompassing utopian ideology, Pope Saint John Paul did tentatively endorse the free-market system as the best available tool for the efficient production and sharing of material goods.

---

[116] Pope John Paul II, *Sollicitudo Rei Socialis*, 1ff.

[117] Pope John Paul II, *Centesimus Annus*, 4ff.

However, the pope recommended the application of the principle of sub-sidiarity in order to balance, regulate, and reduce the potential excess and abuses of these markets, such as avarice, waste, and environmental pollution. In *Peace with God the Creator, Peace with All of Creation*[118] (1989), Pope Saint John Paul insisted that respect for God's natural creation is a key tenet of Christian faith.

In *Redemptoris Missio*[119] (1990), Pope Saint John Paul asserted the unique, indispensable, and universal role of the Son of God in the plan of salvation, a dogma which was reiterated by the Congregation for the Doctrine of the Faith in *Dominus Iesus*[120] (2000). *Redemptoris Missio* also signaled the diverse vital components that comprise the worldwide evangelical enterprise.

The Pontifical Council for Dialogue and the Congregation for the Evangelization of Peoples together further enfleshed the instruction of Pope Saint Paul VI and Pope Saint John Paul II by issuing *Dialogue and Proclamation*[121] (1991) which delineated the five principal elements of mission: 1) presence and witness, 2) social transformation and human liberation, 3) spir-ituality and prayer, 4) interreligious dialogue, and 5) proclamation and catechesis. In the *Catechism of the Catholic Church*[122] (1997), the Congregation for the Doctrine of the

---

[118] Pope John Paul II, *Peace with God the Creator, Peace with All of Creation: On the Occasion of the World Day of Peace January 1, 1990* (Città del Vaticano: Libreria Editrice Vaticana, 1989), 2, 5, 15. Pope Francis I's ecological encyclical *Laudato Sí: On Care for Our Common Home* (2015) expands upon the insights of Saints Francis of Assisi and Pope John Paul II.

[119] Pope John Paul II, *Redemptoris Missio: The Mission of Christ the Redeemer: On the Permanent Validity of the Church's Missionary Mandate* (Città del Vaticano: Libreria Editrice Vaticana, 1990), 4ff.

[120] Congregation for the Doctrine of the Faith, *Dominus Iesus: Lord Jesus: On the Unicity and Salvific Universality of Jesus Christ and the Church* (Città del Vaticano: Libreria Editrice Vaticana, 2000), 5ff.

[121] Pontifical Council for Interreligious Dialogue and the Congregation for the Evangelization of Peoples, *Dialogue and Proclamation*, 2ff.

[122] Congregation for the Doctrine of the Faith, "Part Four: Christian Prayer, Section 2: The Lord's Prayer: Our Father!" *Catechism of the Catholic Church.*(Città del Vaticano: Libreria Editrice Vaticana, August 15, 1997), 2759ff.

Faith correlated each phrase of the Lord's Prayer to the social sins that it seeks to curb.

Drawing upon his own earlier pronouncements, especially *Sollicitudo Rei Socialis* and *Centesimus Annus*, as well as Pope Saint Paul VI's *Humanae Vitae*[123] (1968), Pope Saint John Paul II engendered *Evangel-ium Vitae*[124] (1995) in defense of all human life, from intrauterine babies to chronically infirm and terminally ill patients to feeble elderly folks to political enemies to heinous criminals, insisting that the death penalty is only permissible "when it would not be possible otherwise to defend society."[125] Pope Saint John Paul proposed the Gospel and Culture of Life to counteract the manifold Culture of Death which is rooted in profound materialism.

In the wake of a truly tumultuous year that featured the far-reaching Asian tsunami, Hurricane Katrina, the monumental Pakistani earthquake, the internal Sudanese peace treaty, and the ominous boasts of Iran's president trumpeting the Islamic Republic's aggressive pursuit of nuclear weapons, Pope Benedict XVI offered *Deus Caritas Est*[126] (2005) in order to remind the faithful that love for God and disinterested love for our neighbors are inextricable duties binding upon all biblical adherents.

Within the context of a global economic recession, Pope Benedict penned *Caritas in Veritate*[127] (2009) with the aim of convincing his audience that real charity entails living in relationship and solidarity with marginalized people, not merely sharing our excess possessions. Benedict urged that market structures be reformed to include

---

[123] Pope Paul VI, *Humanae Vitae: Human Life: On the Regulation of Birth* (Città del Vaticano: Libreria Editrice Vaticana, July 25, 1968), 1ff.

[124] Pope John Paul II, *Evangelium Vitae*, 1ff.

[125] Pope John Paul II, *Evangelium Vitae*, 56.

[126] Pope Benedict XVI, *Deus Caritas Est: God is Love: On Christian Love* (Città del Vaticano: Libreria Editrice Vaticana, Decembers 25, 2005), 1ff.

[127] Pope Benedict XVI, *Caritas in Veritate*, 1ff.

"integral human development" as a central objective of the economy. Pope Benedict also encouraged his audience to treat God's natural creation responsibly.

In light of the current horrific wave of genocide against Christians, Jews, Yezidis, Druze, and others, at the hands of Islamic jihadists in Iraq, Syria, Nigeria, Lybia, Pakistan, and beyond, our church's teaching on the legitimate defense of innocents against genocide, pogroms, ethnic and religious cleansing, and terrorism asserts that civil and military authorities are charged with the "grave duty" to protect civilians, even to the extent of wielding "arms to repel aggressors against the civil community entrusted to their responsibility."

This doctrine reaches all the way back to the origins of Christianity as reflected in the instruction of Moses, Jesus, and Paul, and stretches forward in time to Augustine, Aquinas, the Dominicans of Salamanca, the Jesuits of Coimbra, and now is unflinchingly reaffirmed in both the Catechism of the Catholic Church and the Compendium of the Social Doctrine of the Church.[128]

As the Islamic hijrah and jihad expand and accelerate around the world, including into Europe and the USA, the debate over immigration guidelines becomes an increasingly relevant topic in light of our Catholic teaching regarding the obligation to protect the lives of innocent civilians.

Our magisterial Vatican congregations and councils take pains to balance two competing moral demands on behalf of the common good: the need of refugees to emigrate from active zones of warfare and genocide, with the obligation to protect the innocent civilians and the "spiritual heritage" of the shelter countries.

---

[128] Exodus 22:2; Matthew 24:43; Romans 13:4; Augustine of Hippo, City of God; Thomas Aquinas, Summa Theologica; Congregation for the Doctrine of the Faith, "Part Three: Life in Christ, Section Two: the Ten Commandments, Chapter Two: You Shall Love Your Neighbor as Yourself, Article 5: the Fifth Commandment" *Catechism*, 2265; Pontifical Council for Justice and Peace, *Compendium*, 504.

The Congregation for the Doctrine of the Faith wisely affirms that the authorities of the shelter countries may legitimately consider the security needs, material needs, and spiritual needs of their own native citizens when weighing how best to respond to the moral obligation to offer sanctuary to potential immigrants who are being targeted for annihilation in their countries of origin.[129]

The Pontifical Council for Justice and Peace's monumental *Compendium of the Social Doctrine of the Church* (2004) undertook the ambitious task of synthesizing the entire canon of Roman Catholic Social Teaching by reflecting upon its central principles and applying them anew to our contemporary situation.

Generally speaking, CSD critiques a myriad of facets of the contemporary world which the church has discerned violate the essential dignity of human persons and trample upon the requisites of justice and the common good of the global society. Within the context of the exponential augmentation of global mass communication and the advent of ever-novel luxuries and thrill generators facilitated by technological innovations, stubborn injustices like violence, destitution, ecological degradation, exploitation, and even slavery linger and shamefully find new and gruesome manifestations.

The intention of CSD is to guide and equip Christians so that they are better able "to bring about an authentic civilization oriented ever more towards integral human development in solidarity."[130] In its online reflection on the *Compendium*, the staff of the Catholic Social Action Office of Queensland, Australia wisely explains that:

> *CSD does not purport to offer a 'blueprint' for an ideal type of society. Rather, CSD proposes principles aimed at creating 'right'*

---

[129] Congregation for the Doctrine of the Faith, "Part Three: Life in Christ, Section Two: the Ten Commandments, Chapter Two: You Shall Love Your Neighbor as Yourself, Article 4: the Fourth Commandment," *Catechism*, 2241.

[130] Pontifical Council for Justice and Peace, "Letter from Cardinal Angelo Sodano to Cardinal Renato Raffaele Martino," *Compendium*.

social, economic, and political relationships and the construction of social structures and institutions based on justice and respect for human dignity. Inherent in CSD, is the belief that the application of these principles to the structures and institutions of society, both nationally and globally, will enhance human dignity, overcome poverty, and promote and ensure social justice.[131]

The entire corpus of CSD, as typified by the *Compendium*, has always sought to discover the structural causes that create the conditions of poverty and marginalization while courageously proclaiming a preferential love for poor people as a foundation for the pursuit of solutions. The *Compendium* revealed CSD's meta-aspiration of helping to hasten the Reign of God by reminding us that:

[God] himself has entered history in order to enter into dialogue with humanity and to reveal to mankind his plan of salvation, justice, and brotherhood. In Christ, his Son made man, God has freed us from sin and has shown us the path we are to walk and the goal toward which we are to strive.[132]

Not coincidentally, the *Compendium* itself echoed *Mater et Magistra* and *Octagesima Adveniens* in advocating for wider use of the tried and true See-Judge-Act process for applying revelation to our current reality:

Christian communities will be able to look to this document for assistance in analyzing situations objectively, in clarifying them in the light of the unchanging words of the Gospel, in drawing principles for reflection, criteria for judgment, and guidelines for action.[133]

---

[131] Social Action Office, Conference of Leaders of Religious Institutes, Queensland, "An Introduction to Catholic Social Teaching" (Brisbane, Queensland, Australia: sao.clriq.org.au/cst, 2006), 2.

[132] Pontifical Council for Justice and Peace, *Compendium*, 17.

[133] Pontifical Council for Justice and Peace, *Compendium*, 11.

Professor Joe Holland, the president of Pax Romana USA (a multifaceted movement that promotes the study and implementation of Catholic social and ecological doctrine, emphasizes the See-Judge-Act method, and simultaneously serves as a non-governmental organization representing the Vatican before several bodies of the United Nations) declared the *Compendium* to be "a veritable goldmine of wisdom that draws on the biblical, theological, and philosophical dimensions of Catholic Social Doctrine."[134] In fact, Pax Romana is adamant that the *Compendium* "needs to become a core work in the intellectual and spiritual formation of committed Catholics."[135]

Synopsis of CSD/CST

As previously noted, CSD spells out "God's plan of love for humanity"[136] on earth, whose features are: life and dignity for all; striving for the common good; solidarity with the weak; well-ordered societies; just and participatory governance; preferential treatment for families and materially poor people; stewardship of creation; and prophetic resistance to violence.

My Original Claims Revisited & Evaluated

In the first chapter, I delineated my original claims based on my preliminary intuitions regarding the factors that I believed capable of respectively discouraging and encouraging the ongoing post-immersion conversion process of AeA missionaries. It is important here to

---

[134] Edward Joseph Holland, *Compendium of the Social Doctrine of the Church: A Pax Romana Study Guide* (Washington, DC: Pax Romana USA, 2010), 2.

[135] Holland, *Compendium Pax Romana Study Guide*, 2.

[136] Pontifical Council for Justice and Peace, *Compendium*, 11.

revisit these initial claims in light of the findings garnered from my interviews,[137] consultations, readings,[138] and reflections.

My assertion that a lifestyle that features excessive material luxury is blatantly antithetical to the spiritual advancement of missionaries was resoundingly affirmed by both the missionaries that I interviewed and the social philosophers whose written works I consulted. My converse contention that intentional material simplicity or asceticism would lead to the reinforcement of missionary spirituality was likewise roundly buttressed by my research and readings.

Furthermore, my contention that participation in local stateside ministries of direct service to materially poor or abandoned people during the post-immersion stage or the lapse in between immersions would sustain and bolster missionary vocations was confirmed. Several AeA missionaries who noted that involvement in such local social ministries in fact precipitated their initial missionary calls also spoke of its role in maintaining and deepening their missionary values in between immersion opportunities.

I also stated that missionary vocations could be muffled by unrelenting ideological pronouncements by relatives and friends blaming all situations of misery in the world as the fault of the poor. My claim on this score was modified during the conversations with my fellow missionaries who explained that in order to hold onto their missionary vocations they felt obliged to spiritually distance themselves from such vexing influences. Of course, since I only interviewed committed missionaries, my initial intuition was neither fully validated nor invalidated. In order to achieve that, I would have to consult former short-term missionaries who no longer participate in missionary endeavors.

---

[137] See Chapter Three.

[138] See my distillations of Bellah, Madsen, Sullivan, Swidler, Tipton, and Kavanaugh in Chapter Four and of Rambo, Gelpi, Bosch, and CSD in Chapter 5.

Continuing on the theme of familial and interpersonal influences, I originally surmised that relatives and friends who merely showed an unwillingness to listen repeatedly to the immersion and post-immersion narratives of their missionary family member or friend could debilitate the post-immersion conversion process of missionaries. Just as with my previous claim, I now see the need to adjust my contention in this sphere because the committed missionaries whom I interviewed have chosen to distance themselves spiritually from these obstinate relatives and friends in order to maintain their missionary trajectories.

Likewise, since I did not consult former missionaries, I cannot definitively confirm or deny my initial declaration. Nevertheless, my complementary claim, that opportunities and measurable successes in terms of inviting others to discern their own potential missionary vocations by participating in an initial missionary immersion, was strongly affirmed to be an effective promoter of conversion deepening, especially among younger and first-time post-immersion AeA missionaries.

On another related point, I projected that most post-immersion missionaries would express the need for a community of encouraging fellow missionaries and/or family members who would always remain eager to listen to their immersion and post-immersion stories. This intuition was also firmly validated by my research. I even went so far as to assert that friends, relatives, and fellow missionaries who deliberately pointed out in conversations with the post-immersion missionaries' instances of injustices and human rights violations that periodically arise in news reports would serve to foster the continuing conversion of post-immersion missionaries. My research affirmed my preliminary claim.

My final preliminary intuition that encouraging post-immersion missionaries to dedicate time regularly to prayer and liturgy, meditation, and other opportunities for ongoing spiritual formation would advance their conversion was confirmed by all generations of AeA missionaries. Furthermore, numerous young post-immersion missionaries stated that not only did they perceive newly intensified spiritual nourishment from the Eucharistic liturgy, but they also felt that each subsequent Sunday it reconnected them spiritually with both their newfound friends overseas as well as their fellow missionaries.

Implications from Conversion Theology & CSD regarding My Concern

Before proceeding on to Groome's final movement, the decision and response in favor of lived Christian faith, which essentially consists of a renewed praxis aimed at contributing to the Reign of God, I offer a synthesis of my findings from the vital texts that have informed my study, namely: AeA's present praxis revealed primarily in the focus group interviews (as delineated in the first four chapters); the sociological and philosophical texts of Bellah et al. and Kavanaugh (as presented in chapter five); the conversion theology texts of Rambo, Gelpi, and Bosch (as depicted in chapter six); and the magisterial documents regarding the social doctrine of the church that make explicit the vision of the lovingly motivated divine plan for life on earth (also exhibited in chapter six).

The vital text of our present praxis reveals five central post-immersion concerns that must be addressed if missionary conversion is to proceed in an optimal fashion. These five essential issues are: the ongoing need for material simplicity, community, sacramental nourishment, engagement with marginalized people locally, and multiple opportunities to motivate others to discern their own respective potential missionary vocations.

The sociological and philosophical texts most relevant to the goal of post-immersion conversion for North American missionaries, as penned by Bellah et al. and Kavanaugh, reveal that the establishment and maintenance of regular, values-based communal life shared with other religiously motivated missionaries and volunteers is indispensable to the fostering of conversion.

The non-magisterial theological texts most pertinent to missionary conversion, as authored by Gelpi and Bosch, warn that self-centered privatization of any aspect of conversion serves to counteract, weaken, and negate all the other meritorious facets of conversion. This truth is attested repeatedly in the biblical injunction to never divorce our love of neighbor from our love of God or our love of self. Even more concretely, Rambo's text illuminates four factors that radically serve to promote ongoing Christian conversion among post-immersion missionaries: relationships, rituals, rhetoric, and roles. Not coincidentally, these four dimensions of interaction overlap with the five crucial needs that emerge from our examination of the present praxis.

Finally, the magisterial theological texts that comprise CSD portray the crucial constituents of God's loving design for human life on earth and instruct us how to pursue these divinely ordained objectives. As suggested by Gelpi and Bosch, these key components stem from the covenantal, mature, and interwoven love of God, others, and self.

Summation

The integral vision of the Reign of God on earth that CSD painstakingly portrays, coupled with the practical insights shared by the sociologists, philosophers, and conversion theologians, serve to challenge AeA to broaden and deepen our post-immersion praxes. CSD orients missionaries toward our ultimate goal, the expansion of the Reign of the God as revealed in the Bible. Reflection on pertinent aspects of conversion theology in relation to post-immersion conversion experiences has helped us to identify phenomena that either advance or hinder the long-term conversion trajectory of missionaries.

In the next and final chapter, I offer recommendations for a renewed post-immersion praxis for AeA, in light of the wisdom appropriated from the dialectical hermeneutic among AeA's actual praxis, the insights of sociologists, social philosophers, and conversion theologians, and the vision of God's Reign on earth as given to us in the Bible and further detailed by the corpus of CSD.

7

RECOMMENDATIONS FOR

A RENEWED PRAXIS

W e now enter the final phase of this practical-theological study, the renewed praxis which Groome labels the shared decision and response to foster lived Christian faith in service of the Reign of God. Groome's fifth movement exhorts practitioners of theological reflection to leap from study and contemplation into action on behalf of the expansion of God's Reign on earth. Groome encourages the theologian to seize the initiative by applying the wisdom culled via the focusing activity and previous movements to forge a renewed praxis. Groome's culminating movement mirrors the ultimate stage of the magisterially endorsed See-Judge-Act method.

Informed by my own thirty-year history of post-immersion missionary experiences, by attentive listening to my fellow post-immersion AeA missionaries, and by sagacity obtained from sources such as the sacred scriptures, CSD, sociologists, social philosophers, and conversion theologians, I offer recommendations applicable to all spheres of post-immersion spiritual formation with an eye to the promotion and consolidation of conversion in the post-immersion stage.

Our study has identified vital necessities that any post-immersion conversion stimulation program ought to address. Five of these requisites emerged from my interviews with post-immersion AeA missionaries; one arose from magisterial conversion theology literature; and another from non-magisterial conversion theology literature.

These seven needs are: simplicity, community, service, stories, sacraments, deprivatization, and the Reign of God.

Material Simplicity

Need for Material Simplicity

Our research reveals that nearly all neophyte AeA post-immersion missionaries feel intense bouts of guilt regarding the wide disparity between the degree to which creature comforts are available to themselves and those available to their newfound friends overseas in the mission field.

Correspondingly, upon their return to the USA, they naturally feel impelled to waste, consume, and amass fewer material goods. In other words, the missionaries report feeling called to practice asceticism.

The need to practice austerity emerged in all of my focus group sessions as well as in the studies and analyses of Bellah et al., Kavanaugh, Rambo, Bosch, the Pontifical Council for Justice and Peace,[1] and the Congregation for Institutes of Consecrated Life and Societies of Apostolic Life.[2]

---

[1] Pontifical Council for Justice and Peace, *Toward Reforming the International Financial and Monetary Systems in the Context of Global Public Authority* (Città del Vaticano: Libreria Editrice Vaticana, 2011), 1.

[2] Congregation for Institutes of Consecrated Life and Societies of Apostolic Life. *Congregavit nos in Unum Christi Amor: Fraternal Life in Community* (Città del Vaticano: Libreria Editrice Vaticana, February 2, 1994), 35ff.

Recommendations to Address the Need
for Material Simplicity

We discovered that the missionaries find it easier to detach them-selves from the habit of the overconsumption of material goods when they participate in meetings of their missionary communities, engage in community service among local poor and vulnerable people, and increase the frequency of personal and communal prayer.

The iterated need for material simplicity is adequately addressed by the support offered and encountered in genuine community settings where the moral and spiritual values and goals are mutual because the experience of sincere human solidarity overcomes the negative, isolating consequences of our individualistic materialist-consumer society. Furthermore, post-immersion interaction with both margin-alized and like-minded people facilitates integral conversion.

These interactions include forums for sharing of missionary narra-tives and insights as well as mentoring. The spiritual, emotional, and intellectual exchanges among people fill the gaps intentionally cre-ated by the intentional absence of material clutter which previously resulted from an overabundance of economic exchanges.

Community

Need for Community

Our study shows that the majority of AeA post-immersion mission-aries feel impelled to seek the companionship of other missionaries and religiously motivated volunteers. The nightly pattern of shared prayer, debriefing, and reflection that hold the missionary immersion group together, ends abruptly for most of the missionaries upon their return to the USA.

This rupture creates an acute need to continue these marvelous, wis-dom-nurturing communal practices. The imperative of meeting regularly with one's missionary community during the post-immersion phase leaps off the pages of all of my focus group session transcripts and is supported by the findings in the studies and analyses of Bellah et al., Kavanaugh, Rambo, Bosch, Ver Beek, and the Congregation for Institutes of Consecrated Life and Societies of Apostolic Life.[3]

Recommendations to Address the Need for Community for the Archdiocese of Miami

Partially as a result of their genuine interest in our study, our AeA Executive Director Teresita González and Mission Coordinator Mónica Lauzurique have astutely and adroitly chosen to implement several vital components of a more thorough, effective, and consistent post-immersion conversion-inducement plan.

Specifically, our leaders have reinstated the neglected tradition of regular first Friday of the month meetings. These gatherings feature varied themes: some are prayer and reflection oriented; others are more business, planning, and finance oriented; and still others are more purely social in nature.

Furthermore, all of these monthly gatherings are intergenerational, as we are encouraged to attend with our entire respective families. My research shows that this frequent and regular pattern of reunions is absolutely indispensable in the long-term conversion process of post-immersion missionaries; without this component, the research shows that many missionary vocations are squandered.

Finally, our two full-time leaders have wisely launched an AeA Facebook social networking page that welcomes missionaries, collaborators who have never been immersed, families of our missionaries,

---

[3] See, for example, Congregation for Institutes of Consecrated Life and Societies of Apostolic Life, *Congregavit nos in Unum Christi Amor*, 11ff.

friends, interested parties, and potential missionaries. One principal benefit of this page is that folks are now able to share their post-immersion reflections with a sympathetic and fertile audience.

Recommendations to Address
the Need for Community
for the Diocese of Saginaw

On the organizational level, AeA has a formal presence in two US dioceses, Miami, Florida and Saginaw, Michigan. Saginaw is isolated from the Miami headquarters in terms of distance, time, leadership, volunteers, and resources. In a sense, our Saginaw branch operates on a shoestring as well in terms of pre-immersion and post-immersion processes.

The central Miami cell should bolster our Saginaw cell by committing to sending a small team of veteran volunteers on a consistent basis (at least twice annually, during the pre-immersion and post-immersion cycles) to help convene and direct formal pre-immersion and post-immersion meetings and to initiate the implementation of the same enhancements that are implemented in Miami.

Deprivatization of Conversion

Need for Deprivatization of Conversion

My investigations show that spiritual tunnel vision[4] debilitates and nullifies integral conversion because any enduring dichotomy between words and actions is hypocritical, as is any attempt to truly love God without loving other people as well. Our Judeo-Christian sacred scriptures emphasize these points over and over. Therefore,

---

[4] By tunnel vision, I refer to a narrowness that produces two phenomena, both an emphasis on understandings and desires over and against actions that flow from those understandings and desires, as well as an exclusively self-centered spirituality through which one only seeks personal purification and reward.

theology and spiritual practice need to be pursued in communion with others. Furthermore, it is God's will that these pursuits produce genuine benefits for the least of humanity.

The importance of guarding against selfish privatization of conversion is attested to by my focus group interviews as well as the findings of Bosch, Gelpi, Bellah et al., Kavanaugh, Rambo, Pope Saint John Paul II, and the Congregation for Institutes of Consecrated Life and Societies of Apostolic Life.[5]

Recommendations to Address the Need
for Deprivatization of Conversion

My studies demonstrate that an ongoing relationship with a more veteran missionary mentor nearly always produces abundant conversion-oriented fruit.

In addition, a regular and at least somewhat structured habit of daily prayer is a time-tested tool for profound and lasting spiritual growth. Moreover, the serious study of and patient reflection upon CSD is a dynamic engine of intellectual and affective stimulus that has led many missionaries to more profound insights, growth, and committed action on behalf of the expansion of God's Reign on earth.

Finally, many missionaries have found that post-immersion service among chronically poor, suffering, and marginalized people in or near their own respective hometowns has fortified and encouraged the progression of their own missionary vocations.

---

[5] See Chapter Three regarding my focus group interviews; Bosch, *Transforming Mission*, 117-118; Bosch, "Mission in Jesus' Way," 7; Gelpi, *Conversion Experience*, 54; Gelpi, "Converting Jesuit," 4-5; Bellah et al., *Habits*, 142-143; Bellah et al., "Individualism and the Crisis of Civic Membership," 263; Kavanaugh, *Still Following Christ*, 17; Rambo, *Understanding Religious Conversion*, 44-48; Pope John Paul II, *Sollicitudo Rei Socialis*, 38-39; Congregation for Institutes of Consecrated Life and Societies of Apostolic Life, *Congregavit nos in Unum Christi Amor*, 16.

Service

Need for Service

Hands-on service among marginalized and materially destitute folks is a gospel imperative.[6] My investigations show that it also helps to consolidate missionary conversion in the post-immersion stage. Post-immersion missionaries explain that such direct service reminds them of their overseas missionary experiences and somehow mystically reconnects them with the friends they made during their respective immersions.

Along with these memories come reminders of the insights that they initially realized, as well as the resolutions for change that they intensely desired to implement when they first returned home. The transformative value of direct service to indigent people is borne out by my focus group interviews and the findings of Bellah et al., Kavanaugh, Gelpi, Bosch, Rambo, and Popes Paul VI, John Paul II, Benedict XVI, and Francis.

Recommendations to Address the Need for Service among Local Poor People

Countless missionaries recall how they heard their initial respective missionary vocations while serving as volunteers with local domestic community service ministries, agencies, and projects, such as rescue missions, homeless shelters, soup kitchens, orphanages, and home-building ministries. Likewise, the evidence reveals that participation in these same ministries, community service agencies, and projects assists missionaries who desire to continue progressing in terms of their Christian conversion in the period between immersions.

This is so because the face-to-face service both reminds them of their friends overseas and serves to reinforce their mission-oriented

---

[6] Works of Mercy in Matthew 25; Feet Washing in John 13.

insights and resolutions. Time after time, post-immersion missionaries have told me how spiritually renewed they feel when they engage in local service projects, and especially so when they have been able to do so in the company of other missionaries.

Contributing to the Reign of God

Need to Contribute to the Reign of God

Our study has brought to light the enduring longing among missionaries to align our daily lives with divine purposes. We aspire to contribute regularly to the Reign of God, no matter how small the measure. I have found that in order to be able to pursue this divine vision of life on Earth, we need to be constantly informed, inspired, and guided by the wisdom offered by our sacred scriptures, the writings of the saints, and the overflowing treasury of CSD.

The necessity to learn and keep in mind God's vision for life on Earth (known as the Reign of God) is attested to by many of my focus group participants as well as by Kavanaugh, Rambo, Gelpi, and Bosch, along with all of the popes in earnest at least since 1891.

Recommendations to Address the Need to Contribute to the Reign of God

We ought to devise a comprehensive list of questions suitable for both reflection and discussion derived from conversion-related and mission-related biblical passages, relevant quotes from saints and martyrs, and passages from the magisterial documents specifically dedicated to missionary endeavors (many of which we identified in the previous chapter), along with the *Compendium of the Social Doctrine of the Church.*

I emphasize this intellectual component as a stimulus for all of our missionaries to dedicate time and effort to the serious reading, reflection, and study of both of our rich and grand inherited written revelations, the sacred scriptures and our magisterial teaching. Of course, these reflections should always be linked with reflections based upon our missionary immersion and post-immersion experiences, which we should consider as revelatory texts in-and-of-themselves.

Storytelling

Need for Storytelling

My research reveals that novice post-immersion missionaries need many opportunities to recount narratives and epiphanies from their immersion experiences. This exercise serves two purposes. The first is to bolster their own respective conversions. The second is to offer them the role of a stateside evangelizer who speaks in order to inspire, prophetically challenge, and invite others to begin discerning their own latent Christian and missionary vocations.

This need to tell and retell our immersion narratives and attendant insights is demonstrated by my focus group interviews as well as by Rambo, Gelpi, the Pontifical Council for Interreligious Dialogue, the Congregation for the Evangelization of Peoples, and Popes Saint Paul VI and Saint John Paul II.

Recommendations to Address the Need for Storytelling

Post-Immersion Reentry Debriefing Retreat

As I stated above, our AeA Executive Director Teresita González and Mission Coordinator Mónica Lauzurique have wisely and deftly decided to implement several vital components of a more complete, effective, and consistent post-immersion conversion-inducement plan. Specifically, at the end of each summer immersion season, they lead a formal post-immersion reentry debriefing day featuring post-immersion reflections inspired by Jo Ann McCaffrey and employing printed resources for post-immersion reflection and reintegration published by From Mission to Mission.

Expansion of Reentry Debriefing Retreat

My research and reflection indicate that our current annual post-immersion reentry debriefing day ought to be extended to two days in length to facilitate the incorporation of a wider variety of reflective activities, including journaling, drawing, sharing in pairs, large group sharing, role playing, and discussion of missionary conversion resolutions and commitments for the near future. The implementation of the journaling, drawing, and discussion components will serve as training that will equip the post-immersion missionaries with practical tools that they can then employ in order to continue to significantly deepen their transformation.

Retreat for Parents & Families of Missionaries

In order to boost the probability of genuine sustained missionary conversion and commitment, I propose that we implement a formal retreat day directed toward the parents and families of the missionaries. I envision that this day should feature prayer, journaling, large group discussions regarding the families' respective worries and questions, advice talks from the perspectives of both a young neophyte missionary and a parent, and role playing of recurrent post-immersion reentry scenarios, including methods that tend to promote conflict and alternately harmony when dealing with freshly returned missionaries.

This retreat day should be scheduled while the missionaries are still in the field during the annual summer immersion season so that the immediate post-immersion missionaries and their families can enjoy the optimal boost to their respective conversion trajectories.

Mentorship

I include the vital component of mentorship within the storytelling segment for sound reasons. The post-immersion mentoring process is primarily narrative in nature because the novice missionary is encouraged by his or her mentor(s) to describe the post-immersion events and clashes that produce intense emotions and often reveal potential generative themes. When explored collaboratively, skillfully, patiently, and lovingly, these narratives, emotions, and generative themes, in turn, can lead to insights. The insights, especially when they are enhanced with prayer, then generate true spiritual growth, healing, and conversion.

Every post-immersion missionary benefits from spiritual direction or spiritual companionship offered by a more veteran missionary. I propose that AeA identify a pool of experienced missionaries who are able and willing to spare at least a couple of hours every fortnight to either field telephone calls, electronic mail, chat, or text message inquiries from recently returned post-immersion missionaries.

If no one calls or writes during these bi-weekly mentoring "office hours," then these volunteer mentors should initiate the telephone calls, chats, or email correspondence with all of the post-immersion rookies, beginning with the youngest. These mentors should also make it a point to contact missionaries that respective immersion and pre-immersion leaders identify as especially vulnerable to post-immersion depression.

Distance Formation Online for Out-of-Towners

This long-distance formation component that I propose herein is simply one additional facet of the aforementioned mentoring proposal. Owing to the regular phenomenon of AeA missionaries who participate in immersions but who live far away from Miami, usually due to university studies or employment exigencies, in addition to our Facebook page, we need to establish and maintain an online distance component to help foster their ongoing need for conversion. We need to set up an online forum whereby mentors and less experienced missionaries can interact.

Of course, they also ought to use electronic mail and telephone calls when more privacy is needed. Our mentors ought to make ample use of the high-quality resources that are currently available, including the following: We should post general post-immersion advice and wise adages along with prayer and reflection resources, such as links to the daily lectionary biblical readings, to online liturgies of the hours, and to biographical abstracts of valiant missionaries and of the patron saints of each day.

As stated above, online, we ought to compose and post reflection and discussion questions related to missionary conversion drawn from the *Compendium of the Social Doctrine of the Church*, other mission-related magisterial documents, patristic writings, and the Holy Bible. As previously noted, intentional reading, study, and reflection upon official Catholic social doctrine and sacred scripture is a proven way to guide and foster the long-term, ongoing conversion of missionaries.

Enhanced Interactive Social Network to Facilitate the Posting of Reflections

Moreover, it would be fruitful to enhance and expand our online interactive social networking capability. This would allow us to invite new and veteran missionaries to offer both their own reflections as well as advice to our fellow missionaries who may be struggling with a post-immersion sense of isolation or sadness.

Prayer & Sacraments

Need for Prayer & Sacraments

In the course of our study, we learned that post-immersion missionaries often feel an intense spiritual and emotional rupture when the immersion routine, which includes daily shared prayer, debriefing, and reflection, abruptly ends for most of the lay missionaries upon their return to the USA. This sudden separation from the intentional immersion schedule creates an acute need to continue these marvelous, wisdom-nurturing, communal practices. The need for regular prayer, reflection, and Eucharist during the post-immersion phase stood out in every one of our focus group sessions and is attested to in the studies and analyses of Bellah et al., Kavanaugh, Rambo, Bosch, Ver Beek, and the Congregation for Institutes of Consecrated Life and Societies of Apostolic Life.[7]

Recommendations to Address the Need for Prayer & Sacraments

Creation of a Reentry Ritual

My research and reflection demonstrate that whatever ritual we devise needs to be enacted during a post-immersion "welcome back" liturgy. It is evident that this step would also render it necessary to formulate a commissioning and sending forth ritual or to at least correlate the reentry ritual with the already existent commissioning and sending forth ritual, which happens to be a mass that features a special blessing for those about to depart.

These rituals could be simple. For example, the commissioning/send-off ritual could consist of bestowing a blessing, an AeA T-shirt, and a lit candle upon the pre-immersion missionaries and having them

---

[7] Congregation for Institutes of Consecrated Life and Societies of Apostolic Life, *Congregavit nos in Unum Christi Amor*, 14ff.

follow the cross bearer out of the chapel with their candles still lit during the final procession. Then, the reentry ritual could feature all the recently returned missionaries wearing their AeA T-shirts and carrying lit candles in the entrance procession of the "welcome back" or "reentry" liturgy.

Reclamation of our Tradition of Shared Scriptural Reflection during Reentry Eucharistic Liturgy

My research shows that we will significantly bolster the post-immersion reintegration process, and thereby the overall progress of post-immersion conversion, by reestablishing, in consultation with our priest friends, the tradition of a shared scriptural reflection during this annual "reentry" liturgy. Just as this single participatory feature has proven time and again among university students to augment a deeper appreciation of both the mass as well as of the sacred scriptures, it has an even more profound effect upon recently returned missionaries.

Prayer

We ought to compile a bibliography of prayer resources for our post-immersion missionaries. At the top of the list, I would include a Bible, some version of the *Liturgy of the Hours* or *Christian Prayer*, and a comprehensive volume of prayers composed by the saints. We should include short guidebooks that teach silent contemplation and *lectio divina as* well as additional prayer books.

Summation

No missionary organization is perfect. All have something to teach as well as to learn. AeA has certainly matured over the course of four decades. However, by continuing to listen critically to the experiences of our member missionaries, our sacred scriptures, our Catholic magisterium, relevant social philosophers, social scientists, and non-magisterial theologians, we are able to identify inadequately addressed breaches in our praxis. Once we become aware of these gaps, we can begin to devise thorough responses. Our study has discerned and dealt with seven crucial categories of concern for our post-immersion conversion-stimulation program, namely: simplicity, community, service, stories, sacraments, deprivatization, and the Reign of God.

Conclusion

After years of research, reading, study, and reflection on the topic of the post-immersion conversion praxes of AeA missionaries, it has proven remarkable to discover that the preponderance of the insights and subsequent recommendations for a renewed post-immersion praxis which organically emerged from my efforts, closely mirror the sage counsel offered in one segment of one book by one scholar of conversion, namely Lewis Rambo.

Specifically, I point to Rambo's four dimensions of interaction within the matrix of religious transformation (relationships, rituals, rhetoric, and roles) which have proven to be the most enduring yet flexible guidelines available for the solidifying and deepening of the ongoing spiritual transformation of post-immersion missionaries.[8]

- The need for mentoring and for regular gatherings correlates with Rambo's concept of "relationships."

- The idea of embedding simple ceremonies in the commissioning and reentry liturgies echoes Rambo's concept of "rituals."

- The study of and reflection on biblical texts and CSD documents, along with post-immersion storytelling, correspond to Rambo's notion of "rhetoric."

---

[8] Rambo, *Understanding Religious Conversion*, 107-123; See also Chapter 6.

- Participation in service endeavors among local poor people, in conjunction with public expositions of missionary narratives, dovetail with Rambo's conception of "roles."

In this book, we have explored the factors that affect the conversion trajectories of post-immersion missionaries. We have culled the data from focus group interviews and analyzed it from the perspectives of social philosophy, sociology, religious conversion theory, and Catholic social doctrine. We have specifically followed the practical theological method known as shared Christian praxis.

We have detailed the impediments to the subsequent deepening of conversion in the societal, ecclesial, interpersonal, familial, and intrapersonal spheres, namely: post-immersion depression, culture shock, feelings of guilt regarding one's own relatively luxurious living conditions, blaming God for the obstinate pervasiveness of extreme poverty and political injustices, and communication difficulties between the missionaries and their non-missionary family members and friends.

We can conclude that the aforementioned discouraging factors can be effectively countered via attention, during the post-immersion stage, to the missionaries' expressed needs to continue:

- to meet regularly with their respective missionary communities,

- to deprivatize their visions of spiritual conversion,

- to live a less opulent lifestyle,

- to participate in hands-on community service projects in conjunction with local poor and vulnerable people,

- to continue striving to contribute to the Reign of God locally, and

- to speak publicly about their missionary experiences.

We find that guided prayer methods, communal liturgies, mentorship, debriefing retreats for the missionaries and their families, ongoing study of the Bible and Catholic social doctrine, and long-term commitment to the missions, can all be efficacious tools in the promotion of the consolidation and deepening of conversion and the prevention of backsliding.

BIBLIOGRAPHY

Bellah, Robert Neelly, Richard Madsen, William M. Sullivan, Ann
    Swidler, and Steven M.Tipton. *Habits of the Heart: Individualism
    and Commitment in American Life*. Berkeley, CA: University of
    California, 1985.

Benedict XVI. *Deus Caritas Est: God is Love: On Christian Love.*Città
    del Vaticano: Libreria Editrice Vaticana, December 25, 2005.

-----. "Letter of his Holiness Benedict XVI to the Bishops of Latin
    America & the Caribbean," *Aparecida Concluding Document*.
    Aparecida, Brasil. Città del Vaticano: Libreria Editrice Vaticana,
    May, 2007.

------. *Caritas in Veritate: In Charity and Truth: On Integral Human De-
    velopment*. Città del Vaticano: Libreria Editrice Vaticana, June 29,
    2009.

Bevans, Stephen B., SVD. *Models of Contextual Theology: Revised &
    Expanded Edition*. Maryknoll, NY: Orbis, 2004.

Bevans, Stephen B., SVD, and Roger P. Schroeder, SVD. *Constants in
    Context: A Theology of Mission for Today*. Maryknoll, NY: Orbis,
    2005.

Bosch, David Jacobus. *Transforming Mission: Paradigm Shifts in the
    Theology of Mission*. Maryknoll, NY: Orbis, 1991.

Cardijn, Joseph. *Laypeople into Action*. Adelaide, Australia: ATF,
    1964.

CELAM, Episcopal Conference of Latin America and the Caribbean.
    General Conference V. *Aparecida Concluding Document*. Apare-
    cida, Brasil. Città del Vaticano: Libreria Editrice Vaticana, May,
    2007.

Chaplin, Melissa. *Returning Well: Your Guide to Thriving Back "Home" After Serving Cross-Culturally*. Newton, MA: Newton, 2015.

Chinn, Lisa Espineli. *Reentry Guide for Short-Term Mission Leaders*. Orlando, FL: Deeper Roots, 1998.

Chirino, Josefina R. *The Continued Short-Term Mission Among the Poor of the Developing World: An Effective Tool in Ministry to Young Adults of the Developed World*. Miami Shores, FL: Barry University, 2001.

Colburn, Robert. *Coming Home: A Re-entry Workbook for Returned Missionaries and Volunteers*. Edited by Juliet Huntly. Toronto, Ontario: Word Guild, 2000.

Congregation for the Doctrine of the Faith. *Catechism of the Catholic Church*. Città del Vaticano: Libreria Editrice Vaticana, August 15, 1997.

------. *Dominus Iesus: The Lord Jesus: On the Unicity and Salvific Universality of Jesus Christ and the Church*. Città del Vaticano: Libreria Editrice Vaticana, August 6, 2000.

Congregation for Institutes of Consecrated Life and Societies of Apostolic Life. *Congregavit nosin Unum Christi Amor: Fraternal Life in Community*. Città del Vaticano: Libreria Editrice Vaticana, February 2, 1994.

Conn, Walter. *Christian Conversion: A Developmental Interpretation of Autonomy and Surrender*. Mahwah, NJ: Paulist, 1986.

Connors, Maureen Rosemary. *Re-Entry for Volunteer Missioners: The Neglected Side of the Missioning Process*. Vol. 1 of *Lay Mission Handbook Series*. Longmont, CO: From Mission to Mission, 2000.

Connors, Maureen Rosemary and Michelle A. Scheidt. *How Do I Get Over It? Surviving Violence and Trauma Experienced in Cross-Cultural Settings: A Guide for Transitioning Missioners and Volunteers*. Longmont, CO: From Mission to Mission, 2000.

Daley, Mike and Matt Kemper. *Preparing for Your Mission Trip Journey: A Practical and Spiritual Guide for Your Mission Trip*. Cincinnati, OH: Glenmary, 2009.

Dorr, Donald. *Mission in Today's World*. Maryknoll, NY: Orbis, 2000.

Duggan, Robert D., ed. *Conversion and the Catechumenate*. Ramsey, NJ: Paulist, 1984.

Friesen, Dorothy and Mary Ellen Brody, RSM. *Returning Home? Planning Your Return from a Cross-Cultural Experience: A Guide for Transitioning Missioners and Volunteers*. Longmont, CO: From Mission to Mission, 2000.

From Mission to Mission. *Close of Service Workshop for Cross-Cultural Volunteers: Facilitator Manual*. Pinellas Park, FL: From Mission to Mission, 2000.

------. *Close of Service Workshop for Cross-Cultural Volunteers: Participant Notebook*. Pinellas Park, FL: From Mission to Mission, 2001.

------. *Welcome Home? Returning from a Cross-Cultural Experience: A Guide for Transitioning Missioners and Volunteers*. Longmont, CO: From Mission to Mission, 2000.

Gaventa, Beverly Roberts. *From Darkness to Light: Aspects of Conversion in the New Testament. Overtures to Biblical Theology Series*. Philadelphia, PA: Fortress, 1986.

Gelpi, Donald Louis, SJ. *The Conversion Experience: A Reflective Process for RCIA Participants and Others*. Mahwah, NJ: Paulist, 1998.

------. *The Turn to Experience in Contemporary Theology*. Mahwah, NJ: Paulist, 1994.

Gittins, Anthony J., CSSp. *Bread for the Journey: The Mission of Transformation and the Transformation of Mission*. Maryknoll, NY: Orbis, 1993.

------. *Ministry at the Margins: Strategy and Spirituality for Mission*. Maryknoll, NY: Orbis, 2002.

Goizueta, Roberto S. *Caminemos con Jesús: Toward a Hispanic/Latino Theology of Accompaniment*. Maryknoll, NY: Orbis, 1995.

Gregory X. Protection of the Jews. October 7, 1272. http://www.papalencyclicals.net/Greg10/g10jprot.htm.

Gregory XVI. In Supremo Apostolatus: *At the Summit of Apostolic Power: On Slavery*. December 3, 1839. http://www.papalencyclicals.net/Greg16/g16sup.htm.

Groome, Thomas H. *Sharing Faith: The Way of Shared Praxis: A Comprehensive Approach to Religious Education and Pastoral Ministry*. San Francisco, CA: HarperCollins, 1991.

Gunst-Heffner, Gail and Claudia DeVries-Beversluis, eds. "International Service Learning: International Service Learning: A Call to Caution." *Commitment and Connection*. New York, NY: University Press of America, 2002.

Gutiérrez, Gustavo, OP. *A Theology of Liberation: History, Politics, and Salvation*. Maryknoll, NY: Orbis, 1971.

------. *The God of Life*. Maryknoll, NY: Orbis, 1989.

Happel, Stephen and James J. Walter. *Conversion and Discipleship: A Christian Foundation for Ethics and Doctrine*. Philadelphia, PA: Fortress, 1986.

Holland, Joe. *Modern Catholic Social Teaching: The Popes Confront the Industrial Age 1740-1958*. Mahwah, NJ: Paulist, 2003.

Holland, Joe, ed. *Compendium of the Social Doctrine of the Church: A Pax Romana Study Guide*. Washington, DC: Pax Romana USA, 2010.

Holland, Joe and Peter Henriot, SJ. *Social Analysis: Linking Faith and Justice*. Maryknoll, NY: Orbis, 1983.

Huyser-Honig, Abram. "Study Questions: Whether Short-Term Missions Make a Difference." Carol Stream, IL: *Christianity Today* (June, 2005).

Jezreel, Jack. *Just Faith Introductory Seminar*. Miami Gardens, FL: Saint Thomas University, March 2003.

John XXIII. *Mater et Magistra: Mother and Teacher: Christianity and Social Progress*. Città delVaticano: Libreria Editrice Vaticana, May 15, 1961.

------. *Pacem in Terris: Peace on Earth*. Città del Vaticano: Libreria Editrice Vaticana, April 11, 1963.

John Paul II. *Centesimus Annus: On the 100ᵗʰ Anniversary of Rerum No-varum*. Città del Vaticano: Libreria Editrice Vaticana, May 1, 1991.

------. *Ecclesia in America: The Church in America: Post-Synodal Apostolic Exhortation on the Encounter with the Living Jesus Christ: The Way to Conversion, Communion, and Solidarity in America*. Città del Vaticano: LibreriaEditriceVaticana, January 22, 1999.

------. *Evangelium Vitae: The Gospel of Life: On the Value and Inviolability of Human Life*. Città del Vaticano: Libreria Editrice Vaticana, March 25, 1995.

------. *Familiaris Consortio: On the Role of the Christian Family in the Modern World*. Città del Vaticano: Libreria Editrice Vaticana, November 22, 1981.

------. *Laborem Exercens: On Human Work*. Città del Vaticano: Libreria Editrice Vaticana, September 14, 1981.

------. *Peace with God the Creator, Peace with All of Creation: On the Occasion of the World Day of Peace, January 1, 1990*. Città del Vaticano: Libreria Editrice Vaticana, December 8, 1989.

------. *RedemptorisMissio: The Mission of Christ the Redeemer: On the Permanent Validity of the Church's Missionary Mandate*. Città del Vaticano: Libreria Editrice Vaticana, December 7, 1990.

------. *Sollicitudo Rei Socialis: On the Social Concerns of the Church on the 20th Anniversary of PopulorumProgressio*. Città del Vaticano: Libreria Editrice Vaticana, December 30, 1987.

Kavanaugh, John Francis, SJ. *Still Following Christ in a Consumer Society: The Spirituality of Cultural Resistance*. Maryknoll, NY: Orbis, 1991.

Knell, Marion. *Burn Up or Splash Down: Surviving the Culture Shock of Re-Entry*. Tyrone, GA: Authentic, 2007.

Jordan, Peter. *Re-Entry: Making the Transition from Missions to Life at Home*. Seattle, WA: Youth With A Mission, 1992.

Leo XIII. *Rerum Novarum: New Things: The Condition of Workers*. Città del Vaticano: Libreria Editrice Vaticana, May 5, 1891.

Lupien, Julie and Michelle Scheidt. *Remaining Faithful: How Do I Keep My Experiences Alive? A Manual for Reflection, Integration, and Prayer After a Short-Term Experience in Another Culture.* Longmont, CO: From Mission to Mission, 2005.

Malony, H. Newton and Samuel Southard, eds. *Handbook of Religious Conversion.* Birmingham, AL: Religious Education Press, 1992.

McCaffrey, Jo Ann. *At Home in the Journey: Theological Reflection for Missioners in Transition.* Chicago, IL: Chicago Center for Global Ministries, 2005.

McCluskey, Patricia, IHM and Sara Talis. *How Do We Welcome Them Home? A Journey of Transition for Communities Welcoming Missioners and Volunteers Home: A Guide for Parishes, Families, Religious Communities, and Mission Sending Organizations.* Longmont, CO: From Mission to Mission, 2001.

McKenna, Megan. *Blessings and Woes.* Maryknoll, NY: Orbis, 2003.

------. *Not Counting Women and Children: Neglected Stories from the Bible.* Maryknoll, NY: Orbis, 1994.

------. "Revelation and Ministry Lectures." Miami Gardens, FL: Saint Thomas University, Revelation and Ministry Course, IPM 751, January 1995.

Moreau-Jones, Tina M. *Gathering the Fragments: A Survey of Components for the Formation of International Lay Missioners.* Washington, DC: Catholic Network of Volunteer Service, United States Catholic Mission Association, and Saint Vincent Pallotti Center, 2002.

Paul III. *Sublimus Dei: On the Enslavement and Evangelization of Indians in the New World.* May 29, 1537.http://www.papalencyclicals.net/Paul03/p3subli.htm.

Paul VI. *Populorum Progressio: On the Development of Peoples.* Città del Vaticano: Librería Editrice Vaticana, March 26, 1967.

------. Humanae Vitae: Human Life: On the Regulation of Birth. Città del Vaticano: Librería Editrice Vaticana, July 25, 1968.

------. *Octagesima Adveniens: On the80th Anniversary of Rerum Novarum: A Call to Action.* Città del Vaticano: Libreria Editrice Vaticana, May 14, 1971.

------. Evangelii Nuntiandi: Apostolic Exhortation on Evangelization in the Modern World. Città del Vaticano: Libreria Editrice Vaticana, December 8, 1975.

Peace, Richard V. *Conversion in the New Testament: Paul and the Twelve.* Grand Rapids, MI: Eerdmans, 1999.

Pirolo, Neal. *The Reentry Team: Caring for Your Returning Missionaries.* San Diego, CA: Emmaus Road International, 2000.

Pius XI. *Quadragesimo Anno: Reconstruction of the Social Order on the 40th Anniversary of Rerum Novarum.* Città del Vaticano: Libreria Editrice Vaticana, May 15, 1931.

Pius XII. *Exsul Familia Nazarethana: Apostolic Constitution on Migrants.* Città del Vaticano: Libreria Editrice Vaticana, August 1, 1952.

Pontifical Council for Interreligious Dialogue and the Congregation for the Evangelization of Peoples. *Dialogue and Proclamation: Reflection and Orientations on Interreligious Dialogue and the Proclamation of the Gospel of Jesus Christ.* Città del Vaticano: Libreria Editrice Vaticana, May 19, 1991.

Pontifical Council for Justice and Peace. *Compendium of the Social Doctrine of the Church.* Città del Vaticano: Libreria Editrice Vaticana, June 29, 2004.

------. *Toward Reforming the International Financial and Monetary Systems in the Context of Global Public Authority.* Città del Vaticano: Libreria Editrice Vaticana, October 24, 2011.

------. *Peace and Conversion.* Città del Vaticano: Libreria Editrice Vaticana, September 30, 1983.

Pontifical Council for the Pastoral Care of Migrants and Itinerant People. *Erga Migrantes Caritas Christi: The Love of Christ towards Migrants.* Città del Vaticano: Libreria Editrice Vaticana, 2004.

------. *Refugees: A Challenge to Solidarity*. Città del Vaticano: Libreria Editrice Vaticana, October 2, 1992.

Priest, Robert J., Terry Dischinger, Steve Rasmussen, and C.M. Brown. "Researching the Short-Term Mission Movement." *Missiology* 34, no. 4. Wilmore, KY: American Society of Missiology (October 2006).

Putnam, Robert David. *Bowling Alone: The Collapse and Revival of American Community*. New York, NY: Simon and Schuster, 2000.

Rambo, Lewis Ray. "Psychology of Conversion." *Handbook of Religious Conversion*. Edited by H. Newton Malony and Samuel Southard. Birmingham, AL: Religious Education, 1992.

------. *Understanding Religious Conversion*. New Haven, CT: Yale University, 1993.

Rambo, Lewis Ray and Lawrence Reh. "Phenomenology of Conversion." *Handbook of Religious Conversion*. Edited by H. Newton Malony and Samuel Southard. Birmingham, AL: Religious Education, 1992.

Ruffing, Janet. "Socially Engaged Contemplation: Living Contemplatively in Chaotic Times." *Handbook of Spirituality for Ministers: Perspectives for the 21st Century*. Volume 2. Edited by Robert Wicks. Mahwah, NJ: Paulist, 2000.

Scherer, James. *Gospel, Church, and Kingdom: Comparative Studies in World Mission Theology*. Minneapolis, MN: Augsburg, 1987.

Scherer, James and Stephen Bevans. *New Directions in Mission and Evangelization 1, 2, and 3*. Maryknoll, NY: Orbis, 1992.

Schreiter, Robert. *Constructing Local Theologies*. Maryknoll, NY: Orbis, 1985.

------. *Reconciliation: Mission & Ministry in a Changing Social Order*. Maryknoll, NY: Orbis, 1992.

Schroeder, Roger P. *What is the Mission of the Church? A Guide for Catholics*. Maryknoll, NY: Orbis, 2008.

Senior, Donald, CP and Carroll Stuhlmueller, CP. *The Biblical Foundations for Mission*. Maryknoll, NY: Orbis, 1983.

Social Action Office, Conference of Leaders of Religious Institutes, Queensland. "Introduction to Catholic Social Teaching." Brisbane, Queensland, Australia: http://sao.clriq.org.au/cst.html. 2006.

Stiles, J. Mack and Leeann Stiles. *Mack and Leeann's Guide to Short-Term Missions*. Downers Grove, IL: InterVarsity, 2000.

Storti, Craig. *The Art of Coming Home*. Yarmouth, ME: Intercultural, 2001.

Vandergrift, Monica. *Spirituality of Return: Celebrating Our Many Homecomings*. Ann Arbor, MI: UMI, 1991.

Van Engen, Jo Ann. "The Cost of Short-Term Missions." *The Other Side*. Grand Rapids, MI: Association for a More Just Society (January/February, 2000).

Vatican Council II. *Ad Gentes Divinitus: Decree on the Church's Missionary Activity*. Città del Vaticano: Libreria Editrice Vaticana, December 7, 1965.

Vatican Council II. *Gaudium et Spes: Pastoral Constitution on the Church in the Modern World*. Città del Vaticano: Libreria Editrice Vaticana, December 7, 1965.

Vatican Council II. *Inter Mirifica: Decree on the Mass Media*. Città del Vaticano: Libreria Editrice Vaticana, December 4, 1963.

Vatican Council II. *Lumen Gentium: Dogmatic Constitution on the Church*. Città del Vaticano: Libreria Editrice Vaticana, November 21, 1964.

Ver Beek, Kurt Alan. "The Impact of Short Term Missions: A Case Study of House Construction in Honduras after Hurricane Mitch." *Missiology: An International Review* (October 2006): 477-496.

------. "Lessons from the Sapling: Review of Research on Short-term Missions, Study Abroad, and Service Learning Lecture." Grand Rapids, MI: Calvin College, October 4, 2006.

Ver Beek, Kurt Alan and Robert Priest. "Are Short-Term Missions Good Stewardship?" Grand Rapids, MI: *Christianity Today*

Magazine, http://www.christianitytoday.com/ct/2005/julyweb-only/22.0.html (June, 2005).

Wicks, Robert J. *Self-Ministry Through Self-Understanding: A Guide to Christian Introspection.* Chicago, IL: Loyola University, 1983.

Witherup, Ronald D., SS. *Conversion in the New Testament. Zacchaeus Series: New Testament.* Edited by Mary Ann Getty. Collegeville, MN: Liturgical, 1994.

Young, Amy. *Looming Transitions: Starting and Finishing Well in Cross-Cultural Service.* Lawrence, KS: CreateSpace, 2015.

DR. DAVID MASTERS was raised in a big Catholic family who descend from Alsatian-Lorrainian Jews, French Canadians, and indentured-servant Balearic Islanders who arrived in the Timukwa region of the Pascua Florida Peninsula in 1768. David's Kiskeyan wife, Dayane, usually accompanies him on missionary excursions, often along with their soccer- and piano-playing sons, Rubén and Marcos.

Dr. Masters teaches courses on the world's religions, sacred scripture, Christology, Catholic social and ecological doctrine, human rights, peacemaking, reconciliation, missiology, ecclesiology, church history, ethics/morality, marriage and family, sacraments, and youth ministry to high school, university, and adult education students.

Deeply indebted to his mentors and collaborators, young David was initially trained by his parents as a door-to-door Peregrinatio Pro Christo missionary. His missionary destinations have included the Antilles and Central and South America.

David has served enthusiastically for decades at Msgr. Edward Pace High School in Miami Gardens as a theology teacher, retreat director, and campus minister. He has likewise thrived as an adjunct professor of theology and ministry at Saint Thomas University in Florida.

David is active in the Iraqi Christian Relief Council, Amor en Acción, Iglesia en Misión, Misión en Acción, and the Missionalis Societas Ioannes Paulus II. David now focuses on the monumental global struggles against genocide, BDS, and female circumcision.

David earned a BA in journalism, faith, peace, and justice, and African-American studies from Boston College; an MA in practical theology, sacred scripture, and peacemaking from Saint Thomas University; and a DMin from Barry University in sacred scripture and missiology.

He has received accolades from Pax Romana USA (Peter Maurin Award), the Peace Education Foundation (Peace Educator of the Year), and the US Coast Guard's Officer Snook environmental program (Water Pollution Prevention Collaborator).

His previous publications include an analysis of the Miami McDuffie riot of 1980 and a chapter on Catholic doctrine regarding the indispensable role of families, which he and his wife authored jointly for *Pax Romana's Study Guide on the Compendium of the Social Doctrine of the Church*. David has translated and edited articles for an online Spanish language biblical commentary website.

David's avocations are visiting manifold houses of worship, history, hiking, reading biblical commentaries, and probing the etymologies of names.

OTHER BOOKS
FROM PACEM IN TERRIS PRESS

SEEKING GLOBAL JUSTICE & PEACE

Catholic-Inspired NGOs at the United Nations

Emeka Obiezu, 2019

ROMAN CATHOLIC CLERICALISM

Three Historical Stages in the Legislation of a Non-Evangelical,
Now Dysfunctional, and Sometimes Pathological Institution
Joe Holland, 2018

CATHOLIC PRACTICAL THEOLOGY

A Genealogy of the Methodological Turn to Praxis,
Historical Reality, & the Preferential Option for the Poor
Bob Pennington, 2018

SAINT JOHN OF THE CROSS

His Prophetic Mysticism in the Historical Context
of Sixteenth-Century Spain
Cristóbal Serrán-Pagán y Fuentes, 2018

BRETTON WOODS INSTITUTIONS & NEOLIBERALISM

Historical Critique of Policies, Structures, & Governance of the International Monetary Fund
& the World Bank, with Case Studies
Mark Wolff, 2018

THE WHOLE STORY:

The Wedding of Science & Religion
Norman Carroll, 2018

PADRE MIGUEL

A Memoir of My Catholic Missionary Experience in Bolivia
amidst Postcolonial Transformation of Church and State
Michael J. Gillgannon, 2018

277

POSTMODERN ECOLOGICAL SPIRITUALITY
Catholic-Christian Hope for the Dawn of a Postmodern Ecological Civilization Rising
from within the Spiritual Dark Night of Modern Industrial Civilization
Joe Holland, 2017

JOURNEYS TO RENEWED CONSECRATION
Religious Life after Fifty Years of Vatican II
Emeka Obiezu, OSA & John Szura, OSA, Editors, 2017

THE CRUEL ELEVENTH-CENTURY IMPOSITION OF
WESTERN CLERICAL CELIBACY
A Monastic-Inspired Attack on Catholic Episcopal & Clerical Families
Joe Holland, 2017

LIGHT, TRUTH, & NATURE
Practical Reflections on Vedic Wisdom & Heart-Centered Meditation
In Seeking a Spiritual Basis for Nature, Science, Evolution, & Ourselves
Thomas Pliske, 2017

THOMAS BERRY IN ITALY
Reflections on Spirituality & Sustainability
Elisabeth M. Ferrero, Editor, 2016

PETER MAURIN'S
ECOLOGICAL LAY NEW MONASTICISM
A Catholic Green Revolution Developing
Rural Ecovillages, Urban Houses of Hospitality,
& Eco-Universities for a New Civilization
Joe Holland, 2015

PROTECTION OF RELIGIOUS MINORITIES
A Symposium Organized by Pax Romana at the United Nations
and the United Nations Alliance of Civilizations
Dean Elizabeth F. Defeis & Peter F. O'Connor, Editors, 2015

BOTTOM ELEPHANTS
Catholic Sexual Ethics & Pastoral Practice in Africa:
The Challenge of Women Living within Patriarchy
& Threatened by HIV-Positive Husbands
Daniel Ude Asue, 2014

CATHOLIC LABOR PRIESTS
Five Giants in the United States Catholic Bishops Social Action Department
Volume I of US Labor Priests During the 20th Century
Patrick Sullivan, 2014

CATHOLIC SOCIAL TEACHING & UNIONS
IN CATHOLIC PRIMARY & SECONDARY SCHOOLS
The Clash between Theory & Practice within the United States
Walter "Bob" Baker, 2014

SPIRITUAL PATHS TO
A GLOBAL & ECOLOGICAL CIVILIZATION
Reading the Signs of the Times with Buddhists, Christians, & Muslims
John Raymaker & Gerald Grudzen, with Joe Holland, 2013

PACEM IN TERRIS
Its Continuing Relevance for the Twenty-First Century
(Papers from the 50th Anniversary Conference at the United Nations)
Josef Klee & Francis Dubois, Editors, 2013

PACEM IN TERRIS
Summary & Commentary for the Famous Encyclical Letter
of Pope John XXIII on World Peace
Joe Holland, 2012

100 YEARS OF CATHOLIC SOCIAL TEACHING
DEFENDING WORKERS & THEIR UNIONS
Summaries & Commentaries for Five Landmark Papal Encyclicals
Joe Holland, 2012

HUMANITY'S AFRICAN ROOTS
Remembering the Ancestors' Wisdom
Joe Holland, 2012

THE "POISONED SPRING" OF ECONOMIC LIBERTARIANISM
Menger, Mises, Hayek, Rothbard: A Critique from
Catholic Social Teaching of the Austrian School of Economics
Pax Romana / Cmica-usa
Angus Sibley, 2011

BEYOND THE DEATH PENALTY
The Development in Catholic Social Teaching
Florida Council of Catholic Scholarship
D. Michael McCarron & Joe Holland, Editors, 2007

THE NEW DIALOGUE OF CIVILIZATIONS
A Contribution from Pax Romana
International Catholic Movement for Intellectual & Cultural Affairs
Pax Romana / Cmica-usa
Roza Pati & Joe Holland, Editors, 2002

Books from Pacem in Terris Press,

are available for purchase from Amazon at:

amazon.com

amazon.uk

amazon.de

amazon.fr

amazon.co.jp

amazon.es

amazon.it